The Sublime in Everyday Life

Notions of the sublime are most often associated with the extraordinary, and include the intra-psychic, high-cultural and exceptional occurrences of elation and exaltation as part of the experience. Using psychoanalytic and aesthetic theories, this book aims to revitalise the sublime by re-evaluating its significance for contemporary life and, in a unique and fascinating endeavour, opens up a space that explores the sublime in the ordinary, everyday and quotidian.

Through the exploration of familiar (i.e. love, death, art and nature) and unfamiliar (pornography, education and politics) threads of the sublime experience, this book posits the sublime as invoking an ordinary human response which contains minute, inter-psychic, inclusive and even mass-media cultural elements, and carries within it therapeutic and political potential. It explores loving and caring, as well as hateful, traumatic and destructive encounters with the sublime, demonstrating how it can overflow and destabilise our psychological and social symbolic structures and expose their fictional and constructed nature, but also shows it as something we can engage with in order to re-create and heal ourselves, above and beyond what any 'given' form of reality can offer us.

Demonstrating the urgent need to understand the sublime as something that is immanent in our everyday life, a source of energy and inspiration that can be invoked to support our mental health and well-being, this book will be of great interest to psychoanalysts, psychotherapists and art therapists, as well as scholars and students of philosophy and popular culture.

Anastasios Gaitanidis is a Senior Lecturer in Counselling Psychology at Regent's University London. He is also a Psychoanalytic Psychotherapist in private practice and has published several articles and books on psychoanalysis, sociology and culture.

Polona Curk works on intersubjective affective influence and mental health. She has published on autonomy, destructiveness and affective equality in intimate relationships, on the psychoanalytic concept of narcissism, and the notion of insight in mental health.

'The sublime in everyday life, taken from different perspectives, is marvellously demonstrated in this book. Given my experience in the field of psychoanalysis for madness and traumas, I am impressed by the emphasis on unexpected moments of wonder, difficult to share and to name. To call them an encounter with the sublime is a great help which triggers here beautiful accounts of intense meetings experienced as sudden, amazing, and fugitive, beyond words, still opening a brand-new path for untold stories. Longinus, who lived in troubled times, should be delighted by the new use of his word in ours.'

—Françoise Davoine

'Finding the sublime in the realness of the world is an act of great courage and humanity that has been beautifully held together by the editors, Anastasios Gaitanidis and Polona Curk. The wisdom achieved by neither capitulating towards a cold acceptance of death nor an unrelated pursuit of pleasure, but becoming poet-philosophers, is the gift that the authors provide those fortunate to be readers of this dazzling volume of ideas and emotions. I highly recommend it to poets, philosophers, and all seekers of the sublime.'

—Mark Gerald

'The story of Odysseus' encounter with the Sirens in the introduction to this book seems to capture the ambivalent space between mind and world when it comes to the sublime. We may wish to sublimate the world with our minds in a Kantian way but ultimately its mysteries lie beyond our mind's grasp. This book explores many psychoanalytic, philosophical, critical, social and political perspectives on the sublime, with an overarching commitment to relocate the sublime somewhere between the extraordinary and the ordinary or to interweave the two. The origins of the word sublime seem highly suggestive of this ambivalence and intersectionality – given "sub" can mean both up to and under in Latin and the rest of the word is derived either from the Latin "limen" meaning threshold or "limus" meaning obscure. I hope this book will bring sublime enjoyment to many readers.'

—Isabel Henton

The Sublime in Everyday Life

Psychoanalytic and Aesthetic Perspectives

Edited by
Anastasios Gaitanidis and Polona Curk

LONDON AND NEW YORK

First published 2021
by Routledge
2 Park Square, Milton Park, Abingdon, Oxon OX14 4RN

and by Routledge
52 Vanderbilt Avenue, New York, NY 10017

Routledge is an imprint of the Taylor & Francis Group, an informa business

© 2021 selection and editorial matter, Anastasios Gaitanidis and Polona Curk; individual chapters, the contributors

The right of Anastasios Gaitanidis and Polona Curk to be identified as the authors of the editorial material, and of the authors for their individual chapters, has been asserted in accordance with sections 77 and 78 of the Copyright, Designs and Patents Act 1988.

All rights reserved. No part of this book may be reprinted or reproduced or utilised in any form or by any electronic, mechanical, or other means, now known or hereafter invented, including photocopying and recording, or in any information storage or retrieval system, without permission in writing from the publishers.

Trademark notice: Product or corporate names may be trademarks or registered trademarks, and are used only for identification and explanation without intent to infringe.

British Library Cataloguing in Publication Data
A catalogue record for this book is available from the British Library

Library of Congress Cataloging-in-Publication Data
A catalog record has been requested for this book

ISBN: 978-0-367-20296-5 (hbk)
ISBN: 978-0-367-20297-2 (pbk)
ISBN: 978-0-429-26072-8 (ebk)

Typeset in Times New Roman
by Taylor & Francis Books

In memory of Tessa Adams

Contents

Acknowledgements	ix
List of contributors	x

Introduction   1
ANASTASIOS GAITANIDIS AND POLONA CURK

1 Psychoanalytic fictions of the creative sublime   10
TESSA ADAMS AND ANASTASIOS GAITANIDIS

2 The silence of Ajax: Reading Longinus against himself   21
JUSTIN MURRAY

3 The sublime in the everyday: How theatre crafts art out of the ordinary   37
ANNA SEYMOUR

4 Ordinary idolatrous pleasure and the fateful fashioning of an adolescent boy   51
ONEL BROOKS

5 Experiencing the sublime through encounters with the Real   66
JOSEPH NEWIRTH

6 Wisdom through desire: When truth meets love as a sublime event   79
ANASTASIOS GAITANIDIS

7 'How extraordinary that you should exist': On playing and experience of truth   91
POLONA CURK

8 The sublime and the feminine *jouissance*: *A Fantastic Woman*,
   The Untamed and St Teresa   106
   AGNIESZKA PIOTROWSKA

9 The lure of humiliation: Sublime aspects to success in the school
   mathematics classroom   122
   GIRISH JIVAJI

10 The sublime in *Catch-22* as bridge between post-modern
   literature and psychoanalysis   138
   CHRIS VLACHOPOULOS

11 The Diogenes complex: Sublime living in irrational times   152
   DANIEL RUBINSTEIN

   Index   169

Acknowledgements

We would like to thank all our contributors for their wonderful and creative chapters, and for bearing with us for all the delays due to the current rather strange situation in the world. We would also like to thank our editors at Routledge, Russell George and Alec Selwyn, for their guidance and hard work. We are particularly grateful to our deceased friend, Tessa Adams, who provided the initial inspiration for this project and whose imagination and creativity had an enormous impact on the form and content of this book.

Anastasios: I would like to thank my friend and co-editor, Polona Curk, for her tireless work in getting this book completed. I would also like to thank my friend and contributor, Chris Vlachopoulos, for his invaluable editorial assistance and advice. I am also very grateful to all my friends and colleagues (Lorenzo, Alan, Isabel, to name but a few) for believing in me and the importance of this project. Above all, I am extremely thankful to my wife, Sasha, for her 'sublime' presence in my everyday life.

Polona: I would like to thank Anastasios for inviting me to join this thought-provoking book project, for the stimulating discussions around it, as well as for always being a supportive friend and colleague. I would like to thank Nejka, Avi and my friends for always being there to listen and support. I would like to thank Fabian for being an attentive and challenging reader as well as the inspiration for my writing.

We would like to acknowledge and thank for the following permissions:

From *Bluets* by Maggie Nelson published by Jonathan Cape. Reproduced by permission of The Random House Group Ltd. © 2017.

From the script for *The Theory of Everything*, by Anthony McCarten © 2013. Reproduced by permission of Anthony McCarten.

Contributors

Anastasios Gaitanidis (editor) is a Senior Lecturer in the DPsych Counselling Psychology at Regent's University London. He is also a Psychoanalytic Psychotherapist in private practice and the Director of Relational Psychoanalytic Therapy Ltd. He has published several articles on psychoanalysis and psychotherapy in peer-reviewed journals and he is the co-editor (with Polona Curk) of *Narcissism – A Critical Reader* (2007) and the editor of *The Male in Analysis – Psychoanalytic and Cultural Perspectives* (2011).

Polona Curk (editor) works on autonomy and intersubjective affective influence from psychoanalytic and psychosocial perspectives. She has published on autonomy, responsibility, destructiveness and affective equality in intimate relationships, and on the psychoanalytic concept of narcissism (*Narcissism – A Critical Reader* (2007) with Anastasios Gaitanidis). She has contributed to works on determining will and preferences in persons with mental ill health and supporting them in court and currently works on insight in relation to mental health. Polona holds a PhD from University of London in Psychosocial Studies.

Tessa Adams was a Fellow of the Royal Society of Arts and Visiting Fellow of Goldsmiths College (University of London). She was an Art Theorist and practising Psychoanalytic Psychotherapist, holding professional membership with both the Site for Contemporary Psychoanalysis and the Guild of Psychotherapists. She had published widely on psychoanalysis and contemporary art practice and co-edited the volume *The Feminine Case: Jung, Aesthetics and Creative Process* first published by Karnac in 2003 and republished by Routledge in 2018. Tessa died age 79 almost 3 years ago and this book is dedicated to her memory.

Onel Brooks completed a Doctorate in Philosophy before training as a Social Worker and then as a Psychoanalytic Psychotherapist. He is a Senior Lecturer in Psychotherapy, Counselling and Counselling Psychology at the University of Roehampton, London, where he contributes to the Research Centre for Therapeutic Education, Psychology Department. He has held a number of posts as a Senior Counsellor and was a Senior Social Worker and Psychotherapist at the Tavistock Clinic for a number of years. He is in independent practice as a Psychotherapist and Supervisor and is a member of the Philadelphia Association. He is interested in the details of our theoretical models and claims, and the details of what we say and do with clients. He often finds that he is provoked into thinking by psychoanalysis, as well as philosophy and literature, and particularly Nietzsche and Wittgenstein.

Girish Jivaji worked as a Teacher of Mathematics in London for many years. He completed his PhD at Birkbeck College, University of London, in 2011 in which he used a psychosocial perspective to examine some of the processes at work in choosing to be good at school mathematics. He continues to use a psychosocial perspective to think about schooling more generally. He uses a genealogical approach inspired by the work of Foucault to think about the modern day school classroom as a 'social technology'. In addition to this, he uses theoretical ideas from a variety of sources such as Foucault, Lacan and Butler to aid in thinking about the subject of this 'social technology'.

Justin Murray is a Director and Theatremaker whose work has been seen nationally and internationally. He left Durham University with a degree in Classics and has trained extensively through the Young Vic Directors Program. He recently directed The Wizard Of Oz at The Scoop in More London Riverside as part of London's Free Open Air Theatre Season. Justin was Associate Director of Actors of Dionysus for whom he directed Antigone (R&D and national tour). Justin is artistic director of Catharsis and has directed their previous five shows, *Hippolytus* (The Hope Theatre), *Hecuba* (White Bear Theatre), *Purged* (Brighton Fringe), *The Complete Greek Tragedies* (In One Hour) (Rosemary Branch) and *Ashurbanipal* (The Crypt Gallery). As Associate Director: *FILTH* (Camden Fringe) and *Rounds* (Southwark Playhouse/Bolton Octagon). Other recent work includes *Bismillah*! An ISIS Tragicomedy at the Edinburgh Fringe, and an excerpt of *People, Places and Things* by Duncan Macmillan, translated into Lithuanian, as part of the Juozas Miltinis European Directors' Residency in Lithuania. Assisting includes *The Odyssey* at The Scoop in 2016, and *The Cherry Orchard* at The Union Theatre, both for Phil Wilmott.

Joseph Newirth is a Professor at the Derner School of Psychology at Adelphi University. He is a Supervisor at the NYU Postdoctoral Program in Psychotherapy and Psychoanalysis, New York University, and is on the faculty and a Supervisor at the National Training Program at the National Institute of the Psychotherapies, New York, NY. He received his BA from the City College of New York, his PhD from the University of Massachusetts and his psychoanalytic training at the William Alanson White

Institute. He encourages dialogue, critical thinking and opportunities for students and supervises to deepen their understanding of how psychoanalytic theories relate to the practice of psychoanalysis and psychotherapy. He has published numerous articles in professional journals and frequently presented papers at national and international conferences. His first book, *Between Emotion and Cognition: The Generative Unconscious* (2003) received the Gradiva Prize for critical analysis and interpretation in 2004. His second book, *From Sign to Symbol: Transformational Process in Psychoanalysis, Psychotherapy and Psychology* (2018) was published by Lexington Books received the American Board and Academy of Psychoanalysis annual book award for scholarly contributions in advancing the field of psychoanalysis

Agnieszka Piotrowska is an award-winning Filmmaker and a Theorist. She is the Head of School for Film, Media and Performing Arts and Professor of Film and Cultural Studies at the University for the Creative Arts, UK. She is also a Visiting Professor at Gdansk University, Poland. She is best known for her acclaimed documentary *Married to the Eiffel Tower* (2009) screened globally in 60 countries. Piotrowska has written extensively on psychoanalysis and cinema and is the author of the monographs *Psychoanalysis and Ethics in Documentary Film* (2014), *Black and White: Cinema, Politics and the Arts in Zimbabwe* (2017), and *The Nasty Woman and Neo Femme Fatale in Contemporary Cinema* (2019). She has edited four books including *Femininity and Psychoanalysis* (2019) and *Creative Practice Research in the Age of Neoliberal Hopelessness* (2020). She is a Founding Scholar at the British Psychoanalytic Council.

Daniel Rubinstein is a Reader in Philosophy and the Image at Central Saint Martins. He has written books and articles on European philosophy, visual cultures, queer theory, cyber cultures and psychoanalysis. His most recent books are *Photography After Philosophy* and *Fragmentation of the Photographic Image in the Digital Age.*

Anna Seymour, PhD, PFHEA HCPC registered Dramatherapist, is the Professor of Dramatherapy at the University of Roehampton, London. She is Visiting Professor of Dramatherapy at the University of Osijek, Croatia, honorary member of the Societa Professionale di Dramaterapia (Italy) and an international trainer and consultant to several Dramatherapy programmes across the world. She has worked as a Dramatherapist and Clinical Supervisor in the NHS, voluntary sector and private practice. As an adoptive parent she has a particular interest in attachment processes. Anna has a background in professional theatre with and for working-class communities and was associated with more than 30 shows, devising, directing and performing work. As an academic she has taught theatre praxis and given lecture series in the Drama departments of several leading

UK universities including the Universities of Manchester and Birmingham. Former Editor of the British Association of Dramatherapists Journal, she is the Senior Series Editor, *Dramatherapy: Approaches, Relationships, Critical Ideas* published by Routledge/Taylor and Francis

Chris Vlachopoulos has a background is in psychology; he completed his studies at the University of Reading and also holds a Master of Arts from Goldsmiths College in Writing for Performance and Dramaturgy. He is active in the theatre as a Playwright and Dramaturg: he has adapted ancient Greek tragedies for the stage, such as *Hecuba*, and is an associate writer for Catharsis Theatre. He has studied the work of contemporary playwrights extensively, particularly of those adhering to the absurdist tradition of contemporary drama, as well as contemporary writers of post-modernist fiction. In his work he draws on ideas from contemporary research in psychology and evolutionary biology, as well as the theoretical frameworks of Barthes, Lacan and Freud to explore language and the role it plays in shaping our sense of Self.

Introduction

Anastasios Gaitanidis and Polona Curk

This book is first and foremost an attempt to honour the legacy and work of sublime friends, those who have initially dreamt it up as a possibility but could not materialise it as they are no longer with us (especially the exquisite Tessa Adams, our late friend and colleague) and those who have inherited this dream and toiled hard to turn it into reality (the editors and contributors of this book). In addition, this book is an attempt to substantiate the existing aesthetic and psychoanalytic, theoretical and clinical knowledge of the sublime by placing it within the context of everyday life, as well as an ongoing attempt to revitalise the world of our ordinary sensorial and interpersonal experiences by introducing the sublime as part of its mysterious, irreducible and open-ended texture.

This book is not in any sense a rejection of the philosophical and psychoanalytic tradition surrounding the notion of the sublime. It is a plea that the existing philosophical and psychoanalytical perspectives on the sublime acknowledge their rootedness in the same world that we all engage in our everyday lives – that, for all their theoretical and clinical refinements, the various philosophical and psychoanalytic explanations of the sublime remain an expression of, and hence must be guided by, the world of our common human experience.

We now turn to the emergence and development of the notion of the sublime in philosophy and psychoanalysis in order to show how this legacy is taken up and transformed in the manner that endowed the present book with a particular power and relevance for the personal, interpersonal, cultural and political questions that confront us in the 21st century. By proposing a more 'grounding', 'ordinary' way of speaking and thinking about the sublime, we hope that we will be able to reinvigorate the sensuous, mysterious and 'sacred' ways we experience our everyday encounters with the world and each other.

'Aesthetics was born as a discourse of the body', Terry Eagleton (1990, p. 13) declares in his *The Ideology of the Aesthetic*. In the 18th and 19th century, a number of philosophers realised that if post-Cartesian Reason was to retain its legitimacy, it should not leave outside its rule ordinary lived experience, the whole of our likes and dislikes, affections and aversions, of how the world strikes the body on its sensory surfaces – what Immanuel Kant (1914) euphemistically called the 'rabble' of the senses. The material, sensorial underbelly of philosophical thought needed to be revealed and illuminated in its excluded otherness – but only so as to be gradually integrated back into its fold. Aesthetics as the inferior sibling of Reason was thus brought into existence and taxed with the task of creating a cognitive map of the life of the body in order to reconcile philosophical thought with its somatic other.

The birth of Aesthetics therefore signified both a creative turn to the sensuous body, which gave rise to a genuinely emancipatory force, as well as providing the ideological cover for Reason's imperialistic expansion and control. It functioned both as the Master's emissary and the conspirator against him. Aesthetics contained within it a *promesse du bonheur*, a promise that could be fulfilled if the disenchanted, instrumental world of Reason could be transformed into something beautiful or sublime. However, this promise was also deeply ideological as it 'aesthetised' away the legitimate frustrations of the subject in the modern capitalist world. The latter, as Eagleton (1990) argues, was required to perform within an isolating and cruel competitive environment as well as consent to being grouped under a form of state power organised around the notion of formal equality. Aesthetics, as 'the discourse of the body', provided the needed model for a projected ideal of subjectivity. Like the work of art, the ideal modern subject would be 'autonomous' and consent to regulate her/his emotional life whilst at the same time submit her/himself to an environment that was ruled by the antagonistic and unforgiving principles of exchange value.

This requirement for both consent and submission becomes evident in the account of Aesthetics provided by the 18th Anglo-Irish philosopher and politician, Edmund Burke. Both of his main categories of the aesthetics, the beautiful and the sublime, contain elements of submission and consent. The beautiful enchants us with its harmonious, smooth features and produces within us spontaneous consent – we want to submit to it and become its servants because we want to pleasurably imitate it and thus acquire/possess its qualities. On the contrary, for Burke, the sublime is the effect of the threat of terror or violation that culminates in the experience of pleasurable pain or painful pleasure. The terror of witnessing a wild thunderstorm or a tempest at sea, crushes us into submission but, assuming we remain safe, there is delight in being made to feel insignificant (see Burke, 1990).

The theme of submission is also adopted and developed by Kant (1914) in his description of the sublime. One can best understand Kant's account of the sublime if one uses the tale of Odysseus' encounter with the sirens as an example. Odysseus derives a painful pleasure, a kind of masochistic joy out of the sirens' song without endangering himself as he has tied himself to the ship's mast. In order to overcome the terror of nature's sublime call, he had to allow his mind to dominate his own nature/body. Thus, Kant argues, the immediacy, disorder and danger of the natural sublime are overcome by the extreme – almost sadistic (see Jacques Lacan's (1989) *Kant with Sade*) – effort of the mind to assert its autonomy and superiority over nature. Crucially, in this sublime experience Odysseus' subjectivity validates itself in the process of becoming aware of its relationship to nature (inside and outside). However, in a Kantian moment of transcendence, the object of the sublime feeling not only makes him realise that he is subject of (and to) nature, but it also makes him aware that he has the capacity to be more than nature by asserting his freedom from its threatening immediacy and making it submit to the mastery of his reason.

Late 20th-century developments in the discourse of the sublime, such as certain applications of sublimity in the context of postmodernity, attempt to avoid Kant's glorification of self-sufficiency and the mastery of reason as an expression of the modern subject's character structure, and align themselves more with the Kantian emphasis on the limits of representation which the object of sublime feeling underscores. Jean-Francois Lyotard, for instance, is less interested in exploring the sublime from the perspective of how our response to it enables us to control our relationship with the external world, but focuses instead on the sublime as an aesthetic experience of the paradoxical presentation of the unpresentable (see Lyotard, 1994). For Lyotard, the sublime is primarily an ephemeral experience of shock or surprise, suggesting that something 'happens' in a moment deemed uncontrollable and resistant to communicative rational discourse. The sublime is an inescapable, unpreventable 'event' whose both presence and the instance of its 'happening' remain beyond understanding. Lyotard's reading of Kant thus conceives the sublime not only as a challenge to the imagination but as an invitation to embrace both reason's limits of representation and, ultimately, what brushes itself against them, i.e. the sublime as an unpresentable presence, an immaterial materiality.

However, for early 20th-century Critical Theorists, especially Theodor Adorno, the sublime is neither an example of reason's triumph over the overwhelming impact of external natural events (as in Kant) nor an opportunity to welcome the immaterial materiality of these events against the limits of rational comprehension and communication (as in Lyotard), but rather a 'return to nature within the subject'. The major effect of the sublime is described as a 'shudder'. Shudder is of course a physical sensation, belonging to the realm of the body, but for this sensation to be more than self-identical and operating within the body, it needs to remove itself from the experience of nature's threat and attach itself to the process of artistic objectification, i.e. the process of crystallisation of the compositional and formal elements of the artwork. It is through this process that, for Adorno, the sublime relocates itself from nature to the work of art (see Adorno, 1997).

In addition to the process of objectification, art expresses our own and external nature's suffering and pain through a process of mimesis: 'Because the spell of external reality over its subjects and their reactions has become absolute, the artwork can only oppose this spell by assimilating itself to it' (Adorno, 1997, p. 31). If authentic art is the 'negative imprint of the administered world' (ibid.), it also has the power, through its negativity, to point beyond the world in a gesture of utopian semblance and offer a mode of transcendence that appears in an instant in our encounter with the artwork. Art therefore is both a reflection of the current state of the world and how it could be otherwise.

Perhaps with differing levels of awareness, it is likely that people still experience physical reactions to direct or indirect violence within their environments: a knot in the pit of their stomach when they hear that refugees are treated as illegal aliens, a pain in their lower back when they experience someone complaining that s/he is a 'customer' and needs to receive a particular service, acid reflux when they see people flaunting their privilege without any consideration for its effects on their fellow human beings, and losing breath when they can only find scraps of time to spend with their friends and families as they are overwhelmed with useless, mind-numbing administrative tasks. Perhaps, we have all become veritable hysterics! However, unlike the hysterics of Freud's era, we do not have the time to reflect on and process this physicality which, as a consequence, becomes fleeting and transitory. Through certain works of art that manage to arrest this transitoriness and express suffering in ways that we cannot escape from or ignore anymore, we can re-gain the opportunity to encounter it in a different form and process it more effectively.

Apart from works of art, psychoanalysis (and any form of radical psychotherapy) also serves the same aesthetic function – it cultivates a science of sensibility that attends to the suffering mind–body and the current shocks inflicted on it by the totally administered world. It is important, therefore, to understand the psychoanalytic notion of *sublimation*, whether in its cultural or therapeutic dimension, not only as a defensive, repressive process (which is one of the ways that Freud (1905) conceived it) but also as a transformative one (as it is often portrayed in the work of Bion – see Civitarese, 2014). Sublimation can thus serve not only to harmonise the requirements of the social structure to the body by repressing our 'lower' bodily urges, pains and affections and turning them into 'higher' cultural and artistic pursuits, mystifying thus the modern subject into 'mistaking necessity for freedom and oppression for autonomy' (Eagleton, 1990, p. 8), but it could also help us to give form to the body's everyday suffering so as to transform it into a powerful critique of the social systems that oppress us.

As the nightmarish vision of Michel Foucault's (1977) *panopticon* has become an all too frightening reality, and new walls are constantly being erected both between and within us, we, as fellow prisoners, need to find spaces where we are not being externally and internally surveilled so as to develop through a process of emancipatory sublimation a new kind of solidarity which encourage us to believe that this is not the only possible reality.

Psychoanalysis could provide this emancipatory, transformational space, as it encourages us to collect the scraps and fragments of broken messages that we secretly and subterraneously pass to each other in our ordinary everyday life – which usually fall by the wayside – and attempt to put them together into personal and collective songs of freedom, redemption songs, that still have the ability to surprise us and the structures, social, economic or otherwise, that try to control us.

This book is perhaps an attempt to collect these songs of freedom, these 'scraps and fragments' of the sublime in everyday life and give them importance by highlighting their power to move and change us. In the Kantian and Burkean perspectives mentioned above, notions of the sublime have been referring to the topic areas of *extraordinary, intra-psychic* and *high-cultural*, the notion of the sublime as something exceptional that comes from outside the experience of the everyday and unsettles it. However, in this book, we argue that the sublime also resides within and permeates our everyday life. Whilst still locating the sublime at the intersection of psychoanalysis and aesthetics that share the task of finding a way to represent the unrepresentable, this book aims to offer a more broad understanding of our encounters with the sublime, where the latter is understood to include *ordinary, inter-psychic, everyday inclusive*, and even *mass-media cultural* experiences. It is suggested that the sublime can emerge, for example, in the production and exchanges between individuals and popular cultural products as a particular way of sharing in the body social (not unlike Freud's 'oceanic feeling') as well as a similar immersion in nature and solitude. It underlies deep relational experiences of love as well as aspects of trauma, terror and pain.

The sublime can overflow and break down the psychological and social symbolic structures, and yet it is also what can put the human subject back together; it can be, in other words, therapeutic, just as therapy can be a source of the sublime. It can be a source of psychological crisis, but also a catalyst for renewal and transformation. The book aims to provide an understanding of various encounters with the sublime in our everyday lives and share insights on the ways in which we partake in these encounters; that is, how we author, survive and engage with them in order to make meaning, re-create and transfigure ourselves, above and beyond what social and symbolic structures can arguably do for us.

As various threads regarding the sublime in the everyday are interwoven in different, multi-disciplinary ways in all the chapters, we have decided not to divide the book into sections but to have one continuous flow of interrelated themes/perspectives running through the book, starting with an artistic/historical perspective and ending with a contemporary, political one.

The first chapter is written by the late Tessa Adams (and edited, finished and prefaced by Anastasios Gaitanidis) to whose memory this book is dedicated. In this short chapter, Adams warns that the psychoanalytic (i.e. Kleinian and post-Kleinian) and analytic psychological (i.e. Jungian) understanding of the sublime is too prone to subjective interpretation, being able to see artefacts only as either regressive or purposely transformational. This, she argues, is a 'psychological fiction' of the sublime – another attempt, we may add, to understand in a way that masters, determines, controls, rather than leaving art and the artist's role open to engaging with something not otherwise representable. Adams' argument is perhaps that the artist is a vehicle for a (collective) part of psychic life rather than a self-serving individual whose purpose and intentions can be determinedly analysed. Adams strives to keep the sublime at the border of the subjective and the social, imbued by the artist's everyday experience, yet not determined by it. Adams' sublime not only collects from but also extends into the collective psyche in ways that cannot be fully analysed.

In this sense, the sublime cannot be limited by certain structures or people, as various ideologies would often have it. The first attested use of the sublime in history stems from Longinus's treatise written in 1st century AD. His work would seem to be precisely opposed to the idea that sublimity is connected with the everyday. Unpacking Longinus's claims that the sublime pertains merely to the grandeur of literature and even requires a sufficiently sophisticated reader, Justin Murray explores the contradictions in Longinus' text to expose the return of the 'repressed' everyday. He exposes how, even in that seemingly most decidedly 'non-everyday' theory of the sublime, everyday experiences such as nature, theatre, or togetherness, inevitably underpin the sublime experience. Inevitably, too, Murray shows, the views of the sublime are wrapped up in and in turn support the prevalent political ideologies of the time.

Notions of the everyday tend to be relegated to regions characterised by messiness, the mundane and an attendant lack of lofty ideals and ideas, but it is precisely the misaligned usage of the everyday sublime which is uncovered, realigned and explored in the chapters within this collection.

From the perspective of a dramatherapist, Anna Seymour explores how the sublime is rooted in and contingent on both the individual's existent and emergent capacity to experience difficult feelings and the communal, material and cultural/political dynamics people are located in. In these circumstances, the realisation is that the sublime lies in the messy unevenness of life, its unfairness, unpredictability and imperfections, rather than transcendence or the fantasy that one is in possession of omnipotent control – indeed, such attempts to control can lead to farcical, comedic moments. Such moments are manifested in the form of theatre that involves active participation. Exploring the ideological, material and spiritual underpinnings of what can constitute the experience of the sublime, Seymour discloses communal rituals re-enacted in theatre and intrinsically linked with the rituals of everyday life.

It is the active participation at the core of dramatherapy that encourages the creation of sublime moments by letting oneself be present in the experience. Such 'surrender' allows for the shift in perspective and is one of the most often mentioned characteristics of the sublime.

In the next two chapters, Onel Brooks and Joseph Newirth, make sense of sublime moments by weaving experiences from the everyday and their therapy work. Brooks skilfully highlights how patient, continuous attentiveness and thought can transform even the most mundane and minute experiences into an aesthetic object, one that can support a healing gesture towards the representation of loss and love. Newirth uses personal experiences of sublime encounters with nature, and with the self in nature, as a bridge to encounters in clinical work that similarly felt both timeless and beyond speech, gesturing towards the limits of personal subjectivity but also allowing for the identification with larger experiences of being.

It makes sense that exploration of the sublime in everyday life would also include experiences around love. In a sense, all the chapters in this edited collection touch on a longing for connection, acceptance and love. The following three chapters explore these ideas more explicitly.

Anastasios Gaitanidis reflects on love as a sublime event, creating bonds with people that life gives and takes away without one's choosing, forcing one to face loss as well as one's own helplessness and mortality. Rather than making sense of mortality by finding a way 'to learn how to die' as a lover of truth (i.e. a philosopher), or by surrendering oneself to 'addictive' love as a true lover (i.e. poet), Gaitanidis argues that it is essential for truth to meet love (in the figure of the poet-philosopher) so as to be able to acquire wisdom through desire and come to terms with pain and pleasure, loss and happiness. In the next chapter, Polona Curk considers the topic of love in seemingly small everyday moments, highlighting the idea of how the act of playing and wondering with the other, is a conduit through which the sublime can be experienced and created in relationship with the other, if one is indeed prepared to surrender oneself in this way. Accepting that the meaningful cannot be controlled – even in the sense that it cannot be captured in ordinary language – one can sometimes discover in letting oneself go in play or make believe that a certain truth about life and oneself emerges. Agnieszka Piotrowska's chapter provides us with another angle on love, exploring love's influence as depicted in the art of cinema. When the 'everyday' is constructed as difficult, prejudiced and discriminatory, retaining a scope for the sublime requires openings of a different order, including encounters of the transgender, trans-cultural, trans-species and trans-disciplinary kind. Analysing two films depicting, ultimately, reactions to love and loss, the first one finds the sublime in the commitment to one's desire and submersion in music, whilst the second one ends the search in destructive sexual fulfilments.

Perhaps cinema, in opposition to therapy and our personal relationships, is adept at creating sublime moments that one can reflect on as a spectator from a distance: being in and (safely) out of the experience simultaneously, situated at the border between immersion and distance, it can educate one in specific ways. In the next chapter, Girish Jivaji presents sublime moments that are ever-present in 'ordinary' educational experiences. From the moment an individual is situated within socio-cultural, educational contexts, these contexts work to shape and create identities, and one's ambivalent relation to them. These available identities are presented as sublime, ideal objects one should aspire to. Jivaji explores the absurdity within this, and the veiled but immanent presence of shame that any such system deploys to enforce compliance.

Chris Vlachopoulos's chapter engages with the notion of the 'absurd' even more explicitly, relating it to one's obsessions with making sense in a way that would master or regulate uncertainty. He highlights how the absurd can be used as a literary device that allows for an encounter with the sublime by activating our core values, rather than meaningless, bureaucratic, or artificial rules that various institutions subject us to. Vlachopoulos wonders how we could deploy a cross-examination of psychoanalysis and post-modern fiction to interrogate and break the lens through which we view these rules, even if that means a disruption of one's comfort zones.

In the last chapter of the book, we return to the sublime in the political sphere. Examining the sublime as a challenge of the ordered division between 'reality' and 'fiction', Daniel Rubinstein enquires into how the idea of the sublime still relates to our experience of living in the 21st century, where conventional versions of our understanding of the sublime seem to fail. Rubinstein suggests that what is needed is a break with the Enlightenment paradigm and neo-liberal ethics, as the glitches in the symbolic order expose the fictional, ideological and constructed nature of this 'reality'. The sublime is evoked to help us find a response to the state of affairs where we and the world are 'under siege' (even when perhaps the siege is self-inflicted), but this will have to be an alternative response to the 'given' form of reality. Rubinstein deploys the figure of Diogenes the Cynic to remind us that in irrational times, rational responses can be limiting, offering scant possibilities of thought. Diogenes exposes the simulacrum of conventional 'choice' as the only possible option and looks to uphold something more specifically human: the ability for producing, truth-telling, imagining difference. Rubinstein's argues that the sublime can be *formed* as an everyday therapeutic-political agency.

To sum up, the contributors to this collection have touched on many differing themes around the notion of the sublime: some were expected – i.e. love, death, art, nature – and some were more unexpected, such as pornography, education, and openness to encounters of a trans-category kind. The authors have described minute, moving experiences that reveal implicit, buried personal truths as well as immense, overwhelming experiences that render one without words. The contributors have engaged with themes of the sublime that took place in contexts that were personal/political, private/public, and social/cultural. Some authors argued that the sublime allows the possibility to see things anew by illustrating the absurdity of old and cherished ideals. Others demonstrated that the sublime has the power to engage us with otherness, revitalising our sense of awe at the enigmatic power of our interpersonal encounters. In this respect, the sublime teaches us not to be afraid of exiting our ecstatic isolation and encourages a leaning out into the open of meeting the other.

Most importantly, however, all of the contributors in this book attempted to problematise how the sublime relates to the ordinary and the everyday. Within the existing literature, the sublime and the everyday are presented either in opposition or as separate points on a spectrum. One of the main goals of this book was not only to recognise the existence of this spectrum, but also to challenge these predominant notions and offer up a critique in order to recontextualise, revitalise and reduce the distance between the everyday and the sublime. It is our sincere hope that this book has offered multiple passages to the sublime in which privilege is not only given to extraordinary, distant notions of the sublime, but also to the intricate, nuanced, everyday and proximate encounters of the sublime, with their inherent possibility for connection, love, and imagination.

References

Adorno, T. W. (1997) *Aesthetic Theory*. Trans Robert Hullot-Kentor. London: The Athlone Press.
Burke, E. (1990) *A Philosophical Enquiry Into the Origin of Our Ideas of the Sublime and the Beautiful*. Ed Adam Phillips. Oxford: Oxford University Press.
Civitarese, G. (2014) 'Bion and the Sublime: The Origins of an Aesthetic Paradigm'. *International Journal of Psychoanalysis*, 95 (6), pp. 1059–1086.
Eagleton, T. (1990) *The Ideology of the Aesthetic*. Oxford: Blackwell.
Foucault. M. (1977) *Discipline and Punish: The Birth of the Prison*. Trans Alan Sheridan. New York, NY: Random House.
Freud, S. (1905) *Three Essays on the Theory of Sexuality. The Standard Edition of the Complete Psychological Works*. London: Hogarth Press.
Kant, I. (1914) *The Critique of Judgement*. Trans J. H. Bernard. London: Macmillan.
Lacan, J. (1989) 'Kant with Sade'. Trans James B. Swenson. *October*, 51, pp. 55–75.
Lyotard, J.-F. (1994) *Lessons on the Analytic of the Sublime*. Trans Elizabeth Rottenberg. Stanford, CA: Stanford University Press.

Chapter 1

Psychoanalytic fictions of the creative sublime

Tessa Adams and Anastasios Gaitanidis

Editorial note/letter: a sublime friend – the life and works of Tessa Adams

I would like to preface this chapter with a brief introduction to the life and works of my truly 'sublime' friend, colleague and mentor, Tessa Adams. Tessa was a remarkable, unique woman. Determined and obstinate, when needed ... gentle and caring, when her friends needed her. Her spirit was indomitable and her outlook towards life always youthful. She was 65 when I first met her, but I hadn't experienced anyone as 'young' as her. I often find myself thinking of my first encounter with her: I felt as if I was in the middle of a tornado. Her life force was simultaneously exhilarating and exhausting. But when she got to know me better, her power was transformed into this trans-liminal caressing force which protected me from the world's mindless violence. Her magnanimous soul became a port in the storm, a shelter from life's adversities.

She knew how to 'believe' – she realised very early on in her life that trust is a religious affair, not a scientific one. And she took a leap of faith in me. She gave me my first academic job, my first taste of Whitstable – the place she loved so much and inspired her artwork – and handed me the responsibility of finishing this book which was originally meant to be a joint project but was abruptly interrupted by the onset and rapid development of her dementia. She made me believe in hospitality and generosity ... She was the exception to the rule, to the ugliness that condemns most people to a kind of a perpetual miserliness. They are enamoured with it ...

And she hated ugliness: her life itself was a testament to the power of the 'aesthetic'. The beautiful and the sublime were categories she wrestled with as they carried a quasi-ethical dimension for her. 'Aesthetics is the ethics of the future' she used to say. She believed that works of art convey a sublime, sacred message that could be the basis for a moral re-evaluation of the world. That is why she adored religious rituals – this is where the beauty of the sacred song, image and act meet the transcendental, transformative realm of the ethical.

I remember driving on the motorway with her ... There were roadworks everywhere. We were unnecessarily delayed. I was irritated. She said: 'Look, Anastasios! Just look! Aren't they beautiful?' 'What is beautiful Tessa? I don't understand'. 'The road works, you silly. What else?' And she went on to describe the exceptional symmetrical arrangement of the pylons and traffic cones that made the whole artificial landscape so aesthetically pleasing. I was struck by her ability to not simply observe, but to look – really look – and find what is beautiful even in the most mundane (and, frankly, deeply frustrating) aspects of everyday reality. I thought she was blessed with a vision that could make the world sacred again. From that moment onwards, all road works delighted my senses as they were baptised in the pool of a sanctified gaze that could discern the extraordinary in the ordinary, the sublime in the everyday ...

The beautiful, the sacred, the sublime ... and mountains. Tessa loved mountains or, more accurately, mountains loved her. These anarchic perturbations of earth, rock and lava, these awe-inspiring, imposing structures were an unending source of inspiration to her. She enjoyed climbing them but, mostly, she loved painting them. Once I asked her to explain her attraction to them, why she felt so compelled to include them in most – if not all – of her paintings. She said:

> Isn't it obvious? They stand tall and alone, but they're also intimately connected with everything around them. Violent subterranean movements created them but nothing could currently move them. When a storm hits you, you don't want to be in the middle of a turbulent sea; you need to be in the midst of a peaceful mountain. Actually, you need to 'become' the mountain as you will be able to withstand, and not be destroyed by the force of the storm.

I learned to like mountains, but mountains never liked me. I could never replace the blue of the sea with the grey of a Rocky Mountain. I was, and always remain, too Mediterranean. Mountains are a source of sublime terror for me. My Odysseus could have never visited the Himalayas ... Edmund Hillary would have never been his companion.

But I admired Tessa's love for them. I could see why they were so important to her. They were the only thing that could remain solid after everything melted into thin air. Nothing else could survive. Mountains became the symbol of her resilience, the measure of her ability to initially survive the assaults of her mother and then the devastating losses of her twin sister and her beloved father. And she was still able to carry on being thrilled by the sublime nature of life and love in spite of everything.

Yet, there was an assault she couldn't survive ... The assault of this insidious disease on her brave and beautiful mind. She fought against it in the same way that the majestic lions fought against their royal hunters in the Assyrian reliefs exhibited in the British Museum. But it was only a matter of time before she was injured and captured. I felt the intensity of her pain when she finally admitted her defeat to me: 'It is so horrible, Anastasios. I don't want to believe it but I am losing my mind'. I couldn't deceive her: 'Yes, Tessa, it is horrible. But I and your friends will be here for you'.

And most of her friends were there for her. They took good care of her during this turbulent time, as she used to take good care of them when they were fragile and vulnerable. But at the end, I wasn't there for her as much as I wanted to. The gradual deterioration in my late wife's condition and her unavoidable death almost five years ago made it impossible for me to witness and withstand the progressive worsening of Tessa's condition too. Yes, I should have been less scared. I should have become a 'mountain' – but I felt more like a soft rock cliff being gradually eroded by the relentless, unending assault of the sea waves and the constant bombardment of the elements.

But I am here now, keeping my promise to Tessa by finishing this book with the help of another good friend, Polona, and all my friends who have generously contributed to the creation of this book – including Tessa herself who wrote the first chapter, although she never managed to properly finish it and I had to do it on her behalf.

I would never forget my interminable conversations with Tessa about our patients ... how I admired the depth of her care for them, her fearless, creative interventions. 'Do I dare disturb the dust in a bawl of roses?' she said (paraphrasing one of her favourite poets, T.S. Eliot) to one of her patients who didn't want to upset his family with his revelations. Her peer supervision taught me a lot – but it mostly taught me to leave all conceptual tools and rule books aside when faced with the immense pain of another human being. 'It's foolish to believe you could only use reason to explain the affairs of the human heart', she once said to me.

I believed her ... and because of her I have become a better therapist and, hopefully, a better person too. I don't know if there is another life after this one. I would like to believe there is – it is so comforting to know that Tessa could meet all my deceased loved ones and keep them company ... eternally. In the absence of this certain knowledge, I can be partly reassured by the hope that one day the wind will carry my dust and deposit it with hers and theirs into a pile that would produce a sublime artwork, a new life composed by all our dust particles. Until then, I will miss my mentor, my colleague, my friend.

Psychoanalytic fictions of the creative sublime

In the Summer of 2002 Bristol University presented a centenary celebration symposium in recognition of the birth of art critic Adrian Stokes. As a leading aesthete, Stokes developed his life-time project of welding psychoanalytic insight into art practice inspired by his experience (during the 1920s) of intensive analysis with Mrs Klein. It was not surprising, therefore, to find that the papers presented at this symposium demonstrated how psychoanalytic assumptions can service aesthetic judgement; that is, an account of judgement as a feeling-based appreciation and contemplation of the aesthetic.

Stokes' poetic writing, with its fusion of psychoanalytic understanding and art practice, gained him an almost mythical reputation during the period running between 1940s and the 1970s as one of the finest and most discriminating writers on art in the twentieth century. Scholars now see his work as instrumental in the establishment of what has been termed the British School of Psychoanalytic Aesthetics. School, meaning the collaboration and development of the debate that engaged art historians and psychoanalysts in the 'Imago' group, whose membership included Stokes, Segal, Milner and others that secured an on-going exploration of the artist's practice, process and product. Significantly, central to this fertile exchange was the viewer, that is, the way in which an artefact impacts on our viewing experience. In other words, attention was given as to how an affective work might furnish the recall of our earliest unconscious experience, namely, primary process.

From this position, it can be argued that Stokes' Kleinian influence, through his analysis and his personal/professional connection with Hanna Segal and other psychoanalysts, resulted in a large body of work devoted to his thesis, which demonstrates the way in which movements in the Italian Renaissance can be perceived in terms of psychological affect. It is clear that Stokes' engagement with psychoanalytic thinking indicated that aesthetic judgement could include the evaluation of the dynamic of unconscious processes. Furthermore, it was this feature of art criticism that brought psychoanalysts out of the consulting room to claim expertise in assessing 'good and bad art', of which Segal is an exemplar.

Segal's propositions are critical, not only in the way that she revisioned Kleinian theory to accommodate a more specific referent to the genesis of the creative process, but also in her associating aesthetic evaluation with psychopathology. That is to say that she offers a system designed to establish the way that we might distinguish works in terms of 'symbolic equation' and 'symbolic representation'; the former being the product of paranoid-schizoid phantasy, the latter depressive resolution. This is the polarity of classification that virtually locates one category in opposition to the other, as 'good' or 'bad', since she speaks about the oppositions of 'beauty' and 'ugliness' in respect of an artwork in terms of the harmony or disharmony of the artist's 'internal world'. By 1975, Segal was so convinced of her position in terms of authoritative statements about artistic practice that she produced an article for the public published in the *Times Literary Supplement*, titled 'Art and the Inner World' in order to promote her unequivocal mandate that, 'It is [the] internal world, with its complex relationships, that is the raw material on which the artist draws for creating a new world in his art' (Segal, 1975, p. 800). Here the implication is that the prospect of the artist reaching the sublime creation of a new world rests upon the status of the artist's internal world in terms of psychological maturity.

What is historically significant is that Donald Meltzer refers to the Imago group and Stokes' collaboration with Segal some 13 years earlier. This reference which is reported verbatim in Stokes' publication of similar title *Painting and the Inner World* (in which an extensive dialogue with Meltzer is located) advances the proposition that: 'Segal's formulation of the Depressive Position affords the *'mise-en-scene'* for aesthetic creation' (in Stokes, 1963, p. 25).

There are many gems within this erudite exchange from these distinguished men, including Meltzer's claim that Klein posited that 'only by knowing the genius of an object can we be certain of its value' (Stokes, 1963, p. 27). Furthermore, it is notable that Meltzer speaks both of the psychodynamics of 'successful and unsuccessful' art and the function of the gallery experience. 'Contemplating Art', Meltzer tells us, 'is a form of intercourse between viewer and artist – in exact parallel to the sexual relationships between individuals' (in Stokes, 1963, p. 31). Furthermore, he proceeds to discuss the attitude of the viewer on entering the 'gallery'. It is Meltzer's view that the gallery visitor is purposefully charged with an unconscious agenda, namely, seeking to satisfy primitive libidinal needs. That is to say, Meltzer situates the viewer, on the one hand, psychologically at work exposing himself to a situation of intensely primitive (oral) introjection 'through the eyes, ears and touch', while on the other hand, in contrast, 'passively receptive to the prospect of … exposing himself, in a masochistic sense, to the experience of having projected in him a very destroyed object or a very bad part of the self of the artist' (Stokes, 1963, p. 32). What we have here is an analysis of both the active and passive viewer in each case, seeking to be enhanced or repudiated by the artist through the process of projective identification.

We find that Stokes (in reply to Meltzer's propositions) appears to be in agreement with Meltzer's analysis of viewer and artwork in terms of sexual intercourse yet is concerned to ensure that the autonomy of the art object, which Meltzer omits to acknowledge, is not obviated. Stokes (1963) presents his position thus:

> As to sexual intercourse as a process identical in its method with relationship to the art object, while endorsing the interchanges with viewer and picture that you suggest, I would like to add that the relationship exists, as does the parallel, only because of the essential otherness, the character of self-subsistent entity, the complement to the breast relationship, that has been created.
>
> (p. 35)

Now, what is this essential self-subsistent otherness of the object to which Stokes refers to as the quality that he cites as 'the complement to the breast'? Certainly, the Kleinian drama of projection and introjection to which the viewer is exposed, according to analysts such as Meltzer and Segal, from their predictable psychoanalytic focus leaves little room for the concept of the art object as an autonomous agency. Art as object in their view is self-serving with no otherness, and the interaction of viewer and artefact is cast in terms of primitive gratification, or reparation, leaving no room for the trajectory of the artist's canonical gaze. What Stokes is alluding to, of course, is the social basis of art. That is that the artist is a product of art-historical heritage, where the clashes and exchanges of style have passionately revisioned the canon through movements, patronage and ideological alliance. That is to say, although Stokes can be viewed as a respectful ex-analysand of Klein, in his inclusion of the breast, and endorsement of Meltzer's post-Kleinian perspective, he certainly indicates an allegiance to the phenomenological experience of the work that goes beyond the simple trajectories of our internalised infant conflicts.

What seems to be the case here is that Stokes, as art theorist, would prefer to acknowledge the prospect that there is an aspect of the artist's engagement that cannot be accounted for – a social, collective dimension – that endures through time, pertaining to the mother's body but not wholly dominated by it. The way that Stokes' conception provides the object with autonomy is to suggest that there is 'a mechanism in art ... that forges the safety for the object' (Stokes, 1963, p. 25), a position that doubtlessly challenges Meltzer's (Kleinian) assertion that, 'There is no such thing as safety in object relationships' (ibid.). Thus, we see Stokes, drawn to adopt the object relations psychoanalytic aesthetic, fears that the baby (the artistic sublime) will be thrown out with the bathwater. That is to say, within the dialectic of the libidinal tensions of introjection and projection, Stokes situates the prospect of safety through a third state, termed 'resignation'. Elucidated in his publication, *A Game That Must Be Lost* (1973), the state of 'resignation' is described as allowing the art object to exist, as it were in its own right.

In mapping this highly influential interface between art theory and psychoanalysis which typifies the concerns of the Imago group in their struggle with the aesthetic, the question arises as to the place of Jungian thinking within the history of this movement's focus on the problematic of the visual arts. We know that Jung was acquainted with Klein, yet there seems to be no certainty that he either met Stokes or read his work. Clearly, the Imago group were meeting at the end of Jung's life, and Stokes' key publications *The Quattro Centro* and *Stones of Rimini* where available in 1932 and 1934, just at the time when Jung was exploring Picasso, Ulysses and forwarding his view of 'the Artist'. What is interesting is that Jung certainly would have shared Stokes' view that it is art's role to go beyond the gratifications that Meltzer's art/viewer intercourse proposes, in order to serve the society that it represents. For it was in 1950, at the time that Marion Milner (also a member of the Imago group) had formulated her thesis of free expressive drawing, that Jung (1934–1950) explained the task of the artist thus:

> The Work of the Artist meets the need of the society in which he lives, and therefore means more than his personal fate, whether he is aware of it or not. Being essentially the instrument of his work, he subordinates himself to it.
>
> (p. 15/161)

In fact, Jung goes as far to indicate a sublime purpose to the artist, whose calling is selfless and enduring, telling us that the artist is simply agency by stating: 'The artist is not a person endowed with free will who seeks his own ends, but one who realises its purposes through him' (Jung, 1934–1950, p. 15/101). So is this the 'mechanism' to which Stokes refers to, an objectivity that 'forges' its presence without insistence on projective identification? At this point, we can wonder about the poignancy and seeming insularity of Jung's position. It is almost as if he implicitly warns us not to meddle with the artist whom he casts as beyond reach. For instance, we are instructed not to appeal to the artist to divulge their artistic intention to us:

> We have no right to expect [the artist] to interpret (his art) for us. He has done his utmost by giving it form, and we must leave the interpretation to others and to the future.
> (Jung, 1934–1950, p. 73/161)

As we can see, this position leaves the viewer with a task, in contrast to Meltzer and Stokes who see the work in terms of 'intercourse'. From a Jungian position, the work is paramount – the artist has laid the table for our feast and departed. If he exists at all, he *is* the work. This is exemplified by Jung's following explanation that the artist is:

> in the highest degree objective, impersonal, and even inhuman – or superhuman – for an artist he is nothing but his work, and not a human being.
> (Jung, 1934–1950, p. 15/101)

Importantly what must not be overlooked is that Jung's higher sublime calling for the artist is specifically attributed, since Jung identifies the visual artist in two categories which indicate a virtual contrast of the sacred and the profane. These categories are deemed 'modes' of functioning, namely, 'visionary mode' and 'psychological mode' and it is to the artist of the 'visionary mode' that Jung attributes the 'other worldly' capacity. The artist of the 'psychological mode' is seen as drawing from the world, rather than creating anew.

This elevation of the 'visionary' artist as an ambassador of the sublime and the sacred, of course, is different to Milner's placing of all artistic activity as the, 'Primary identification of the living experience of the body' (Milner, 1987, p. 183). The artist's task is, in her terms, 'to give life to the bit of dead matter of the external world which is the chosen medium' (ibid.) The objectivity to which Jung refers to is entirely missing in Milner's analysis, since her site of creative experience is the body. And from this position, she makes the claim that the work:

> Must be an externalisation ... of the unique psycho-rhythm of the person making it. Otherwise it would have no life in it whatsoever, for there is no other source of its life.
>
> (Milner, 1987, p. 191)

Thus, for Milner it is the fabric of the body that informs the creative act. Just as our body products pre-occupied us in the ecstatic reverie of infancy, so too the artist is drawn to manipulate and transform media. Milner's sublime is located in what she terms the infant's 'orgiastic' pleasure of 'spreading the imaginative body' which depends, in her view, on the primary illusion that the infant has created itself.

What we find is that Jung's elevation of the artist as heroically objective has been little discussed in contrast to the psychoanalytic aesthetics forwarded by Segal, Milner and other Post-Freudians. Perhaps it is Jung's hesitancy, exemplified by his paper on Picasso, that creates academic unease, since in the opening statement Jung demonstrates a certain embarrassment in associating with the popular interest in Picasso of that day. As a psychiatrist, he tells us, 'I almost feel like apologising to the reader for becoming involved in the excitement over Picasso', and he follows by warning,

> If I venture to voice an opinion on the subject at all, it is with the express reservation that I have nothing to say on the question of Picasso's 'art' but only on its psychology. I shall therefore leave the aesthetic problem to the art critics.
>
> (Jung, 1934–1950, p. 15/204)

As we can see from Jung's statement, he is not prepared to engage in the prospect of aesthetic analysis, and from this we can assume that the project of the Imago group would have held no interest for him. However, ironically there is an element of aesthetic judgement within Jung's remark. For we find that the word 'art' of Picasso is written within inverted commas, indicating that Jung potentially doubts whether Picasso's work should be fully thought of as 'art'. It could be argued that with such reluctance to fully engage with the art project, it is an irony that it is commonly stated that, in contrast to psychoanalysis, the visual image stands privileged by Jung and Jungianism. This reluctance must be set against the legacy of Jung's involvement with pictorial representation. As he states before embarking on Picasso, 'For almost twenty years, I have occupied myself with the psychology of pictorial representation of psychic processes [he is now 57] and therefore I am in a position to look at Picasso's pictures from a professional point of view' (Jung, 1934–1950, p. 15/205).

We could imagine that Stokes might respond to this by asking: 'What is a 'professional point of view' when it avoids aesthetic evaluation deriving from the social-historical context of the work?' Or perhaps Stokes would cast

Jung's 'professionalism' as no more developed than that of Freud's, who modestly indicated that his intention was to avoid touching upon the problematic of the aesthetic when he stated. 'In the face of the creative artist psychoanalysis must, alas, lay down its arms' (Freud, 1928, p. 177). It could be argued that, in contrast to Stokes, both Freud and Jung use and revere the artist without meeting the substantial basis of their work: Jung in conceiving the sublime sacrifice of the artist, Freud in formulating his thesis of sublimation in relation to his analysis of Leonardo. Yet, equating Freud and Jung as equally distant from the substance of the artefact becomes problematic, since as stated, Jung's 20 years of exploration of the psychology of pictorial representation of psychic processes, sets him apart from Freud. Freud was simply unfamiliar with visual processes, while, as is recognised, the making of imagery, and the use of imagery were integral aspects of Jung's work.

However, it is significant that Jung illuminates his reluctance to engage with the aesthetic, by the nature of his explanation for his lack of full engagement with Picasso. We are told that to cover Picasso's work more fully, would be 'too wide, too involved' and 'too difficult' (Jung, 1934–1950, p. 15/204). Although Jung also cites the brevity of his essay as a limitation in being able to explore Picasso, his use of the word 'difficult' in my view is striking. Surely, this 'difficulty' precluding Jung from engaging with Picasso might be better understood within the context of how Jung situates the artist. With his emphasis on 'the super-human, the nonhuman and the distant artist', perhaps Picasso represents a breaking away from the system that Jung had constructed. It is as though this 'difficulty' in fully engaging with Picasso points to the potential of Jung being daunted, almost faltering at the enormity of the task of this kind of aesthetic comprehension. As we have seen, Jung holds that the 'visionary' artist is an agency of the sublime, with no will, simply a conduit for a higher purpose. As he elaborates:

> As a human being [the individual] may have moods and will and personal aims, but as an artist he is a 'man' in a higher sense – 'he is a collective man', a vehicle and moulder of the psychic life of mankind.
> (Jung, 1934–1950, p. 15/157)

Within this deification of the artist (the profundity of which Stokes would have most certainly felt a connection), we hear a resonant echo of Jung's poignant awe in discovering painting at the age of six. Of his life in the arsonage, he recalls:

> I particularly remember an Italian painting of David and Goliath ... a landscape of Basel. Often I would steal into that dark, sequestered room and sit for hours in front of the pictures, gazing at all this beauty. It was the only beautiful thing I knew.
> (Jung, 1995, p. 31)

What, then, is this Jungian legacy if the question of aesthetic judgement lies firmly in that darkened room? The answer seems obvious – for Jung the artefact remains split. The artist remains outside the room, to be revered, to produce the elevated work, inviting contemplation, which cannot be fully possessed. The image is to be canalised to service interpretation. It is interesting that we meet this split in the Art World of today. For although the discourse of Art Theory has integrated psychoanalytic insight, this is in contrast to the discourse of Art Psychotherapy which, by privileging process, has primarily eschewed aesthetic evaluation.

At this point, it is important to note that Jung would have been impacted by John Ruskin – the leading art critic and theorist of the Victorian era – and his approach to art. As we can see, Jung equally locates the artist and their work as both inspired and socially responsible – and, like Ruskin, the agent of change. As we have seen, this parallel is confirmed by many of Jung's statements about the artist, such as: '[The artist] plunges into the healing and redeeming depths of the collective psyche', and 'On the one side [the artist] is a human being with a personal life, while on the other he is an impersonal creative process' (Jung, 1934–1950, p. 15/161 and p. 15/157). The artist is not a person endowed with free will who seeks his own ends, but one who allows art to realise its purposes through him.

What we have here is a much more robust prospect for both the creator and the product. For Jung, in a similar vein to Ruskin, frames the artist as a cypher, sufficient to the task. Creative inspiration in both cases is received from a higher source. In Ruskin's case, it is engendered by God (the sublime creator) while for Jung it is engendered by the collective psyche of human purpose. There is a level of autonomy, particularly emphasised by Jung's comment that 'the [visionary] artist is one who allows art to realise its purposes through him' (Jung, 1934–1950, p. 15/157). Although Jung stresses that this mode '[a]lways takes its materials from the vast realm of human experience – from the vivid foreground of life', he emphasises that this process 'transcends the bounds of psychological intelligibility' (Jung, 1934–1950, p. 15/140).

According to Jung, visionary work derives its existence from the hinterland of man's mind that suggests the abyss of time separating us from pre-human ages, or evokes a superhuman world of contrasting light and darkness. Continuing in this vein, Jung suggests that works of the psychological mode never 'rend the curtain that veils the cosmos' – while those of the visionary rend it from top to bottom (Jung, 1934–1959, p. 15/141–143).

This brings us to considering what Jung would have made of Hans Holbein, whose portraits simply challenged notions of the sublime during the mid-1500s in order to offer a genre of unparalleled psychological portraiture that anticipated photographic realism. The distinction of Holbein's accomplishments owed less to the prospect of individual sacrifice, than to the fact that as a boy apprentice he had followed his father (an accomplished artist) whose techniques had been passed on to him. What is significant to this discussion is that notwithstanding his extraordinary painterly skill, Holbein's most celebrated painting, *The Ambassadors*, tells of the division of the church with the emerging preterits that provided, not only a division of nations, but the onslaught of death that would ensue in the failure of brokering a resolution. Thus Holbein, in irony, places at the feet of the sumptuously dressed Ambassadors an optical illusion of a skull. This skull appears – from the full-frontal view of the painting – to be merely an abstraction of something unknown, and at worse confusing, while from the painting's right-hand side, shocks the viewer into the urgency of its message.

How can Holbein's political artifice be seen beyond the extravagance of its intent? A mystery to art historians, his work is doubtlessly ground-breaking in that it courts no outcome; it simply and elaborately brokers a political warning.

The warning that Holbein's work demonstrates in turn exemplifies our own warning, which points to the potential for the psychoanalytic and the analytic psychological understanding of the artistic production of the sublime to suffer from subjective interpretation, from which position the artist is relegated as virtually redundant. Instead, we find that the Freudian and post-Freudian analysis of the artefact seems to map out in them the terrain of psychological functioning in which these works are either cast as regressive or, in contrast, purposely transformational. This rendering of artwork is (as illustrated above) potentially reductive, as it does not account for the idiosyncratic nature of artists nor the ability of the artwork to exist in its own right framed by the (art-)historical and political context within which its sublime creation takes place.

References

Freud, S. (1928) 'Dostoyevsky and Parricide'. *Standard Edition of Complete Psychological Works, Vol.* XXI, Trans J. Strachey. London: Hogarth Press.
Jung, C.G. (1934–1950) *The Collected Works of C.G. Jung*, Vol. 15, Trans R. F. C. Hull. London: Routledge & Kegan Paul.
Jung, C.G. (1995) *Memories, Dreams, Reflections.* Trans R. Wilson & C. Wilson. London: Fontana Press.
Milner, M. (1987) *Suppressed Madness of Sane Men: Forty Years of Exploring Psychoanalysis.* London: Routledge.
Segal, H. (1975) 'Art and the Inner World'. *Times Literary Supplement*, No. 3827.
Stokes, A. (1963) *Painting and the Inner World.* London: Tavistock.
Stokes, A. (1973) *A Game That Must Be Lost.* Cheshire: Carcanet Press Limited.

Chapter 2

The silence of Ajax
Reading Longinus against himself

Justin Murray

Introduction

Scholarship frequently pays lip service to Longinus as the first word on the sublime in Western thought. His treatise *On the Sublime* is the first attested use of the word in history – though it was not a word or concept Longinus coined himself. He is, however, rarely analysed in any great detail outside Classical scholarship. He is generally thought of as lacking a certain incisiveness which removes him from the centre of contemporary debates about the sublime. Often we see Longinus' broader definitions of the sublime invoked, without his specifics being analysed in any great detail. This chapter aims to redress this balance somewhat, conducting a close reading of *On the Sublime*,[1] with particular focus on some odd loose ends and seemingly extraneous details of Longinian content, in order try and discover whether Longinus' work *On the Sublime* allows for the possibility of the sublime in the everyday; and if not, why not.

Particular attention will be paid to the wording of Longinus' criticism of different authors' writing, in order to reveal the unconscious biases of the author. The aim is to read Longinus through the lens of Freud, or Lacan, as a literary critic would perform a Freudian or Lacanian reading of a fiction text, as well as highlighting points where Longinus anticipates or disagrees with these ideas. The many instabilities, contradictions and nuances of language in Longinus make it ripe for this kind of analysis, as has previously been recognised. As Macksey puts it: 'The story of the reception of [*On the Sublime*] has been one of renewed engagements with the author's subversively unstable oppositions between nature and art, the spoken and the unspoken, genius and craft, simplicity and complexity, concealment and dazzling exposure' (1993, p. 931).

This chapter does not work from one specific definition of the sublime, seeking instead to place Longinus' definition in dialogue with a broad range of contemporary sensibilities. In accordance with the focus of this volume, at all times the attempt will be to relate the analysis of Longinus back to the possibility of the sublime in the everyday – or, as we shall see, the possible reasons why Longinus is so set against this possibility. Since encounters with the sublime are dependent on whether the percipient recognises them as such, (see Vlachopoulos' chapter in this volume) and are by definition subjective – particularly when we are speaking of the sublime in the everyday – when a possible avenue toward encountering the sublime is mentioned, examples will be drawn primarily from my own lived experience.

Nothing is really known about the writer of *On the Sublime*: he would more properly be referred to as pseudo-Longinus. Theories about his background have ranged from his being a Greek freedman writing in the Roman world, to being a Hellenised Jew (due to his referencing the Old Testament alongside Classical sources, making *On the Sublime* an early example of comparative literature), though any hypothesis of this kind is based on conjecture. His name is Roman, but his treatise is in Greek – though this is in an age when it would not have been uncommon for Greeks to take Roman names and citizenship. A date of publication of around the 1st century AD is now generally agreed; previously, due to the claim of a 10th-century medieval manuscript, he was linked to either Dionysus of Halicarnassus or a 3rd-century Cassius Longinus, though few would now argue these cases (Macksey, 1993, p. 915).

The treatise is introduced as being addressed to a friend and fellow philosopher, Terentianus, and as being in response to a Caecilius, whose own treatise on the sublime Longinus is primarily responding to. This offers proof, if any were needed, that the concept of the sublime is not Longinus' coinage. Whatever conversation there was on the topic before Longinus, however, is lost to us – and several lacunae in the manuscripts of Longinus disrupt our understanding here too. Longinus begins by offering his thesis defining the sublime as 'a certain loftiness and excellence of language' (I.2) and mentioning a few general vices which frequently divert authors from the true sublime, before outlining the five elements he believes will lead to work that is sublime, which are, in order:

- A certain grandeur or loftiness of ideas
- Treatment of the passions; pathos
- Artifice in the employment of figures of speech
- 'Dignified expression', including word choice and metaphor
- Majesty and elevation of structure (particularly in reference to word ordering)

Longinus makes clear that the first two entries on this list are innate abilities, whilst the latter three can be acquired or learnt. For Longinus, the ability to create and experience the sublime arises from a combination of nature and nurture: it is 'a faculty rather natural than acquired, nevertheless it will be well for us in this instance also to train up our souls to sublimity, and make them as it were ever big with noble thoughts' (IX.1). The discussion is interspersed with scholarly tangents, including one extensive digression in which Longinus defends flawed genius over competent literary craftsmanship.

At the end of the treatise, however, Longinus takes a surprising turn. A sort of final coda responds to an imagined question from a fellow philosopher asking whether the sublime is possible in an autocratic world. Longinus responds to this with a short and highly rhetorical defence of autocracy, primarily on the grounds that the minds of today are too divided and runaway for independent, democratic thought, and that an autocratic leader is necessary to pull us onwards to a better age. As we shall see, this autocratic slant in Longinus' thinking and his politics of the sublime are inextricably linked.

Longinus' methodology is generally to mention a feature, and give an example of it he feels particularly apposite from the corpus of great authors from the very earliest (Homer) to those of less than a century's vintage (Cicero). 'Bad' examples, which for Longinus do not live up to standards of sublimity, or demonstrate an author falling short of or accidentally exceeding the mark, are also frequently used. Curiously, he takes examples from Demosthenes and Cicero as much as from Homer and Sappho: for him, an encounter with the sublime is equally as possible in hearing a piece of legal oratory as it is hearing a poem.

Some preliminary observations would do well to be stated at the outset.

1 Longinus' conception of the sublime is entirely literary in character: he has no interest in encounters with the sublime in nature or in any other source. 'How much more do these principles apply to the sublime in literature, where grandeur is never, as it sometimes is in nature, dissociated from utility and advantage' (XXXVI.1). It is this strategic positioning of grandeur that privileges the literary sublime over simple, useless natural beauty.

2 This restriction extends even to other areas of art: a sizeable portion of the text is devoted to arguing why literature achieves a higher degree of sublimity than sculpture or other art forms. He describes the effects of music on listeners, for instance as 'mere shadows and spurious imitations of persuasion, not ... genuine manifestations of human nature' (XXXIX.2).

3 For Longinus, there is an ideal reader of literature. In the discussion of his current depraved age, he asks: 'how can we expect, in the midst of such a moral pestilence, that there is still left even one ... critic, whose verdict will not be biased by avarice in judging of those great works which live on through all time?' (XLIV.10) As we deteriorate, it appears, we will lose the ability to judge the sublime from the ridiculous, and any hope of encountering the sublime in great literature, much less in the everyday, will be lost to us.

4 The sublime is something akin to an objective truth, which 'sways every reader whether he will or no' (I.3).

Together, these arguments seem to form a total barrier to the possibility of experiencing the sublime in the everyday in this the first treatise on the sublime in Western culture: the sublime, by this analysis, appears totally confined to an ivory tower of higher, elite literary forms, accessible only by a highly select few readers with sufficient learning and preparation – readers who may perhaps not even exist in our day and age.

Longinus' point of view is perhaps a natural consequence of the connotations of the Greek word translated as sublime, *hupsos*, a term which in Greek connotes loftiness or supremacy. (Our word *sublime* descends from the Latin *sublimis*, the term used in antiquity to translate *hupsos* (Macksey, 1993, p. 926).) This conceptualisation of the sublime as lofty, or heightened, is bound to dictate how it is understood. Indeed, the feeling of the sublime as something elevated or higher seems to coincide with the way the sublime has been analysed within the realm of psychoanalysis, which sees the sublime as *that which has been sublimated* (Saint-Cyr, 2012, p. 16). From the psychoanalytic point of view, encounters with the sublime could be any ordinary impulse, or even a 'lower' sexual or aggressive urge which, for whatever psychological reason, is sublimated and elevated into being perceived on a 'higher' cultural, scientific or artistic plane; 'the object raised to the dignity of the Thing', as Lacan puts it (1959–1960, p. 112). Many articles in this volume would argue that everyday actions, behaviours, thoughts or feelings that are neither 'higher' (cultural or artistic pursuits) nor 'lower' (immediate satisfaction of urges) can constitute encounters with the sublime, making the sublime part of the everyday rather than always something precisely 'higher'. The connotations of *hupsos*, however, only permit interest in the higher realms, and it follows perhaps naturally that this the only area Longinus is interested in.

Quite why Longinus is so against the idea of connecting the sublime with nature is unclear. Whether he is enlarging on previous discussion of the sublime or is a reactionary voice within a lost broader debate remains uncertain. Caecilius seems to have preferred 'flawless' works to the flawed masterpieces Longinus advocates (XXXIII.8). Longinus sets up voices within the treatise which offer other views on the sublime (e.g. II.1), though these may simply be straw men. Certainly, there is no lack of discussion of natural beauty in the literature and poetry that populated Longinus' world. There was a growing tradition in Roman poetry at the time to aim for condensed, learned poetry on obscure subject matter. Part of this movement included technical treatises in poetic form on subjects involving the natural world. Virgil's *The Georgics*, essentially a series of poems about specific areas of farming, which almost take the form of a technical treatise, participate heavily in this trend. Longinus' emphasis on the 'lofty' and the flawed masterpiece rather than the technically perfect short poem suggests an unstated bone to pick with this style of poetry; certainly, other poets from the neoteric school, such as Callimachus or Catullus, do not appear in the treatise. Longinus favours the epic over the everyday in his pursuit of *hupsos*; this may also explain his critique of Apollonius' *Argonautica*, a long-recognised 'Callimachean' epic, in his work (XXXIII.4) The idea that Longinus might be subtextually connected to Horace is nothing new (de Jonge, 2012, p. 291). It is possible, then, that Longinus' objections to the sublime in nature are more historically, contextually, determined than they initially appear.

However, as we shall see, it is taking Longinus a lot to sustain this highly constructed viewpoint, and the strain of maintaining such a stringent perspective leads to a sort of Longinian textual unconscious, comparable to the Freudian concept of the repressed, which will come back to haunt him in unexpected ways. Indeed, we may notice at first glance that argument (4) appears to contradict argument (3): how can the sublime be manifestly obvious as such to all men at all times when our ability to experience it is being lost to us? These are the sorts of internal inconsistencies this discussion will look to in order to deconstruct the text's outward appearance of stability. As we progress, ideas from the Lacanian psychoanalytic critic will also begin to filter into the discussion.

The sublime and power: turning to Freud

In order to justify this leap into a discussion of the Freudian repressed, and its return, let us examine the quote we used to raise Longinus' proposition (4) outlined above, where he describes readers affected by sublime content carried by forces beyond their control:

> To believe or not is usually in our own power; but the sublime, acting with an imperious and irresistible force, sways every reader whether he will or no.
>
> (I.3)

Already we see the language of power relations become central to the discussion – a context which prefigures Longinus' defence of autocracy and promotion of the aristocratic ruler. The notion of words enacting power over their readers is a concept Longinus owes at least in part to 5th-century rhetorician and sophist Gorgias of Leontini, an author he shows awareness of elsewhere (III.2). In his *Encomium of Helen*, Gorgias asks 'What cause prevents the conclusion that Helen, against her will, might have come under the influence of speech, just as if ravished by the force of the mighty?' (Gorgias, quoted in Dillon and Gergel, 2003, section 12) It is in Gorgias that we first see this conceptualisation of speech as force articulated. Gorgias is using this argument to emphasise the power of rhetoric (his own art), arguing Helen's blamelessness for the Trojan War on the grounds of her powerlessness in the face of words. Longinus here takes the concept and applies it more narrowly to the sublime.

It is also in this intertextual link that this dialogue of power relations acquires a gendered connotation, Helen of Troy representing the archetype of woman perhaps more than any other character in mythology. This strengthens the sexual interpretation of this passage: 'whether he will or no' introduces the issue of consent. Longinus' linguistic choices (or slips) are so remarkably sexual in nature – and there are more to come, as we shall see – as to merit the inclusion of Freud in analysing him. The equating of rape with encountering the sublime is a gift to the Freudian critic. His attempt to enact over-compensatory sexual violence on the reader is a classic behavioural response to repression, perhaps prompted by Longinus' apparent hate of his own generation's morals, as mentioned above.

Killing Homer: or, the inevitability of the nature comparison

Another example of Freud's return of the repressed may be found in Longinus' analysis of the sublime in Homer. For Longinus, the *Iliad* fulfils the criteria of *hupsos* better than the *Odyssey* does: 'Homer in the *Odyssey* may be compared to the setting sun', Longinus says: 'he is still as great as ever, but he has lost his fervent heat'. A few lines later, another example: 'Like the sea when it retires upon itself and leaves its shores waste and bare, henceforth [Homer's] tide of sublimity begins to ebb' (IX.13). His priorities lead him to a different conclusion from most modern readers, who find the *Iliad's* formulaic and interminable battle scenes much less accessible than the *Odyssey*, which strikes many as much more novelesque and approachable. However, neither Longinus' judgement, nor the fact that his proposal is founded on a debunked conception of Homeric authorship, need concern us.[2] What matters is the language in which he expresses his judgement. If there is one stylistic device that Homer is known for, it is the extended, or epic, simile. Many authors in *On the Sublime* are summed up in a simile – Demosthenes is similarly likened to 'a whirlwind or a thunderbolt', whilst Cicero is 'like a widespread conflagration' (XII.4) – though Homer is the first.

This phenomenon is not particular to Longinus: one would be hard-pressed to find an author in the ancient world who does not use similar comparative phrases which would have been seen as right and proper for all sorts of discourse, but in this particular context, the choice takes on a unique resonance. It is fascinating that Longinus frames his critique of Homer with the very device used by the author he is critiquing, whether deliberately, or else that the language of Homer has so infected him that no other choice seems available. The unusually literary quality of Longinus' treatise has long been recognised.[3] Gibbon questions 'which is the more sublime, Homer's Battle of the Gods or Longinus' apostrophe ... upon it' (quoted in Holroyd, 1837, p. 450). We can perhaps evaluate Longinus in the light of this reception. A Homeric simile is generally characterised as being extended and involving several details within the comparison. Here is one famous example from the Cyclops episode of the *Odyssey*:

Its crackling roots blazed and hissed, as a blacksmith plunges a glowing axe or adze in an ice-cold bath and the metal screeches steam and its temper hardens – that's the iron's strength – so the eye of the Cyclops sizzled round that stake.

(Homer, 2003, IX. 390ff)

All at once, we are picturing the blacksmith at his forge, then without warning we are back in the narrative of the Cyclops. And another from the *Iliad:*

As a snake in the hills, guarding his hole, awaits a man – bloated with poison, deadly hatred seething inside him, glances flashing fire as he coils round his lair, so Hector held his ground, filled with latent power, his bright shield resting on a jutting outwork.

(Homer, 1992, XXII. 91ff)

In these two examples we notice some of what are generally regarded as the defining qualities of the Homeric simile: length; intense vividness; the source of the image being drawn from the natural or everyday. Often, as here, it feels as if the simile is in danger of running away with the narration. Longinus' comparisons feel as if they are aiming for these conditions in several respects: comparing the Homeric corpus to one type of sun, followed by another, they create a mini-narrative across several clauses likening the ageing author to the progress of the sun through the sky, and with multiple elements of the comparison mentioned (light, heat, etc.).

It seems Longinus, like all in the Classical world, cannot conceive of literature without recourse to Homer, who cannot describe the world without recourse to nature, and in turn Longinus, try as he might, cannot conceive of describing the sublime without recourse to nature either. If we interpret Longinus' unspoken preoccupation with disallowing the possibility of sublime encounters with the natural world as a Freudian unconscious of the text – a repression of the possibility of a more general, demotic appreciation of the sublime – then these constant comparisons of authors to natural phenomena would signify a Freudian return of the repressed, a veritable arrival of Birnham Wood at the Dunsinane of his conscious mind. The Freudian critic might even interpret Longinus' obsession with Homer in a pseudo-Oedipal fashion. A Classical world obsessed with imitating and refashioning poetic forms between generations was indisputably hyper-aware of the *Anxiety of Influence* identified by Harold Bloom (1997). Homer was almost universally regarded as the father of Greek literature, and perhaps even of Greek (and by extension Roman) society more broadly.[4] In subjecting his literary forefather to critical analysis, therefore, Longinus symbolically 'kills' the father figure. However, it is an unsuccessful symbolic murder since he appears only capable of phrasing it within Homeric idiolect.

This is all to assume, of course, that Longinus' treatise is truly concerned with 'the sublime' rather than simply 'effective creative writing' – perhaps the fashion of the time was to write advice on writing under the name of sublime. Rhys Roberts (1907) has argued that sublime is a misleading translation of what is intended by *hupsos*. But let us apply the principle of charity here. Longinus could have titled his treatise *On the Literary Sublime*; he did not, let us take him at face value on this. But having shown no interest in the sublime in nature, three-quarters of the way through the treatise we read this:

> And this is why nature prompts us to admire, not the clearness and usefulness of a little stream, but the Nile, the Danube, the Rhine, and far beyond all the Ocean ... not to think that tiny lamp more wondrous than the caverns of Aetna, from whose raging depths are hurled up stones and whole masses of rock, and torrents sometimes come pouring from earth's centre of pure and living fire ... [Man] keeps his homage for what is astounding. How much more do these principles apply to the sublime in literature, where grandeur is never, as it sometimes is in nature, dissociated from utility and advantage.
>
> (XXXV.4)

This phrase would seem to allow the possibility of the sublime in nature much more than the rest of the discussion would suggest. However, though the style and eloquence of the passage would seem to be promoting the idea of the natural sublime, it only crops up within an argument that the great old writers of yesteryear knew that nature has a plan for us all, and planned that we should strive for what is good. It is as if Longinus' style is creating a separate argument from his content, one that runs counter to his premises. The obstacle is cleared, then, for the possibility of encounters with the sublime in such everyday circumstances as a sunset, or any other natural phenomena.

Literary criticism as psychoanalytic criticism: metonymy

We saw in the previous section how Longinus' use of comparisons for Homer belied his prohibition of encountering the sublime in nature. This Longinian obsession with comparison (and indeed, with all literary and figurative techniques) can be analysed further here with reference to another major field of psychoanalytic theory; namely, the work of Lacan. In Lacanian psychoanalytic criticism, comparison, or metaphor, is the linguistic correspondent of Freudian compression, when multiple symbols are condensed into one object. (Let us for the moment assume that simile and metaphor are performing the same job of conceptual substitution.) Now, of course, Longinus has no conscious interest in psychology, but Lacan's reframing of the unconscious as a language offers a bridge whereby we can bootstrap Longinian literary criticism and repurpose it as psychoanalysis. Interpreting Longinus in this unintended sense, if well-chosen metaphor creates a literary encounter with the sublime, this would suggest that the sublime can be encountered in everyday moments of psychological compression, when a series of external stimuli corresponds to our own internal symbolic landscape.

Lacan also argued that metaphor's primary function was to suppress (Lacan, 2004, p. 456), which supports the previous argument that Longinus' Homeric comparisons were symptomatic of his own repressions. Comparing Homer's writing to various natural features might be seen as betraying Longinus' ambition to defeat or surpass the father of Greek literature, whilst also rendering his opinions more palatable than if he had simply stated he was just a little past it by the time he sat down to write the *Odyssey*.

The other linguistic function which for Lacan also works on a psychological level is metonymy, the substitution of a part of something for the whole (Lacan, 2004, p. 453). This is the Lacanian psycholinguistic correlative of Freudian psychological *displacement*: an idea or person being signified by one of its attributes (Lacan, 2004, p. 455). Helpfully, Longinus also devotes a section to the discussion of metonymy, or, as he refers to it, 'the contraction of plurals into singulars', which 'sometimes creates an appearance of great dignity' (XXIV.1). For Lacan, the function of psychological metonymy is to connect along the chain of signification. This further shores up the link between Longinus and Lacan's conception of metonymy. In this fusion of Longinian literary criticism with Lacanian psychoanalysis, we have uncovered another way that Longinus might allow us to experience the sublime in the everyday: we can encounter the sublime when a stimulus is encountered which stands in as a constituent part of our own psychological language.

I recall, for example, a moment I might describe as an encounter with the sublime when first arriving at New York City. I feel a shiver down my spine; a rush of adrenaline that lasts for several hours and carries me through a breathless trip through the NYC subway and a first evening's hours of exploration. I associate with it a feeling of being very present, or alive. The New York skyline is not a clear-cut example of natural beauty, but silhouetted against the setting sun it stands in metonymy for all the associations I have with cultural products set in New York which I grew up with. It is these associations, connected to the visual stimulus, that gives this moment its meaning. The example of metonymy Longinus himself uses is a passage of Herodotus where 'when Phrynichus brought a drama on the stage entitled *The Taking Of Miletus*, the *whole theatre* fell a-weeping ...' (XXIV.1).[5] Here, the signifier of the theatre space stands in for the assembly of spectators. If we can read meaning into Longinus' choices of examples, perhaps it is symbolic that the example he has chosen is one of connection: the feeling of togetherness an audience feels in reaction to a sublime shared experience.[6] Is this theatrical event an example of an encounter with the sublime itself? It is entirely possible for an experience to have this effect on a group of spectators without being sublime. We may gain more information from Herodotus' (2003) context of the quote:

> and the people sentenced him to pay a fine of a thousand drachmas, for recalling to them their own misfortunes. They likewise made a law that no one should ever again exhibit that piece.
>
> (Histories, VI.10)

This famous anecdote suggests the Athenians did not entirely enjoy their experience of collective mourning – indeed, they were sufficiently scared of it to put measures in places to prevent a repeat of the experience. This perhaps pushes the moment more into the realm of the sublime than the simply sentimental. Whether the event actually occurred is neither here nor there (Herodotus' attitude to historiography pays little attention to verifiable fact), the point is Longinus' use of it. With the completed context, this would be an example not of metonymy, but of metaphor, as described above: the Athenians saw their own situation mirrored in the action before them onstage, and the combination of this with the shared-ness of the experience provoked a sufficiently intense experience to encourage them all to vote never to repeat it. The dynamic does not have to be entirely restricted to artistic experiences, however: everyday experiences are just as likely to create psychological metaphors of this type. Again, we see Longinus showing an implicit awareness of encounters of the sublime beyond what his own rules will permit.

Quite apart from anything else, this choice of example, an encounter with the theatrical sublime being presented to us as an example of the literary sublime draws attention to the possibility for encounters with the sublime in the shared experience of theatre as mentioned elsewhere in this volume (see Seymour's chapter in this volume). Theatre as, by definition, a multidisciplinary art form creates a problematic space for any attempt to ring-fence written literature as superior to other media. The water is further muddied by Longinus' examples from playwrights such as Euripides elsewhere: a modern performance theorist would lambast Longinus for drawing a line in the sand between Euripides on the page and Euripides in performance. Certainly, Longinus' own example, and his use of metonymy in describing it, opens the door for encounters with the sublime in shared experience, or at least for the togetherness of the experience to be a necessary condition of its intensity. The Freudian literary critic might argue this is Longinus sabotaging himself, choosing an example which does not bear out his own arguments. If so, this would constitute another return of the repressed in relation to proposition (2), the prohibition of experiencing the sublime in any medium other than literature.

The silence of Ajax

We have seen here how rereading Longinus' literary analysis through the lens of Lacanian psychoanalysis can help us destabilise him, allowing for conceptions of the sublime beyond the stringently literary. There is another phrase in *On the Sublime* which is a gift to the Lacanian critic. It appears in Longinus' discussion of the importance of 'loftiness of mind' in creating and experiencing the sublime:

> Sublimity is, so to say, the image of greatness of soul. Hence a thought in its naked simplicity, even though unuttered, is sometimes admirable by the sheer force of its sublimity; for instance, the silence of Ajax in the eleventh *Odyssey* is great, and grander than anything he could have said.
> (IX.2)

There is something of the postmodern to this idea, which, taken out of context, might seem to relate much more to the way the sublime is seen in chapters within this volume, where a silence, or even a thought, could be allowed to be an encounter with the sublime. Again, this feels like another source of instability within the treatise. Surely, whilst nobility is seen by Longinus as allowing us to understand more complex, lofty ideas, the sublimity in simple forms is actually something more widely available? Ajax's own nobility would probably be considered by Longinus prerequisite for this nobility of thought, but the emphasis on 'simplicity' belies this.

Let us interrogate Longinus' example a little more closely. The moment he is referring to is a point in Book XI of *The Odyssey*, when Odysseus is meeting the ghosts of his fallen comrades in the Underworld, and finds Ajax's shade is still angry with him over the events that led to his death:

> I spoke to his ghost in calming words: 'Ajax, son of faultless Telamon, even in death can you not forget your anger with me, over those fatal weapons? ... Come closer to me, my lord, so you can hear my speech. Curb your wrath: restrain your proud spirit'. He chose not to give a single word in answer, but went his way into Erebus to join the other ghosts of the dead departed.
> (XI.540ff)

In a sense, there is no genuine silence here. A genuine pause in literature (comparable to a moment of total silence in music) is rare, and would only be found in poetry or the postmodern novel.[7] By analysing this moment in the way he does, Longinus collapses the difference between a *mention* of silence, and a *genuine silence*, as if the Homeric bard had inserted a Pinteresque pause at this moment in his poem; in reality, of course, this just a series of words like any other. A pause in music or theatre would constitute a more genuine silence than this, but Longinus' overstatement of this example draws attention to the importance of the *idea* of silence here. This is not to say that all forms of silence are avenues to the sublime. However, once again the example opens the door for a broader, more everyday conception of the sublime: in moments of quiet reflection, these sorts of psychological transactions can be allowed to occur, perhaps, as with the silence of Ajax, when we have allowed something important to be left unsaid. This further problematises Longinus' own focus on literature: if words are presence and silence is lack, or absence, the idea of the sublime in silence should be anathema to him.

The Freudian critic, moreover, cannot resist analysing the choice of words here: the thought is not only simple, it is 'naked'. Although this is clearly meant to emphasise its honesty or simplicity, it could be reinterpreted as a slip, betraying a secret sense of shame at the idea described. The characterisation is repeated at XVIII.2, suggesting a significant level of penetration in Longinus' psyche. Longinus even refers directly to the genitals elsewhere as something to be hidden: when arguing that good writing should not 'stoop to what is sordid and despicable', he invites us to 'take a lesson from nature, who when she planned the human frame did not set our grosser parts … in our face, but as far as she could concealed them, [lest she] mar the beauty of the whole creature' (XLIII.5). It seems that, for Longinus at least, the very idea of associating an everyday thought or moment of silence with the sublime is shameful. We have here then another return of the repressed: Longinus is so concerned with the loftiness of literary content, so against the demotic, that he feels unconsciously compelled to describe the beauty of this moment of silence in terms that he elsewhere associates with shame. It is as if Longinus has sublimated the very notion of the narrow literary sublime itself; placed it on such a lofty pedestal that any slight allowance of a broader, more accessible sublime has to come with language he detests.

The political sublime

In the above section, we saw a destabilisation of Longinus' proposition (3), the restriction of experiencing the sublime to the idealised, learned reader. If the simplest of unvoiced thoughts can access the sublime, how can the sublime be so restricted?

As we mentioned earlier, Longinus argues we need to make ourselves ready for the sublime; most of the time our minds are too divided to activate our own genius or appreciate that of others. This triggers a defence of benign autocracy. It is not an area we might have expected focus on in a treatise on writing. It is a viewpoint he inherits heavily from Plato, who in Book IX of *The Republic* [8] likens mental division with the divided state under democracy. For Plato, the form of governance of a state mirrors the state of mind of the average individual within it. In his enumeration of the different types of state governance, he describes democracy as 'a charming form of government, full of variety and disorder, and dispensing a sort of equality to equals and unequals alike' (VIII.556c). Plato's problem with democracy is its tolerance of the less-than-lofty, which risks diluting the ideological purity of the aristocratic rule he idealises. Longinus inherits this in his coda-discussion of the relation of the sublime to society where, as we mentioned earlier, he fears for the future of the minds of today. 'I fear that for such men as we are', he says, 'it is better to serve than to be free. If our appetites were let loose altogether against our neighbours, they would be like wild beasts uncaged, and bring a deluge of calamity on the whole civilised world' (XLIV.10). Longinus appears to imply that the only escape from this is through a benign aristocratic sovereign, who, like Plato's philosopher-king, will be able to lead the kind of men that we are to a brighter future, and it is only through the intervention of this kind of figure that future encounters with the sublime will be possible and the genius of today's writers will avoid being frittered away. Indeed, his loyalty to Plato is enough to make him sink his teeth into Caecilius for having unfavourably compared Plato's style to that of Lysias (XXXII.10).

Unlike the Athenian democracy of Socrates and Plato, the world of the 1st century AD was one of dictators and autocrats: as of 31 BC, Rome's first Emperor, Augustus, ruled the known world, including all Greece, and had been hailed first as the son of a god (the divine Julius Caesar) and then as divine himself; and as of his successor Tiberius, his (adopted) son, the dictatorship had become hereditary. Either for reasons of necessity or genuine ideological commitment, Longinus' treatise props up the dominant ideology of his time (not that it probably needed him to). Žižek, following Lacan, argues that the sublime plays a key role in mediating political ideology. He uses the historical examples of the divine right of kings, or Stalin describing the Communist as made of 'special stuff' ... as examples of political creations of 'sublime bodies' beyond one's physical presence. The sublime, for Žižek, props up political fantasies (Žižek, 1989, pp. 162–163). In 2 AD Augustus was awarded by the senate the title of *pater patriae*: Father of the Nation, a perfect embodiment of Žižek's principle of the sublime body personifying (or here generating) the state.

I carry a vivid memory from my time in my school's Army Cadet Force unit; marching down Kensington High Street as part of the borough's Remembrance Day parade. The sense of being totally in step with a larger body in the context of a patriotic moment the crowds of onlookers, combined with the winter air of a cold November day and the music of a marching band, elicited an intense moment in my subjective landscape which I would class as an encounter with this sort of political sublime. The example illustrates that one does not have to live in an ultra-fascist dictatorship, or a Stalinist dystopia, to encounter this sort of sublime. We saw earlier how Longinus' power dynamics of the sublime are inextricably linked to his idealisation of a ruler who, like the sublime, will carry their lesser subjects kicking and screaming into a brighter future, *whether they want it or not*. Perhaps even Longinus' subtextual discomfort with silence observed above might be seen as an extension of autocratic regimes' well-known discomfort with the private internal lives of their citizens. Once again, it seems as if Longinus' definition of the sublime is not as confined to literature as he would like it to seem. Indeed, it seems Longinus depends on the sublimation of a benign messianic dictator for his views on the sublime to have any productive future meaning for the world in which he perceives himself to live. We encounter the sublime, then, when engaging actively in political discourse; but more problematically, for Longinus, when we submit ourselves to particular political discourse.

Conclusions

We aimed in this chapter to discover what Longinus' take would be on the possibility of the sublime in the everyday; and, if he were against it, to assess the validity of his reasons for this, and try to uncover any possible ways forward. Longinus would see this notion as absurd. However, as we have seen, there is a broader view revealed by reading the text against itself in the way that we have done. The Freudian analysis has helped us perceive Longinus' repressions in relation to the sublime as such, perhaps in relation to his literary forefathers' authority, whilst the Lacanian material allows us to open up more legitimate windows for reframing Longinus' precepts than he will consciously allow. We have seen how Longinus makes four key assertions which work against the notion of the sublime in the everyday. It is in relation to these assertions that we see his most egregious returns of the repressed, and it is by deconstructing each of these that we have encouraged Longinus to unconsciously permit experiencing the sublime in the everyday or removed the barriers from this.

This method has offered us a series of possible avenues touched on by Longinus (though by no means an exhaustive list) to experience the sublime in the everyday. We might find it in encounters with nature and natural beauty, the commonplace sunset as much as the extraordinary volcano. We might encounter it when experiences fit within our internal dynamics of metaphor and metonymy. We might find it in moments of meaningful silence or quiet reflection. We may also be somewhat unwittingly swept up in its force in political discourse.

One final internal contradiction may become apparent from all of this. As we have seen, there is an iconoclastic bent to Longinus' literary criticism – neither Homer, nor Plato, nor any of the other greats are spared his critical knife. The appearance of the 'return of the repressed' we identified in his literary analysis betrays a wish to rebel against authority. This strikes a contrast with his political engagement with the sublime, which, as we saw, seems to prop up the dominant ideology of his time. Perhaps this might be said to betray a subconscious insecurity even with his own proposed political programme.

One might question the value of returning to Longinus in the way we have done, or to bother examining thinkers of the past in too much detail. In a sense, the only reason to look back to Longinus, or any thinkers from the past, is to see how they relate to or affect our current or future thinking. Whilst we presume ourselves not to think of Longinus as too central to current debates on the sublime, when the notion of the sublime was rediscovered in the 18th-century Longinus was in many ways a foundation stone for thinkers such as Burke and Kant. Some of his connotations of *hupsos* have certainly persisted into the present day. As we have seen, however, that foundation stone is not only internally shaky, but has also signalled the connection between restrictive, value-charged definitions of the sublime and right-wing ideologies. Why not, then, fling open the doors to the sublime in the everyday?

Notes

1 All references to and translations are from Longinus (1890) *On the Sublime*. Trans. H. L. Havell.
2 Few scholars would now dispute the fundamentals of what is known as the Parry-Lord hypothesis, which places Homer at the end of a long tradition of formulaic semi-improvised oral epic poetry, and challenges the notion of one poem having been composed before the other (Graziosi and Haubold, 1995).
3 Macksey (1993, p. 914): 'Its style, range of reference, power of explication, and stunning reversals of conventional oppositions all clearly set it apart from other pedestrian treatments of diction or regional rhetorical effects.'
4 Cf. Herodotus (2003): 'It was Hesiod and Homer who first explained to the Greeks the birth of the gods, gave them their names, assigned them their honours and spheres of expertise, and revealed their appearance' (Histories, II. 53. ll.2–3).
5 In a literary sense, this is of course an example of synecdoche (the whole standing in for the parts), rather than metonymy, but since on a broader level metonymy applies to any form of conceptual substitution of this kind, perhaps this need not concern us.
6 Hertz (1983) has in a similar vein analysed Longinus' sequence of quotations and found patterns of meaning in his choices of passage.
7 E.g. in *The House Of Leaves* by Mark Danielewski, the author restricts us to one word per page to illustrate the feeling of a chase sequence; in *Filth* by Irvine Welsh, the introduction of the character of a tapeworm is signalled by several pages of '0's interspersed with the word 'EAT' at intervals.
8 All references and translations are from Plato (2007) *The Republic*. Trans. H. D. P. Lee.

References

Bloom, H. (1997) *The Anxiety of Influence: A Theory of Poetry*. Oxford: Oxford University Press.
Dillon, J. and Gergel, T. (Trans) (2003) *The Greek Sophists*. London: Penguin Books.
Holroyd, J. (1837) *The Miscellaneous Works of Edward J. Gibbon*. London: Bell Yard.

Herodotus (2003) *The Histories*. Trans A. de Sellincourt. London: Penguin Classics.
Hertz, N. (1983) 'A Reading of Longinus'. *Critical Inquiry*, 9, pp. 579–596.
Homer (1992) *The Iliad*. Trans Robert Fagles. London: Penguin Classics.
Homer (2003) *The Odyssey*. Trans D. C. H. Rieu. London: Penguin Classics.
Graziosi, B. and Haubold, J. (2005) *Homer: The Resonance of Epic*. Bristol: Bristol Classical Press.
de Jonge, C. C. (2012) 'Dionysius and Longinus on the Sublime: Rhetoric and Religious Language'. *The American Journal of Philology*, 133, pp. 271–300.
Lacan J. (1959–1960). *The Seminar, Book VII, The Ethics of Psychoanalysis*. London and New York, NY: W. W. Norton & Company, 1992.
Lacan, J. (2004) 'The Instance of the Letter in the Unconscious or Reason since Freud'. In Ed J. Rivkin and M. Ryan, *Literary Theory: An Anthology*. Oxford: Blackwell, pp. 447–461.
Leitch, V. B.*et al.* (Eds) (2001) *Longinus. The Norton Anthology of Theory and Criticism*. New York, NY: W. W. Norton & Company, pp. 135–154.
Longinus (1890) *On the Sublime*. Trans H. L. Havell. London: Macmillan.
Macksey, R. (1993) 'Longinus Reconsidered'. *MLN 108 Comparative Literature*, pp. 913–934.
Plato (2007) *The Republic*. Trans H. D. P. Lee. London: Penguin Classics.
Rhys Roberts, W. (1907) *Longinus on the Sublime*. Cambridge: Cambridge University Press.
Saint-Cyr, V. M. (2012) 'Creating a Void or Sublimation in Lacan'. *Recherches en psychanalyse*, 13, pp. 15–21.
Žižek, S. (1989) *The Sublime Object of Ideology*. London: Verso.

Chapter 3

The sublime in the everyday
How theatre crafts art out of the ordinary

Anna Seymour

Introduction

In his book *Nine Ways the Theatre Affects Our Lives*, dramatherapist Roger Grainger (2013) asks:

> So why do we go there? Why, in fact, do we keep going there? The answer is of course, that this is a world that has welcomed us before. We embark on our own journey in the expectation that by doing so we will be rewarded. The experience of theatre has left us feeling enriched, even when we have not been emotionally shaken by what we have been involved in – not in spite of these things, but actually because of them, our pain carrying us to the heart of the storm so we may know the calm that follows.
>
> (p. 81)

Grainger captures the paradoxical invitation of theatre which we will be engaged with in this chapter. Like the concept of 'the sublime' itself, at its heart lies contradiction and as such the themes of this book are both a delight and a provocation. The concept of 'the sublime' evokes lofty, awe-inspiring, extraordinary experiences of perception and feeling, whereas here we are invited to engage with the ordinary. What a relief!

The entanglements of philosophical or indeed psychoanalytic discourse are seductive but ultimately need to land within the materialism of encounter. Written from the perspective of a dramatherapist and theatre scholar, the first part of this chapter will draw on an eclectic mix of examples taken from different types of dramatic performance to argue that there is an ideological and material underpinning to any conception of what constitutes the sublime. In doing so, it makes a case for the continued need to consider the contexts in which therapeutic or artistic encounters take place and asserts that we cannot deracinate the experience of 'the sublime' from the material circumstances surrounding it. Equally it will argue that there is a dialectical relationship between what is a subjectively experienced or individually produced and common shared experience.

Therapy happens in temporal, material contexts, between people. In therapy, as in artistic *encounter*, a dialectic is engaged between the constructed nature of the meeting, which frames the encounter, and the explorative relationship of therapist and client which of itself continually plays with the 'constructed' and the emergent. It is this tension, core to the creative process, that produces change. The nature of 'the play' that takes place is of course conditioned by the orientation of the therapeutic approach and we could think about the play both as a process: playing, being playful, or as an object: creating 'a play'. In dramatherapy both are true. As a practice, it is predicated on working with the dramatic metaphor 'the thing in between' which the philosopher Jacques Ranciere describes as 'the thing that belongs to no-one' (Ranciere, 2011, p. 15).

In therapy, whilst moments are consciously or unconsciously 'constructed' via narrative, familiar patterns of behaviour, and feeling responses, which provide containment, there is an 'inbetween-ness' at work that defies categorisation and can only be experienced at a level which we might at times describe as 'the sublime'. It is where we arrive at a profound sense of self-knowledge or being, which defies articulation.

Thus, there is an 'extraordinariness' already at play in both therapy and our relationship with artworks which asks us to step by the side of 'the ordinary', in order to encounter something *different* that seeks to provoke change. Both demand a willingness to experience the discomforts of engaging with some difficulty or other and encourage our commitment to take part. Yet self-evidently, the depth and capacity of our engagement is conditioned by the circumstances and the histories that we bring to bear.

In the second part, the chapter will reflect on the roots of drama as a collective art form, in ritual healing and religious practices with a brief reference to contemporary religious ritual. Whilst these practices can be considered 'extra'-ordinary insofar as they exist 'outside' of everyday life or in a special, reserved place and time, they are nonetheless *crafted* out of ordinary experience and imbued with the hopes and expectations, perhaps even fear of those who take part. Some of this fear will be to do with the allocated roles in ritual and the ceremonial conventions which become socially embedded. Spaces and actions are delineated. For instance, in the Catholic mass, it is considered an honour for a member of the laity to carry the bread and wine to be consecrated to the altar and this must be done with reverence and humility. Only certain members of the congregation may enter the sanctuary established around the altar in specific roles and only speak at specified times. The priest is the sanctified conductor of worship. A sense of awe is created and an expectation of ways of behaving that can carry the fear of 'getting it wrong'.

The anticipation of an elevated experience mixing wonderment with potential anxiety typifies descriptions of the sublime, and it could be that precisely the fear associated with imaginatively or bodily entering into an unfamiliar role or landscape is what exacerbates its potency. The mixture of relief and elation that actors often describe after performance can often be accompanied by a sense of forgetfulness of 'what really happened', since the pressures and exposure of performance can lead to a sense of entering another world, a detachment from everyday reality into dramatic reality. As Susana Pendzik (2006) states:

> Dramatic reality is imagination manifested. It is an *as if* made real, an island of imagination that becomes apparent in the midst of actual life. Dramatic reality involves a departure from ordinary life into a world that is both actual and hypothetical. It is the establishment of a world within the world ... Dramatic reality exists between reality and fantasy: it partakes of both and belongs to neither.
>
> (p. 272)

This chapter argues that the sublime exists and emerges within the 'messiness', contradictions and tensions of everyday life. These are the concerns of theatre and dramatherapy because it is only through engaging with the risks of conceiving that things could be other than they are that change can take place. The striving towards 'something other', beyond what can be presently perceived is an act of hope and it is this which dramatherapists believe is the source of healing through the active engagement of the client.

This requires a measure of sensitivity in appreciating the client's cultural referents, a lack of snobbery in recognising different tastes and an awareness of how we acquire a cultural 'vocabulary'.

Context is everything

Debates in the contested territory of high art and popular culture have been well-rehearsed since the late 1960s, by cultural theorists and political activists rejecting the pretensions of bourgeois art and asserting the capacity for there to be 'art for all'. No longer should we regard the capacity to appreciate a fine voice or a felicitous turn of phrase as only appreciable by those of 'finer sensibilities', i.e. those of the middle classes. And yet questions of availability, accessibility, value and power remain. Glyndebourne opera, for example, is accessible to the very few as live art and its cultural trappings from dress code to cloaked ushers to the champagne picnics on the lawn in the extended interval ensure its class presumptions. The fact that the 'bad boy' of opera Peter Sellars chooses to regularly direct there merely ensures that it can boast a 'cutting edge' mentality whilst at the same time preserving its elitist charm. In contemporising classical texts, Sellars' work forms part of the ever-renewing capacity of theatrical re-invention, but how is this conditioned?

Plays and performances capture metaphors that reflect the collective concerns of their times yet their life continues, much like Winnicott's concept of 'the projective object', as available 'containers', other worlds and narratives which can hold experience. Metaphors, as Lakoff and Johnson (1980) point out, in the title of their seminal book are what 'we live by' but often provide a cloak of safety when difficult things need to be expressed or explored. This is the process of dramatic distancing, a core concept of dramatherapy practice where, in the boundaried space of dramatic reality (created by client and therapist) fictional truths are respected as an imaginative extension of everyday truths. In this respect we experience theatre's capacity to both universalise and personalise. Metanarratives are lived subjectively and shift accordingly and they may account for the persistent nature of classic texts to be vehicles for continual interpretation. In testing their durability fresh meanings may emerge. From Shakespeare to Ibsen's 'problem plays' there is no shortage of revivals we can turn to from the classical canon appearing in contemporary stagings. At the time of writing, the UK National Theatre is enjoying considerable success with a musical version of Ibsen's Peer Gynt (2019) whilst the Royal Opera House revives *The Marriage of Figaro* (June/July 2018–2019 Summer season).

Peter Sellars' production (1988) was designed to represent the 52nd floor of Trump Tower. In a 2016 interview in the New York Times, Sellars refers to the astonishing parallels between the opera and what was emerging with the now *President* Trump. In the opera, Count Almaviva debates whether or not to claim his ancient right of 'droit de seigneur' whereby he can demand to 'take' the maid Susanna, who is betrothed to his servant Figaro, before their wedding night. In the context of Trump's locker room talk about 'grabbing women by the pussy', the setting becomes all too real – crudely 'ordinary'. On the one hand, there is acclaimed 'sublime' music, whilst at the same time the contents of the opera engage with serious, uncomfortable issues, and the narrative examines power and hierarchy, whilst affording a sense of democracy in the music as servants are given arias and trios as much as their masters. Thus, the contradiction heightens the potentiality for sublime moments as the musical aesthetic resides within the awfulness of dark matters. This is a relational principle that is both therapeutic and aesthetic: by going through pain, by being with what we fear most, there is a possibility to move forward by 'being differently' with that pain. As Roger Grainger (quoted in Andersen-Warren and Grainger, 2001) puts it:

> To discover what hurts us so much, the very thing that cuts us off from other people and makes us feel different, rejected, inferior, hopeless, is in fact the pledge of our belonging … (it) dignifies our suffering in a way that nothing else can.
>
> (p. 148)

This 'dignifying' I would argue is the job of art whereby the expression of raw emotional defencelessness becomes somehow 'exquisite' elevating experience to what could be described as sublime.

Thus, theatre makers focus our attention in new ways. The seemingly inconsequential events and exchanges of everyday life when crafted into the fictional reality of a play or performance can be valued differently. *The Marriage of Figaro* after all begins with Figaro measuring the bedroom to see if the bed will fit in. With mistaken identity, disguise and farcical concealments in wardrobes, behind plant pots and statues, the serious nature of the core plot is 'played with'. The imperfections of life provide dramatic tension but highlight anticipation of what might come.

So the argument I am threading through this chapter is an obvious one, but worth stating, that artworks are constructed and 'positioned' just as audiences are, but they are open to interpretation, appropriation and transformation. Towards the end of *Marriage of Figaro* there is a moving duet between the Count and his wife, which precedes the final chorus, 'chori en tutti'. In it the Count begs forgiveness from his wife. Sellars chose to interpret this as a 'sublime moment of transformation' wherein there could be reconciliation, followed by the final jubilant, some might say raucous, chorus. How believable this decision was is up to the judgement of the individual; nonetheless, in theatrical terms the narrative closure brings a 'happy ending', a beckon to healing and hope. Directorial decisions, however, can only guide an audience towards their intentions; how they are experienced will be subject to all the factors we are discussing, and this is the potentiality of theatre to create meanings 'in spite of itself'.

Is there a case then for thinking about 'the sublime' as something that is based in opportunity? Not simply 'being in the right place at the right time' but conditioned by life opportunities that have been available, that enable individuals' capacity for empathy and emotional connectedness? Each one of us carries a vocabulary of metaphorical reference points that we refer to and these again are developed through life experience. Metaphor becomes a 'shorthand' way of describing how things are.

But dramatherapy goes beyond the notion that by analogy we can observe human life through the metaphors of theatre, i.e. that our clothes are 'costumes', we all have 'life scripts' etc. Dramatherapists fashion and invite drama into the therapy room with an intentional purpose to use its processes for healing. The therapeutic relationship can be conceived through the dynamics of drama and the aesthetics of theatre, based on the understanding that drama is a fundamental part of human development and existence. As the same time theatre is not only about reproducing life in another form but about playing with the artifice of theatre in absurd, grotesque, maybe even profane ways. Because it is constructed and relies on the commitment of its participants to achieve believability, the self-conscious use of theatre which draws attention to its own constructedness is part of its vocabulary. From the use of 'direct address' to the audience to the Shakespearian 'play within the play' in *Hamlet*, *Macbeth* or *Taming of the Shrew*, there is a complicity created between stage and audience which is thrilling when it challenges conventions. Theatre can invite risk and fantasy because it is both 'real and not real'.

Therapists may apply dramaturgical principles when they think about the structuring of narrative, the attachment to 'things', the bodily presentation of clients. The therapy room can be regarded as the *mise-en-scene* where in each object and embodied moment, the presence of therapist and client(s), can be reflected on through theatrical analogy or in the case of dramatherapy, entering into dramatic reality more or less formally.

Nonetheless, despite the attention to its own constructed nature, we can still observe the cultural influences on how we speak about ourselves and explain ourselves to ourselves. If we can see the influence of genre on story-telling, we can ask what kind of story is being told and how it is being told. What linguistic tropes do we find easy to associate with? What is alien to our expression? What might be considered 'natural', 'normal', 'real'?

Naturalism and realism

The concept of 'as if' the stage action is real life, is primarily associated with Stanislavski's (Merlin, 2014) work in the Russian theatre, at the turn of the 20th century. It marked a revolutionary turning point in dramatic representation. Through this 'suspension of disbelief' it enabled the audience to settle down into a comfortable relationship with plays that were a step away from ordinary existence but invited identification. Paradoxically, Hamlet's dilemma of 'to be or not to be' could be, to borrow from dramatherapist Robert Landy (1991, pp. 7–15) reframed in aesthetics terms as 'to be *and* not to be'. In other words, it could be what Winnicott might describe as 'same but different'. Theatrical artifice was replaced by 'given circumstances' and Stanislavski's quest for authenticity and truth required actors to research the possible 'real' background to fictional characters as well as create believable emotion on stage. They were to draw from everyday observation rather than from the previously codified gestural patterns of staged emotion. If actors could not achieve this then they were to draw on what he termed 'affective memory' (Merlin, 2014) whereby accessing their own emotional responses from a comparable situation, the actor might transfer feelings from their personal lived experience onto the character they were playing. In effect, this could be compared with psychoanalytic notions of transference. Stanislavski was highly influenced by the work of psychologist Theodore Ribout (quoted in Benedetti, 2008) in applying the concept of affective memory.

However, naturalism, once revolutionary, became corrupted in a number of ways, most significantly in the assumption about what we take to be self-evident. Both aesthetically and politically we can see this in populist movements that purport to represent taken for granted truths and deny critical appraisal. The other danger of naturalistic acting is the intensive focus on interiority and individual psychology where the emphasis on individual's process begins to take precedence over the other elements, most notably the given circumstances. We have two problems here: the 'taken for granted' can lead to determinism, where the outcomes become inevitable, the given circumstances already teleological; and the focus on individual psychology which can become individual responsibility or pathology. In these senses the 'natural' becomes 'unnatural' in so far as the systemic constructedness of relationship and context is lost. The excesses of expressionist movement provided a counterfoil.

Then came Brecht, who like Stanislavski argued in his essay 'The Popular and the Realistic' (Brecht, 1980) for 'truthful representations of reality'. He stressed the urgency of the matter in the face of rising populism which resulted in Nazism. Brecht developed a theatre of realism 'for the scientific age', by which he intended to provoke the audience into critical reasoning rather than be overwhelmed and therefore incapacitated by feeling. Yet this is not to say that he created a theatre devoid of feeling and, as this chapter argues, the sharpness of his critical acuity and aesthetic crafting produces the potential for searing and profound feeling emerging out of 'ordinary' circumstances. In his plays, Brecht was at pains to reveal 'society's causal networks', to use theatrical aesthetics not as illusion but metaphorical pathways to deeper understanding of how human relationships are conditioned by the political context. His major plays were all written in exile as he fled from Germany to escape a death sentence.

His final play *The Days of the Commune* (Brecht, 1978), which was not performed until after his death in 1956, marked a distinct change from Brecht's other plays. It is the only play based on an actual historical event and he drew heavily on Lissagaray's (2012) eyewitness account. The play combines real and fictional characters and thus there is a blend of created dialogue and actual reportage taken from archival records. He also drew on Marx's (2014) *Civil War in France*. The play presents moments where the extraordinary achievement of the communards is celebrated but always in the shadow of its temporary nature. Their spirit and determination is always accompanied by intense debate and a whole range of political opinion is laid out in detail, ranging from the cautious to the reckless. The characters are neither sanctified nor valorised. They are flawed and uneven, struggling to make sense of things unfolding but holding onto a vision of a different society.

The intimacy of *the ordinary*, small, everyday things and exchanges is exemplified in a scene set days before the final crushing of the Commune where individuals were lined up and shot. (This event is still commemorated at the Mur des Fédérés in the Pere Lachaise Cemetery in Paris). To celebrate Whitsun, the ancient Madame Cabet who has been to church but sewn four extra sandbags for the barricades to compensate for her absence, wishes to preserve the tradition of distributing gifts to her comrades and yet there is so little to share. Thus, she itemises and distributes what she has: a mouthful of wine, an apple to be shared, two buns and a tie she has made (though the flag is now shorter, she wryly states). Finally, one person remains for whom she has nothing; her hands are empty. And so she gives a handshake, acknowledging this is all she has to offer.

Brechtian aesthetics, working in the modernist tradition, do not seek to smooth out experience but rather, through juxtaposition, montage and drawing attention to the constructed nature of the drama, open up critical questioning. Indeed, at the end of his life Brecht wrote about how theatres might become like law courts where the audience could sit in judgement deciding the outcomes of the drama. How might this connect with 'the sublime'? Could it be through the exhilaration of finely crafted argument, intellectual gymnastics? The rhetorical flourishes of persuasive argument or the cool refinement of making judgement, which, appealing to a universalised sense of what 'social justice for all' might ideally afford, offers a profound and simultaneously transcendent affirmation of humanity. The Brazilian director Augusto Boal (1998), working in the Brechtian tradition, created *Legislative Theatre* as part of what he termed the 'arsenal of the oppressed'. Along with Forum theatre, image theatre and other methods he invited the audience to come onto the stage and step into the role of the protagonist in order to change the ending of the play, but also to rehearse possibilities. Witnessed in the collective context the potentiality of such a form for community engagement is obvious and is now well known across the world.

Brecht, of course, explored the question of judgement in any number of ways but most strikingly in the judge's determination in *The Caucasian Chalk Circle* (Brecht, 2007) In this play, the 'natural mother' and the adoptive mother of a child are pitted against each other with the child placed in the centre of a chalked circle. They are invited to each take his hand and pull, the victor to be awarded custody. Grusha, the servant girl, refuses to pull, and is thereby designated the true mother to the child since she will take a risk to preserve the child. (In deriving this story from Solomon in the Old Testament we could say that Brecht himself was occupied with 'contemporisation' of a classic text). The conclusion of the play is that things should belong to those who can best take care of them. In this sense it refutes the inevitability of 'the natural'. This attitude challenges assumption about a teleological view of dramatic structure. At the same time, Brecht knowingly announces in his plays how things will unfold and end. There is a 'playing with' what might seem inevitable because it is a crafted drama and the ending could be changed. If not in the actual circumstance, as in the case of *The Days of the Commune*, then in another time, another story, or in real life.

What is apparent from this discussion is that 'the natural' is not always 'natural', as Fredric Jameson discusses in *Brecht and Method* (Jameson, 1998), even if we are describing an encounter with nature, which might be argued holds the potential for an unpolluted or pure experience of the sublime. At the point of contact, the situation of our subjectivity within the natural environment is imbued with the preconditions of our material circumstances. For instance, growing up in an industrial city, nature can seem very far away, maybe even boring, perhaps frightening – how do you know where you are without continual visual signposts? The actuality of landscape must be acknowledged which cuts against a romanticisation of 'the countryside'. A brief mention of John Berger is important here, and his celebrated discussion of Gainsborough's *Mr and Mrs Andrews*, in *Ways of Seeing* (Berger, 1972). In his introduction to Berger's *Landscapes*, Tom Overton quotes Simon Sharma's view that 'landscapes are culture before they are nature' (Sharma, 1995, quoted in Berger, 2016). Berger locates the painting within its particular phase of capitalist development whereby oil painting is tangible evidence of the substantial place of the couple in society. Their composure is marked as Berger points out by the fact that they are not in danger of being shot at, whipped or chased off the land. They *own* it. But we could go further in contemplating how their opulent clothes, intricate hairdos and elegant footwear are maintained. Not by themselves, we can assume. Their appreciation of the magnificent landscape they inhabit will be somewhat different therefore from the farmworker hunting for a rabbit for dinner. There is a visual drama in the placing of Gainsborough's two figures in the landscape and of course Berger encourages us to engage in the multiple *ways of seeing* how this is being enacted. Though the surface is two dimensional, its perspective invites us into the landscape. We might imagine sitting in the landscape, too, but only in imagination.

Theatre uses this capacity for an audience's projection, 'projective identification' as we have seen, to achieve different ends. The critical attitude embedded in this first part of the chapter is an argument for *the ordinary* to not become *the taken for granted*. The rationale for this argument lies in the power of human agency to fashion material reality, which challenges the conservatism of naturalism. It offers hope where we can see that what we do and make can be changed. Nothing is inevitable, as Brecht says, 'Everything Changes' (Brecht, 1976).

The roots of drama in ritual

Theatre is profoundly connected with communal rituals that are linked with the rituals of everyday life. The final section of this chapter is devoted to the earliest roots of drama, whose foundations derive from the classical period.

The earliest forms of theatre are invariably intertwined with accounts of religious practice. It is not difficult to see why. Within religious rites there are so many elements that point to theatricality, from the donning of special robes, to demarcation of particular places within rituals may take place, the adoption of particular roles and witnessing of the enactment. The role of ritual in *traditional* societies has been well chronicled by seminal anthropologists such as Turner, Van Gennep and applied to dramatherapy (Grainger, 2014; Jennings, 1995; Mitchell, 1998; Schrader, 2012; Snow, 2009). In the dramatherapy literature, attention has been paid to how ritual functions: as part of everyday life on a daily basis, as a developmental process in rites of passage but also within the shared experience of social gatherings.

Frazer's controversial but seminal text *The Golden Bough* (Frazer, 2003) charts how the understanding of human and natural phenomena developed from magic, via religion, to science – in other words, from 'the irrational to the rational'. Fundamental questions of causation, responsibility and what to do about anything from failed crops to plague may render a population more or less helpless. How do we explain our existence, ourselves to ourselves? As we have seen, the theatre, where 'the old' can sit alongside 'the new', has the capacity, unlike religious rite, to invite critique and therefore offers the potential for new and different meanings and knowledge to emerge as in the therapeutic process. Shared public narratives, which find some form of cultural expression, whether through religious rite, ritual practices or witnessing performance in the theatre, provide the comfort of shared meaning. As classicist Mitchell-Boyask (2009) points out:

> Because of traditional associations between song and healing in Greek culture, tragedy becomes a form of therapy for the diseased *polis*, (*or the people*) that is projected onto the space of the theatre, a space overlooked (at the Acropolis) after 420 by Asklepios a hero/god of healing.
>
> (p. 3)

In classical Greek society the theatre was celebrated in the annual City Dionysia in honour of the god of wine Dionysus as harvest too was enjoyed and civic concerns expressed. However, the theatre was also linked with the cult and healing rituals of the god Asklepios. I will look at both of these and their links next.

Aristotle's proposal that drama provides an emotional *catharsis*, a purging or cleansing, is well known. But when this psychological perception of tragedy is set aside, the psychosomatic nature of the activities of the Asklepion, the full *therapeutic nature* of the drama and the rituals surrounding its performance in Athens, become apparent. In the 5th century BC, following a plague which killed between one third and a half of its population, the citizens of Athens stood between the old and the new. The cult of the god Asklepios, originally based in mythology, ritual healing practices and the metaphors of dreams, was further developed, even transformed, through the emergent scientific experimentation of Hippocrates, based in empirical research. The priests of Asklepios interpreted their patients' dreams. Hippocrates argued that the images created in sleep were indicative of defects in, or imbalances between, the 'humours' within the body that could be treated with drugs or physical exercises as well as by prayers and sacrifices.

For dramatherapists in the contemporary world, where 'hard evidence' is sought for the healing power of working with ritual and metaphor, this narrative is compelling. However, they will also conclude that *the active involvement* of the patient/client in the image-making process of both the healing dream in the sanctuary and the dramatic narrative in the theatre *was, and is*, a powerful process for both diagnosis and recuperation, with or without specific medical interventions. This is where the client, though the power of their creativity, is able to access their own healthy aspects and metaphorically take their healing into their own hands.

We know that the etymology of the term 'drama' is derived from Greek roots which mean 'doing' and dramatherapy embraces the potentiality of this 'doing' in the creative process, rather than the idea of the client being given something to be 'consumed', that will enable healing. Acknowledging the dialectic between production/consumption there is an implicit political aesthetic at work too. The activities of the Asklepion required patients to be active participants in the process. After purification rites and taking part in paeans to the god, they needed to 'produce' the dream in which the god of healing would appear.

Sanctuaries devoted to the god Asklepios were situated next to theatres in a number of places, including, significantly, in Athens at the foot of the Acropolis in view of the Theatre of Dionysus. David Wiles (1997) notes that the cult of Asklepios was linked to the Festival of Dionysus not only topographically but also in terms of civic celebration when the feast and procession of Asklepios coincided with the preliminary day of the festival.

The Great Dionysia of Athens is remembered today as a drama festival of tragedies and comedies, but it had several other important civic functions. Nine tragedies dramatised stories that clearly reflected contemporary concerns (war and peace, political responsibility, the relationship between individuals and political power, trade, disease and family law). As Jean Pierre Vernant argues (quoted in Wiles, 1997), 'the city turned itself into a theatre and acted itself out. Tragedy was born when myth started to be considered from the point of view of the citizen'.

At Asklepios's birthplace of Epidaurus, the great theatre is actually situated within the sanctuary. It is here that the journey of suppliants seeking a cure can be mapped out. Their pilgrimages can be compared with those to contemporary Christian shrines in Europe, such as Lourdes, where processional hymns and prayers are offered and the sick bathed in the spring waters emanating from the site of the Virgin's apparition. At Epidaurus, paeans to the gods preceded 'purification' by washing. These rituals prepare for individuals to enter a 'higher state of being' which is simultaneously embodied and transcends the body.

Lourdes continues to be both an imagined and literal place for contemporary Roman Catholics. In every parish in the UK there are images of 'Our Lady of Lourdes' who smiles benignly with an expression of detached and consummate tranquillity. She embodies the unattainable, a serenity unachievable, an example of 'the sublime' to be venerated and appealed to. She is at once a familiar presence and yet her sanctity is to be feared. The sacred context appeals to a primitive instinct of what we must fear because it is beyond our comprehension: the divine. From birth, Catholics are schooled in the subservient role human beings must play in relation to the sacred, which will be mediated by its priests who have been called by God in intangible ways to fulfil this role. This hierarchical positioning casts the roles in processions which lead to the actual shrine. There is an order in which pilgrims may process and hymns are sung which are learnt from childhood. They now take on a magical dimension when sung by candlelight at the fading of the day after many months of daily preparation, and travel to arrive at the place where they believe the apparition of the Virgin took place. For a working-class person with little experience of travel, let alone to a foreign country the anticipation of arrival is febrile. Unworthiness is a constant theme and yet we are invited to enter the sanctuary and make our supplications, and so on. These are moments where hope for the sublime experience are ubiquitous, where deep respect and humble optimism prevail.

The grandeur of these public rituals inspires awe and the sheer scale of a theatre like Epidaurus is commanding, yet despite its proximity to the temple, there is no evidence of a direct relationship between the Asklepion and the performance of actual plays, so we are left to assume that a symbolic relationship has been established between healing and the multiple roles of theatre. If, arguably, the essence of Asklepion healing was *psychosomatic* – the physical illness of the individual being revealed through dream images – then the therapeusis of drama lay in the *psychosocial* depiction of inter-relational conflicts – within the family, in the 'polis', and in warfare between cities. Quoting Vernant again: 'watching a play is part of "reality" and is a lived democratic practice, the pursuit of politics by another means' (quoted in Wiles 1997, p. 209).

In the civic context of the theatrical Dionysia and the religious context of the Asklepion we see the processes of theatre: shared witnessing and active participation rooted in familiar ritual experiences that 'make sense' of things whilst at the same time providing the potentiality to transcend them.

Conclusion

To conclude: this chapter has argued against the universalising of the concept of 'the sublime', but rather proposes that experiences of the sublime are contingent on the given circumstances of individuals' existent and emergent capacity to experience such feelings. However, this is not an argument for a subjectivist reading of individual experience. Rather, it has aimed to locate the discussion in the cultural/political dynamics of dialectical materialism.

In this respect the main argument does not propose the sublime as the synthetic harmony of transcendence, but rather suggests that precisely because of the messy, unevenness of life, its unfairness, unpredictability and imperfections, moments of what we may refer to as 'the sublime' become precious, as they emerge out of these struggles.

In the first part of the chapter, the contemporisation of classical texts is cited to exemplify our dialectical relationship with the past and how the enduring metaphors of theatre continue to be available 'containers' of experience that reassure in their robust crafting but then allow for fresh interpretation to meet new times. Thus, the past and the present are simultaneously in dialogue and this conversation is precisely what we are engaged with in the therapeutic process in dramatherapy whereby in the present we attempt to come to a rapprochement, and with hope, even heal past wounds.

In the second part of the chapter, the social foundations of theatre in civic, ritual celebration and healing rites is explored, drawing attention to the capacity for theatre to both represent and critique human experience. It implicates the political dimensions of collective gatherings whereby audiences and individuals are allocated roles. It argues for the power of human agency when active participation is encouraged. It looks at how this may be harnessed when, in the 'extraordinariness' of therapy, clients may be supported to discover their own healthy/healing capacity and potentially reach moments of 'sublime' communion in relation to themselves, and others. The aesthetics of ritual practices are referred to in the context of the social construction of roles and expectations with a glance towards the seminal work of John Berger who encouraged us to see beyond surfaces for deeper political/structural meanings in artworks.

In a review of Terry Eagleton's (1990) book *The Ideology of the Aesthetic*, the reviewer Kate Soper (1992) states

> the aesthetic has figured in bourgeois thought both as a symbol of its *aspired to syntheses* of mind and body, of the cognitive and sensual, of individual freedom and social harmony, and as a kind of bad faith, a way of refusing to come to terms with the fact that the material divisions of society cannot be miraculously rendered into a tensionless whole by purely artistic or spiritual means.

This statement captures the contingent nature of the aesthetic. It is always rooted in the materiality of social division and therefore in spite of attempts to synthesise experience into the 'sublime' can fail. Human creativity as expressed through the therapeutic endeavour of using artistry in dramatherapy enables all the contradictory aspects of life to have a place of expression and beauty, and even the sublime may emerge but not in ways that can be predicted. The ordinariness of human experience is embraced, valued and therefore dignified. To quote the provocative art critic Robert Hughes (quoted by Basciano, 2012): 'a Gustave Courbet portrait of a trout has more death in it than Rubens could get in a whole Crucifixion'.

Nothing is inevitable and Courbet was a supporter of the Paris Commune.

References

Andersen-Warren, A. and Grainger, R. (2001) *Practical Approaches to Dramatherapy*. London and Philadelphia, PA: Jessica Kingsley Publications.
Basciano, O.www.chanel4news.com, 7 August 2012.
Benedetti, J. (2008) *Stanislavski, An Introduction*. 4th Edition. London: Methuen Drama.
Berger, J. (1972) *Ways of Seeing*. London: Penguin.
Berger, J. (2016) *Landscapes: John Berger on Art*. London and New York, NY: Verso.
Brecht, B. (2007) *Caucasian Chalk Circle*. London: Penguin Modern Classics.
Brecht, B (1978) *The Days of the Commune*. London: Methuen Drama.
Brecht, B. (1976) *Brecht Poems 1913–1956*. Eds John Willett and Ralph Manheim. London: Eyre Methuen.
Brecht, B. (1980) *Brecht on Theatre*. New York, NY: Hill and Wang.
Boal. A. (1998) *Legislative Theatre*. London: Routledge.
Eagleton, T. (1990) *The Ideology of the Aesthetic*. Oxford: Blackwell.
Frazer, G. (2003) *The Golden Bough*. London: Dover Press.
Grainger, R. (2013) *Nine Ways the Theatre Affects our Lives*. Lampeter: Edwin Mellen Press.
Grainger, R. (2014) *Ritual and Theatre*. London: Austin Macauley Publishers.
Jameson, F. (1998) *Brecht and Method*. London: Verso.
Jennings, S. (1995) *Theatre, Ritual and Transformation: The Senoi Temiars*. London and Philadelphia, PA: Jessica Kingsley Publishers.
Lakoff, G. and Johnson, M. (1980) *Metaphors We Live By*. Chicago, IL: University of Chicago Press.
Landy, R. (1991) 'The Drama Therapy Role Method'. *Dramatherapy*, 14 (2).
Lissagaray, P. O. (2012) *History of the Paris Commune 1871*. London: Verso.
Marx, K. (2014) *The Civil War in France*. London: Ostara Publications.
Mitchell, S. (1998) 'The Theatre of Self-Expression'. *Dramatherapy*, 20 (1), 3–11, doi:10.1080/02630672.1998.9689467.
Mitchell-Boyask, R. (2009) *Plague and the Athenian Imagination. Drama, History and the Cult of Asklepios*. Cambridge: Cambridge University Press.
Merlin, B. (2014) *The Complete Stanislavski Toolkit*. London: Nick Hern Books.
Pendzik, S. (2006) 'On Dramatic Reality and its Therapeutic Function in Dramatherapy'. *The Arts in Psychotherapy*, 33 (4).
Ranciere, J. (2011) *The Emancipated Spectator*. London: Verso.
Soper, K. (1992) 'Review of Eagleton's The Ideology of the Aesthetic'. *New Left Review*, March/April.
Schrader, C. (2012) *Ritual Theatre. The Power of Dramatic Ritual in Personal Development Groups and Clinical Practice*. London and Philadelphia, PA: Jessica Kingsley Publishers.
Snow, S. (2009) 'Ritual Theatre and Therapy'. In Eds R. Emunah and D. R. Johnson, *Current Approaches in Dramatherapy*. Springfield, IL: Charles C. Thomas Publishers Ltd.
Wiles, D. (1997) *Tragedy in Athens*. Cambridge: Cambridge University Press.

Chapter 4

Ordinary idolatrous pleasure and the fateful fashioning of an adolescent boy

Onel Brooks

The therapeutic encounter as an aesthetic object

In the first edition of *The Gay Science*, Nietzsche, quoting Emerson, writes, 'To the poet and the sage, all things are friendly and hallowed, all experience profitable, all days holy, all men divine' (Nietzsche, 1974, p. 8).

In beginning with this echo of Nietzsche echoing Emerson, this chapter raises the possibility that like beauty, uninteresting ordinariness and sublime experiences lie in the eye of the beholder. Nietzsche might be heard as saying that those who are – or try to be – conscientious, subtle and sensitive with words and those who are – or try to be – astute and thoughtful, are able to experience all things as welcoming, a source of wonder, as divine. 'Poets' and 'sages' might serve as terms for people who do not habitually fail to be attentive, thoughtful and reverent. For the rest of us – somewhere between poet and sage on the one hand, and on the other habitually dead to ourselves, others and the world around us – there are ways or practices that take the ordinary and everyday and try to help us to wake up. Cameras, images – such as paintings and drawings – writings, or psychotherapy might encourage us to take notice and consider significance, tone, nuance and style. But images, other aesthetic objects and practices that may have the power to awaken us, may also serve to put us to sleep, even to help to fashion our dreams.

To be in or write about a therapeutic encounter could be a way of taking what seems to be everyday and transforming it into an object of our attentiveness and thought, into an aesthetic object. It could also be a way of showing us that we sleep with our clients often, in the sense that we are asleep with them, happily tucked up with the idols given to us.

This chapter shows and says that our speaking – our ability to make noises to ourselves and to others – is easily overvalued but often fails us in the face of intense experiences. For it is a mistake to think that the experience is what we are able to say of it. Written in fear of abstract nouns, generalisations and the conflating of the experience with what we might say of it, this chapter does not try to present or argue with accounts of 'the everyday', 'the aesthetic' or 'the sublime' in psychoanalysis, nor does it focus on warning the reader about abstract nouns, generalisations and mistaking the words for the experiences. It is an account of a series of encounters with one client, ordinary encounters, but two people relating is an aesthetic matter, as is any account of this. It does not seek to explain why so much as show something of how these two people speak to each other; it does not seek to explain why the speaking falters or stops so much as to say that it does and something about how. Perhaps it also helps to illustrate Nietzsche's claim that all our encounters may reveal what is sacred, divine or sublime, if we are able to welcome rather than turn away, if we are able to be attentive and thoughtful.

This chapter suggests that love and loss escape representation and put us in touch with our being small, finite, mortal and dependent; and our introduction to love and loss (including loss of faith and painful disappointment) happens in the vulnerability of childhood. But the marks and noises we use – words – might be regarded as necessary, indispensable, although very poor conveyers of experience. They are reliable ways to fail, reliable ways to be unreliable, to gesture ineffectually towards our experience.

If we present 'the sublime' as that which escapes representation, or, what is experienced as overwhelming in its vastness, power, intensity or strangeness, a source of awe and wonder, we might say that we begin life wordless and wide-eyed, and immersed in 'the sublime', before we are charmed into the ways of those who speak and perhaps overvalue words. Although a wordless creature can say nothing about feeling small, finite, limited and dependent, we might want to say that our experience of the sublime in love, awe and fear has much to do with echoes of these early experiences. And in the face of experiences of love, passion and loss, words often fail us, as if reducing us to the child we were. However, it is not just 'the sublime' that challenges our ability to speak or represent. If language gestures towards but cannot reach and do justice to 'the sublime', it also struggles in the face of 'the beautiful' and 'the ugly', 'the quaint' and 'the dingy'. It also fails in 'the everyday', and this is a failure we live with every day.

First encounter

Asked to see a 14-year-old boy for once-weekly therapy for up to two years, I am told that he is aggressive and violent at school and on the streets, and often inappropriate to the female teachers and the girls at his school. I am told that he may have an undiagnosed learning disability, then asked whether I know anything about how to work with people who have learning difficulties. Most therapists and counsellors, I am told – especially psychoanalytically orientated ones – tend not to know what they are doing with people like this, often making the mistake of treating them as if they are like people without learning issues. (Should I hear treating them as if they are 'normal'?) The referrer also communicated that the boy had some counselling before that, focused on giving him information about relationships and sex, drawing up family trees and making some sort of book that detailed what had happened to him. I was being warned not to be stupid but to work with him responsibly: do as you are told; psychoanalysis is useless or harmful here. I was being warned that my not seeing and working with him as if he has some sort of cognitive disability would be to refuse to recognise not only my own limitations but the limitations of psychoanalysis. Experts on working with learning disabilities have spoken. An image or idol – professionally fashioned – threatened to push its way into the sessions.

Clearly, we are already involved in aesthetic and ethical issues: matters of taste and judgement and ideas about what is a good life for this particular person.

The boy who came to see me had a raw restless energy. He was loud, he shouted, would not or could not stay in his seat, so he got up and walked around the room sometimes. He also wanted to talk and hear from me, clearly curious, as well as suspicious about me and what was supposed to take place in the room. I found myself thinking that he was like a much younger boy and in need of more socialisation. Then I worried about what that word means. Does it mean 'compliance'? Does it mean taking away his rawness, his lust for life?

He told me in our first meeting that he had seen a film on the television very late at night. A boy's mother left when the boy was very small. When the boy grew into a young man, he was out at a bar late at night, met an attractive older woman and went to bed with her. The sex was great and after a while they decided to marry. But one night the boy's father saw them together; later his father told the boy that he could not marry that woman, because she is his mother. I showed some interest in this apparently loaded dreamlike story and his question to me, 'Could this happen?' I wanted to know what he thought.

My client's mother had been seriously ill most of his life, spending most of her time in bed. His father did not live with them, but he was very present in their lives. I remarked that his mother's illness would be tough for him, his brothers and his sister, but he said – with some impatience – that they were used to it, and that he did not want to talk about that. I dropped it, but of course I thought he was telling me where it hurts, where the experiences and longings were that were too raw and intense to come to words without much effort and pain.

He then asked me about a 'star', 'superstar', 'celebrity', an 'idol' who had been accused of inappropriate conduct with boys. Tom wanted to know whether I thought this figure did it. I said I did not know whether he did it and asked Tom for his thoughts. Tom said to me, 'You are not much good to me if you don't know about things. What would be the point of my coming here?' He wanted to know why a grown man would want to have 'sleepovers' with young boys, if he was not up to something sexual with them. I wondered to myself what to make of his asking me about this in his first session. He was the celebrated first child before illness began to steal his mother, and siblings added to the rate of his fall from being the first and the most important. He could be heard as being concerned with 'inappropriateness', a fall from grace and the question of guilt or responsibility. Without pretending to know what I do not know, I said something about this celebrity's childhood with its disruptions and inappropriateness, and wondered whether his interest in boys had anything to do with this. I told him that I did not know; I just wondered about whether these things were connected.

'Why?'

In the second or third session, I began to understand that he spent hours each night watching pornography. When he could get away with it in the day, he would watch more pornography. Single-minded and dedicated to this world of 'porn stars', a devotee not an expert or connoisseur, he spoke rapturously about his intense nightly vigil.

Listening carefully to what he had to say, I would ask what it was about this particular scene, this particular scenario, this particular woman that seemed so important to him. He would try to say something about this but would quickly become inarticulate or incoherent, finding himself without the words to put to the intense feelings stirred up by his viewing. Often, he would just talk about big body parts doing things with big body parts. As well as listening carefully and thoughtfully, I waged a mischievous and vicious campaign against his seriousness and reverence, his idolatry. I was, I said, not surprised that he might watch pornography and even a lot of it, but so much every day? Does he get a bit bored sometimes? Not even a little bit? He insisted that it was never boring.

Like a small child who is able to ask 'why' indefinitely, he persistently questioned me about 'porn stars'. One of his favourites was why men in porn had 'big ones'? Yes, I told him that I did not know why and wondered what he thought. No, he did not like that sort of response. He thought they used drugs. Maybe surgery. Eventually I said that I did not know why, but that I imagine that if you go to an interview for one of these movies, they do not say 'Do you have GCSE English?' They probably say, 'Let's have a look then!' And if it is big you get the job; if it is not big you don't. So is it a mystery? In this way we would go from his earnestly and insistently asking me for answers to his questions – as if seeking initiation into a mystery cult – and irritated by my attempts to hear his thoughts and to question his questions, to seeing pornography as something that is calculated, commercial and at least a little comical, to exchanges that were more irreverent and critical.

Another example is that he wanted to know how 'porn stars' could have intercourse for hours without ejaculating (but these are not his exact words). After listening to this for weeks and trying to get his thoughts, I said with some mischief that he seems to believe what he sees on the screen. How does he know whether these men really have sex for hours or that what he is seeing was not filmed over days, even weeks, then edited to look like one protracted act of intercourse? Clearly this had never occurred to him.

When he remarked with some apparent disgust that some women have pubic hair, I said with some puzzlement, 'What's wrong with that?' Being educated solely by pornographic images, he said as a retort and confidently, 'Well you wouldn't have sex with a woman with pubic hair, would you?' I looked at him without expression. With horror, he exclaimed, 'My god, you would!' Thus, he diagnosed me as a deviant.

For quite some time he confided in me that his ambition was to be a 'porn star'. He took great pleasure in imagining himself as part of this pantheon: those who are like gods in the giving and receiving of sexual pleasure. And the set of a pornographic film was spoken of as if it must be a heaven. 'No', he insisted, seeing and sensing my reaction, 'I mean it'. For a long while I said nothing about his idealisation of the life of people in the porn industry, but during one session I began to say that it did not sound so great. He said I was talking nonsense, but I thought it was high time that I tried to topple the image he had set up for worship. So I said that I imagined that it could be the case that you do not really desire the person they want you to have sex with. He insisted that he would want to have sex with any woman: he did not care who. Aware of his mounting irritation with my nonsense, I said that he might find that he did not really like her, which is different from desiring her. He was more incredulous. I was being stupid. Liking does not have anything to do with it. I said that I thought it would not be so great to have sex with someone that you might not be that attracted to, you might not even like, and with all of those other people around. What other people? I said that there would be a cameraman, probably a director who tells you what he wants you to do at what time, putting you off, and the scriptwriter – the one who is responsible for the dialogue. His protests got louder around here. Okay, no scriptwriter, but there would probably be other people around. I don't know: other people who are porn actors, somebody operating the lights?

At one stage, after a long monologue, from him, about the beauty of pornography, I said something about how the problem with all of his understanding about sex coming from porn is that there is a lot that pornography does not show. It seems as if it shows you everything, but it does not show much about what it means to be in a relationship with someone. It does not really show you sex either, because sex is more about feelings and touch rather than about looking. It is an intense experience rather than a show. Perhaps there are things that pornography *cannot* show? (I would say now that sexual acts can be represented easily enough, but experiences of giving and receiving erotic pleasure and how this reverberates throughout what we are, is much more difficult to represent.) He would look at me, look puzzled, unable to speak, then eventually resume his ritual worship. I would again listen and weigh up whether he was going to get something like sympathetic interest in and comments about how he was gripped by pornography and taking these actors as idols, or comments that invited him to see a ridiculous side to it.

Looking back now, I can see that this was likely to get me into trouble, but of course, at the time, I did not see it coming, so to speak.

Experience and what we say of it

It did not occur to me then that he might say to his school or the social worker that we just spent all our time talking about porn. Of course, as well as his love of pornography, we spoke about school, what he was up to on the streets, including the fights he had been in where the police were called, his mates and certainly his family. He could not say more than a few sentences about his mother's health. He had a mission. He wanted me to help him to make it in the world of porn. I was instructed to find out for him how to do it. I of course wanted him to tell me more about why he thinks he might want to do this for the rest of his life.

A particular scene in one of the pornography films held him firmly within its embrace for weeks, capturing him. He spoke about it on and off for weeks, with my being interested in why just this scene, and his struggling to tell me, but quickly coming to the limit of what he could say about his interest and excitement. Eventually, he could let us both know that there was something about the expression on the woman's face. It seemed adoring as well as amorous, leading us onto mothers and babies. He began the next session mobile phone at the ready. I did not understand immediately. He had brought in the incredibly exciting scene for me to watch because he found that he could not tell me what there is about it that really got to him. 'Perhaps if you saw it, you might get it'. He began to stand up to come across to show me.

I heard myself say – as I went from not understanding what was happening, to anxiety after my realisation, to a strangely calm and curious place – 'I wonder what I would be doing if I were to be in here watching pornography with you? What would it mean? I know that there have been problems at school. I know that your mother is very ill and it is hard for you to talk about this. So what would I be doing sitting here watching porn with you?'

My being puzzled and curious about his idea that we might watch porn together seemed to stop him. He sat, phone in hand, looking puzzled too. I meant but did not say that part of my wondering was about what he was inviting me into by this offer. I added, 'I am not sure it is even legal for me to watch porn with you'.

> 'What? How old do you have to be to watch porn?'
> 'Eighteen, I think. You are not even sixteen yet. So what would I be doing?'
> 'Eighteen? Can you join the army at sixteen or seventeen?'

'I think that might be right'.
'And can you get married at sixteen or seventeen with your parents' permission?'
'I think you might be able to do this'.
'So you can fight in a war and die, you can get married, have sex and have a baby, but you can't watch porn! That's fucked up!'
'No, you certainly have a point there'.

Not bad for a boy who supposedly has learning difficulties.

Due to my frequent reminders that there is an important difference between the experience and what we say of it, I may be more vulnerable to the claim that I should have looked at the scene with him. Indeed, it might be said that here and generally with this client, I am representing an unreasonable adult demand – colluding with the tyranny of words – insisting that he finds words to convey how he is moved and why, by what he is drawn to, yet knowing full well that, like the rest of us, he is likely to find it very difficult to say much about the things that are most important to him. However, with this client, and clients in general, valuing, encouraging and leading into speaking seems to be far from an arbitrary, oppressive exercise of power. It is a privileging of speaking (hence, thinking and being awake to what might be important to us) over finding ourselves just acting in certain ways, over being resigned and wordless in the face of what moves us. What may be most important to us may not be easily put into words, but it may be crucial that we try and do not retreat in the face of what is unspoken or feels unspeakable.

Interestingly, he claimed that his phone would not work, so he could not show me the scene. I was not sure whether this was true or a way of retreating from something with me. He said to me, 'You're lucky!', as if I had been let off something. He did not raise the issue again or try to show me anything on his phone at a later date.

What things might mean

As well as watching pornography, there was some interest in women and girls. For example, he found one of the young women teachers at his school extremely attractive and exciting and had asked her if she would go out with him. She had looked him up and down then asked him his age. He was fourteen at the time. She said, 'Well, maybe if you were older'. At the point of his telling me this, he was approaching his 15th birthday, and trying to convince me, as well as himself, that she had said that she would have sex with him when he was older. He was planning to present himself to her for sex, as he was now older.

After listening to this and other interactions with this and other women teachers in his school, I felt as if I did not want to keep quiet anymore, and that it would not be responsible of me. So soberly and dryly I said something like 'You know, I think you are very good at thinking about what you would like things to mean, but you are not so good at thinking about what they might mean'.

He laughed at this and said something like, 'You come out with some things. I forget the exact words, but I've got to remember to tell my mates that one'.

I said that I could not know, but I think that his teacher was being considerate about his feelings when he asked her out. She could have made a complaint about his doing this. She could have laughed at him, or said something like 'You? No way!' But she was kind. She might have meant that as she was a woman in her 20s she might be interested in someone in their 20s or older, not a 14-year-old. He listened quietly and carefully to me. I said I thought that it is best that he does not try to have sex with the women at school. It would be better if he found a girl who was about his age who wanted to have sex with him.

When he was due to go away with a group of girls and boys, he devised a plan – fantasy? – to trick one of the girls into spending the night with him. I asked him how he thought she would feel when she realised that she had been tricked, and suggested that even if she had been interested in him, she might be quite anxious and upset about being tricked into spending the night with him. He listened carefully. He changed his plans.

Coming closer

He became very angry with me sometimes. One was to do with my trying to stop him from using the phone in the room to ring the emergency services. He stormed out, threatening not to come back. He missed a few weeks before he returned, apologetic. Another was his deciding that we needed to have our therapy session in the local fast-food establishment near where we met. I wanted us to talk about this, about eating and about how that kind of space would mean that he could not speak to me about the things that he often spoke to me about. He walked out. Another was his opening the cupboards in the room and interfering with art objects he found in them. I asked him firmly to stop and to put them back. He was furious and, as he stormed out, threatened to open all of the doors to the other therapy rooms on his way out of the building. I felt that had I gone after him to try to prevent him doing this, then he would have done it. I sat in my chair and waited, as I had done on the other two occasions when he got up and left me. It felt important that he was giving me this experience of being left, abandoned, discarded, testing me to see if I would follow him or whether I could cope with being treated like this.

I tried to speak to him about what the emergency was – on a number of occasions he had saved his mother's life by calling the emergency services. We could not manage to speak about this or the other two occasions when he walked out. He insisted that he was just messing about: none of it was important.

In spite of his initially seeking to place the issue of his mother off-limits – closing the door on it – mothers and illness sometimes turned up in the session and, as we worked together, I began to see that many things might be linked to his mother and her serious illness. I would take my opportunity, following the principle that 'less is more', touching on but not insisting on this connection.

Early in our meeting together, when he was telling me about watching porn late at night, I said that I imagined that he was very concerned about his mother's health, and that watching porn late into the night regularly was perhaps a way of his trying not to think about or be aware of what this stirs up in him. He would look quite frightened when I said things like this. In response to something about the noises people make in porn, I said that I imagined that these noises might be easier for him than the noise of his mother gasping for breath downstairs. He confirmed that he could hear her sometimes. He became more able to acknowledge concerns about his mother's health, but here, again, words tended to fail him.

A development of my comments about his watching porn so much and so compulsively was the suggestion that he was trying to keep other things out of his mind, that he might be frightened by what may come into his mind at times, and that he was also afraid of falling asleep and dreaming. This meant, I suggested, that he was always tired and irritable, in no place to approach his schoolwork.

I remarked on other occasions that as long as his computer or phone is working, he will be able to plug himself into porn; but other people, well, I imagine that this feels a lot riskier. When the computer dies, you can recharge it.

One of the hopeful things was that he had a group of mates who got up to quite ordinary adolescent things, such as playing football, playing games online, trying to get alcohol, trying their luck in terms of picking someone up and doing a bit of school work too. I asked at one stage whether they watch as much porn as he does. He was clear that he was the one who watched the most, and he also spoke about it most.

At the beginning of one session, as we approached his sixteenth birthday, he came in showing more despair than he had before. He said: 'My head is fucked! I think about porn all the time, and always want to talk about it'. He acknowledged that he thought he watched so much porn to keep other things out of his head; he could say little about what these other things were, but there was something about his fear that some of the thoughts he was keeping out were 'mad'. He told me that his mates sometimes ask him what is wrong with him. They claim that they watch quite a bit of porn, but they spend a lot of time doing lots of other things, and they do not talk about porn all the time. This concern about his mind lasted for a few sessions. He stopped talking about pornography so much in the period that followed. There were more stories about hanging out with his mates, playing football and computer games.

Prior to our final session, I received a message from his referrer who informed me that his mother had died days before the session, that the whole family was in chaos and grief and I should not expect to see Tom.

The final session

Tom was on time for his session. He looked like a boy who was carrying something heavy but managing to keep going. He asked if I had heard, and I replied that I had heard that his mother had died. He told me a little about this, soberly, interrupted by silences, and my making comments about how this had been hanging over them for years, but now it has happened. I expected that this would be how we would spend the whole session, in a mournful respectful and reflective silence, punctuated with a little speaking. Eventually Tom said, 'It's very sad, but there is nothing I can do about it. I want to tell you something, though'.

He then told me about being out the previous weekend with his mates and meeting a group of girls. He found that he really liked one of the girls. She was attractive, but that was not all: he could not say why, but he was really into her. He reported making a conscious decision not to behave 'like a lunatic', the way that he usually behaved, loud, wild, 'over the top'. He started a conversation with the girl he liked, and she seemed happy to speak to him. They got on really well. Some of his mates wondered what was up with him because he was behaving differently. A small group of them ended up around someone's house, and he was alone with the girl he liked in a room. He said that he wanted to 'jump on her', then he worried that she might not like it, but he could not work out how he was supposed to know if she was really interested. He decided to ask her if she wanted to have sex. She said yes, and they did. It was great! He had wanted to tell me about it because he has not really been able to tell anyone about it. Yes, his friends know, but he did not really tell them or talk about it.

I acknowledged that this was important, that he had liked her, had asked her, rather than just taking it for granted that she would want to. Two things bothered him though. She had pubic hair. He had not reacted because he thought it might hurt her feelings, but he was shocked. The other thing is that he could not keep going for a long time. It was over in seconds. He could not have sex without limits. Although she did not seem to mind, he felt disappointed with himself. He had telephoned her after a few days and she seemed happy to hear from him. They were planning to meet for a second time.

After thanking me for seeing him for such a long time, he left his final session, not excited and giddy, but quietly, like someone who is aware of having a little bit of good fortune after a significant loss. I wished him well.

Finding transformational objects

If the term 'aesthetic' is concerned with sensory experience and the feelings aroused by it, then a written account can be responded to as if it is an aesthetic object. If what is presented above is a series of encounters between two people with their own styles and idiosyncrasies, then this chapter has made some attempt to say or show something about 'the aesthetic'. Yet it has not been explicit about 'the sublime', nor about psychoanalytic theory in relation to 'the aesthetic', 'the sublime' and the client work outlined above. But is it clear that we should aim to be explicit, rather than subtle, about 'the sublime' or about what we do with psychoanalysis – or what it does with us – when we are alone together?

This ordinary encounter with an adolescent boy, that becomes a matter of aesthetics and values when we look more closely, was not about preaching to him that pornography is 'bad', 'evil' and must not be watched. I sought to disrupt the worshipping – the idolisation of – a way of depicting what people do together when they are alone with each other, and equating this experience with its representation in pornography.

Pornography might be said to have much to do with valuing quantity and measurement over quality – bigger, longer, faster – seriously sticking to the formula, sameness, and doing it like everyone else does, as opposed to what is idiosyncratic, novel or whimsical. It might be said to be a feeling entitled to see everything and have it all at our disposal, an earnest no-nonsense belief in explicitness, leaving no stone or any other body unturned, being certain, absolute, definite, unambiguous and categorical. We might say that much of our modern world is pornographic, seducing us into pornographic values as if these are the only values. More to the point, if I dare to be so explicit, it may be possible to speak about taking a pornographic attitude to anything, including psychoanalysis. With respect to psychoanalysis, this may refer to celebrating its explicit use as theory and in interpretations to people, as if more explicit, bigger and longer, more certain, definite and insistent, more exact, rigorous, scientific and systematic must be better than an approach that is more restrained, reserved, tactful, sceptical and equivocal, that, following Nietzsche, likes to push and sound out idols from time to time.

One criticism of this chapter could be that it is not explicit enough: that it talks about pornography whilst, like the session it describes, failing to allow any to be shown, whilst failing to be pornographic enough. That is, it does not parade enough psychoanalytic theory; it does not make explicit claims about the internal processes in my client and in me. It does not drive its points home. It might even be said that this chapter could be clearer and surer about what is really relevant to the sublime and the experience of this client. It lingers too much on the surface of things, on the tone, texture and context of our speaking together – which might be regarded as preliminaries – and does not say more about what was really going on, what was really important. My hesitations or reluctance here is related to a concern about a knowingness and an insistence that may take us in a direction opposite to that indicated by Nietzsche: that we may not be so open to the sacred or sublime but look largely to confirm what we think we already know or believe.

And yet clearly psychoanalysis does help me to think about this particular client and to say something about 'the aesthetic' as well as 'the sublime' in relation to him. Winnicott's work (for example, Winnicott, 1960) and the use that Bollas (1987) makes of it, helps me to say the following sort of things about my client. His mother was less ill when he was born and when he was an infant, and there were some robust and passionate interactions between them in the form of feeding and playing. Bollas, following Winnicott, writes of the mother being an object that actually transforms the infant, through her feeding, playing and management of his environment. Some of her care for him becomes part of his caring for himself, but she is known less as a separate person or object; she is more an embrace or holding that facilitates a process of transformation. The mother, Bollas claims, is known as a transformational object, as that process of change, as a 'powerful metamorphosis of being' (Bollas, 1987, p. 17). Bollas states:

> The mother's idiom of care and the infant's experience of this handling is one of the first if not the earliest human aesthetic. It is the most profound occasion when the nature of the self is formed and transformed by the environment. The uncanny pleasure of being held by a poem, a composition, a painting, or, for that matter, any object, rests on those moments when the infant's internal world is partly given form by the mother since he cannot shape them or link them together without her coverage.
>
> The infant has his own intrinsic 'form', given the design of his inherited disposition, and his own cognitive abilities (ego capacities) bias his subjective experience of reality. But as I have said earlier, these internal transformational abilities are identified with the mother. This first human aesthetic informs the development of personal character (which is the utterance of self through the manner of being rather than the representations of the mind) and will predispose all future aesthetic experiences that place the person in subjective rapport with an object.
> (Bollas, 1987, pp. 32–33)

For Bollas, our lives fundamentally involve a search for this object or its echo that we know only by the transformations it has facilitated in us. It makes sense to me to take Tom's preoccupation with pornography as a search for a transformational object that will therefore continue what she has started, and as a way of sustaining his tie with his earliest object – his mother. It was as if this world of passionate unreserved intimacy with a woman was held on to and re-sought in his nightly ritual worship of bodies locked in a kind of intimacy. If the aesthetic is concerned with the sensory experience of being with and being transformed by the mother, what might we say about 'the sublime'? Do we need to distinguish these terms? Is the sublime part of the aesthetic?

Many things might be said about what the sublime is. They may not all be consistent with each other, nor may they fit easily with what I am saying about my work with this client. Feagin (1999, p. 886), for instance, claims that the sublime is to do with a feeling brought on by our encounter with objects that are infinitely large or vast or overwhelmingly powerful. But what is infinitely vast or powerful need not be restricted to the raging torrent of a waterfall: we often stumble on raging torrents within us, words and actions from the other that take us out of ourselves and leave us less sure of who or what we are. If it makes some sense to say that 'the aesthetic' is the trace of the embrace of the mother transforming the infant, 'the sublime' might be thought about as a sense of encountering that which is beyond and responsible for the initiation of the fateful change that fashions our being. This includes the mother as an all-powerful incomprehensible force, encountered by the raw wordless infant who is largely other than what psychoanalysis refers to as 'the ego'. The mother appears here, Bollas seems to tell us, as the source of notions about gods and fate, as the mysterious background that makes all things possible. This is our experience of being in the presence of and dwarfed by something intense, powerful and ineluctable, whether we locate its source in others, objects or in ourselves.

However, to say this about Tom is not to make a statement about all of us, including all of our involvement with pornography. It is not to claim to know that all aesthetic and sublime experiences are only to be considered as the echo of fateful changes in us or a sense that powers beyond our comprehension are at work. To know this might be to know too much, and to be less open to what each individual experience might suggest. Here, again, is the fear that if we think that we know too much about how something is 'holy' or 'divine', rather than approach it with more humility and reverence, we make it less likely that it will reveal itself to us. Here is the idea that a knowing and reductive use of psychoanalysis that is confident about what the sublime is, is different from an attitude of welcome to all things and people that may lead us to the divine or sublime.

The sublime and the beautiful

Feagin writes that the 'postmodern sublime' involves the argument that whilst beauty can be represented, on the other hand, 'the sublime is associated with the formless, that which is "unpresentable" in sensation'. This seems to be consistent with the account given above in which the infant has its experience of transformation but cannot present or represent the mother; and in which my client, caught up in his experiences of transformation, searches assiduously for ways of representing this in pornographic images.

For Feagin (1999, p. 886), a political reading of the sublime and the beautiful emphasises that beauty is related to 'existing forms or structures of society', presumably related to societal norms; the sublime, on the other hand, is connected to resistance to what is dominant. Perhaps this takes us to Wittgenstein's lecture on ethics, in which he includes aesthetics in ethics, as 'the general enquiry into what is good' (Wittgenstein, 1929, p. 4). So instead of separating aesthetics from the sublime, as Feagin seems to, Wittgenstein helps us to keep these two notions together and close to 'ethics', which is for him an 'enquiry into the meaning of life, or into what makes life worth living, or into the right way of living' (Wittgenstein, 1929, p. 5). In his paper, Wittgenstein makes the argument found in a number of writers associated with 'existentialism' who argue that even when we have gathered all the facts – all the true propositions, 'evidence' – we still need to make decisions about what we value and the life we want to lead. Unlike the propositions of science or any system, our words being designed primarily for a more crude (and this chapter says pornographic) use – what is bigger than what, what can easily be represented or looked at – fail us or become less clearly useful when it comes to matters of values. We come close to the limit of what we can do with words.

> It seems to me obvious that nothing we could ever think or say should be the thing. That we cannot write a scientific book, the subject matter of which could be intrinsically sublime and above all other subject matters ... Our words used as we use them in science, are vessels capable only of containing and conveying meaning and sense, natural meaning and sense. Ethics, if it is anything, is supernatural and our words will only express facts; as a teacup will only hold a teacup full of water and if I were to pour out a gallon over it.
>
> (Wittgenstein, 1929, p. 7)

Wittgenstein means by 'ethics' an experience: 'when I have it I wonder at the existence of the world' (Wittgenstein, 1929, p. 8). Perhaps this takes us back to where this chapter began, to Nietzsche quoting Emerson.

Ability to wonder

Ordinary idolatrous pleasures are widespread and may reduce our ability to wonder at anything. As good members of society and the same as everyone else – everyone who is 'not ill' or 'abnormal' – we may – just like everyone else who matters to us – have idols that give us pleasure. A craving for systems, certainty and being like the others around us might make it difficult for us to see how we too might be caught up in such pleasures. If knowing and being able to see, understand and even control, are part of our ordinary idolatrous pleasure, then there are ways of having a relationship with psychoanalysis that may be caught up in this, rather than helping us to think about and undermine our ordinary idolatrous pleasures.

Winnicott worried about psychoanalysis being presented as a system, presented in a dead language regarded as orthodox, true and universally applicable. He objected to dogma. Robert Rodman, the editor of 'The Spontaneous Gesture', a collection of Winnicott's letters, writes the following of Winnicott in his introduction to this book: 'In objecting to dogma in the psychoanalytic endeavour, he is recommending obedience to the Second Commandment' (Winnicott, 1999, p. xxii).

The Second Commandment is about not making and bowing down to 'graven images' of God. I understand Rodman as saying that a dogma in psychoanalysis, or any system, is a graven image of our experience of living and we are always in danger of worshipping or fetishising the image. But in our devotion to the dogma, the actual experiences of people are at risk of falling out of the picture, and the dogma can be used to challenge and distort the experience. This was and is the danger with Tom.

This chapter shows something of what it means for a client to have intense experiences, feel fascination and a sense of relatedness, to feel firmly embraced or held by an object; but it does not say how we might differentiate between ordinary idolatrous pleasures and 'the aesthetic'. It does not help us to distinguish between psychoanalysis as a passionate intensity, and on the other hand, a pornographic peering into what is usually concealed and unseen, into the quiddities of our being. Perhaps such distinctions are not easily made. But the chapter does suggest that these intense experiences – whether idolatrous or aesthetic – may be used both to evade or deepen our experiences – that is, defensively or they may set us on the path of wonder or reverie.

The words we can use to speak of our desires, hopes, aesthetic experiences, including of 'the sublime', are other than the experiences we have; more words do not necessarily close the gap between experiencing and speaking. Being too sure, insistent and explicit can crush people and their experiences. Words, categories and concepts are unavoidable if we speak and write, but the poet and the sage do not restrict themselves to how others speak, they are singularly concerned with our experience of living and what makes life worth living.

References

Bollas, C. (1987) *The Shadow of the Object: Psychoanalysis of the Unthought Known*. London: Free Association Books.
Feagin, S. L. (1999) 'Sublime'. In Ed Robert Audi. *The Cambridge Dictionary of Philosophy, Second Edition*. Cambridge: Cambridge University Press, pp. 886.
Nietzsche, F. (1974) *The Gay Science*. New York, NY: Vintage Books.
Winnicott, D. W. (1960) 'The Theory of the Parent-Infant Relationship'. In *The Maturational Processes and the Facilitating Environment*. London: Karnac.
Winnicott, D. W. (1999) *The Spontaneous Gesture. Selected Letters*. London: Karnac.
Wittgenstein, L. (1929) 'A Lecture on Ethics'. *Philosophical Review, 74* (1) (January 1965), pp. 3–12.

Chapter 5

Experiencing the sublime through encounters with the Real

Joseph Newirth

As an analyst, I have understood my job as helping patients put into words their unspoken and unarticulated experiences and thoughts. I think of this as a transformational process (Bion, 1965, Civitarese, 2014, Newirth, 2018) in which the concrete thoughts and actions of the paranoid-schizoid experience are transformed into the symbolic thoughts of the depressive position. I have thought of this within the context of the psychoanalytic theory of therapeutic action which has evolved from a one-person theory of interpretation, remembering and the reconstruction of past events, into two-person, intersubjective approaches which focus on experience near therapeutic processes of holding, empathy, reverie and the development of transitional experiences all of which emphasise the creation of meaning. These two-person intersubjective modes of analytic participation have developed largely within the context of relational, intersubjective and contemporary Kleinian theories.

And yet, I want to begin this chapter by describing a clinical experience that I had in which my understanding of the psychoanalytic process seemed totally inadequate and in which I felt completely dumbfounded, in a state of shock, or as described in the Old Testament being struck down in a state of awe. I felt as if I was looking into the infinite void. We can think of states of 'awe' as subjective, urgent moments, which from an abstract perspective represent concepts of the sublime. The concept of the sublime has typically been used to describe literary, artistic or philosophical ideas that describe an extremely powerful positive or negative experience where a person feels overwhelmed by reality, exceptional beauty or absolute horror, experiences which go beyond our capacity to express ourselves, to put into words our inchoate experiences of being overwhelmed by something outside of the self. How can we approach these experiences in psychoanalytic practice and everyday life?

Clinical illustration: staring into the void

I had been working quite well with Jane, a married professional woman who had three children. One day she arrived in a state of shock and told me that her daughter had just been diagnosed with a potentially fatal form of cancer.

As she told me the details of her meeting with the oncologist I felt horrified and became progressively distressed, unable to speak. It was as if my mind were shattered; I could not think or even find an empathic, consoling, human thing to say. It was as if I, like my patient, was looking into an infinite void, a black hole in space which sucks all energy and life out of the universe. I became silent and my patient and I looked at each other with terrified, dead eyes. The only thought that emerged was that there was nothing I could say to my patient that would be either meaningful or compassionate. Finally, I apologised for being unable to speak in the face of such devastating news.

After the session, I tried to understand my experience. As I thought about this experience of awe, I realised that I had experienced the Lacanian Real, a concept that I, as many other people, have struggled with understanding and now had experientially grasped it as representing the limits of my capacity to understand, create meaning, symbolise and even believe that we live in a world that has rules, in which we have some form of agency, as opposed to being a speck of dust pushed and pulled like anything else in the chaos of the universe. I began to think about psychoanalytic concepts of reality and how they relate to experiences of awe, such as my experience with my patient facing the horror of a child being diagnosed with cancer. Experiences of awe and the sublime seem to represent a moment of contact with an unexpected reality, which exceeds what we believe we know and could meaningfully symbolise.

Psychoanalytic concepts of reality have evolved in parallel to the development of other aspects of psychoanalytic theory, from one-person to two-person theories, from an emphasis of adapting to a fixed external reality to viewing reality as a construction of the individual within a particular culture and/or as an intersubjective experience between a patient and therapist or a parent and child. In the following section, I will review psychoanalytic concepts of reality first in order to explore the relationship between reality, positive and negative experiences of awe, and then the nature of the sublime and its implications understanding critical moments in the clinical encounter with the sublime.

Psychoanalytic concepts of reality

Reality as the objective external world

Freud was a positivist, a nineteen-century scientist, who thought of reality as constituted by the natural world, the objective context that we both live in and which we had to adapt to. For Freud the problem was not the nature of reality but rather the avoidance of reality through infantile, narcissistic and pathological wishes which deny reality and attempt to make the world conform to our wishes. Freud's (1911a) paper, 'Formulations on the Two Principles of Mental Functioning', describes the relationship between the individual and reality, between the pleasure principle and the reality principle, between primary and secondary thought process. He begins this paper with the following statement in which he defines the core problem of neurosis:

> We have long observed that every neurosis has as its result, and probably therefore as its purpose, a forcing of the patient out of real life, an alienating of him from reality. Nor could a fact such as this escape the observation of Pierre Janet; he spoke of a loss of '*la fonction du réel*' ['the function of reality'] as being a special characteristic of neurotics, but without discovering the connection of this disturbance with the fundamental determinants of neurosis.
>
> (p. 218, italics in original)

For Freud and generations of analysts after him, our task was to help patients accept reality and to give up their infantile wishes. At the same time that Freud was writing his paper on the pleasure principle and the reality principle, he was also writing the paper on the Schreber case (Freud, 1911b), which could be thought of as his first challenge to the primacy of the pleasure principle. In his paper on the Schreber case, Freud speculated that the concept of projection could function as an alternate dynamic to repression, which would have changed, as Klein later suggested, the relationship between the individual and reality, emphasising the constitutive effects and importance of the individual's internal fantasy rather than the impact of external reality. Although Freud seemed fascinated by the possibility of understanding the dynamics of projection, he did not follow this theoretical line and question the fundamental place and importance of objective reality.

After the horrors of World War I, Freud (1920) began to seriously question the relation between the pleasure principle and the reality principle. Suddenly, reality could not be seen as simply a benign or neutral context to which we had to adapt. In *Beyond the Pleasure Principle*, Freud (1920) draws a picture of reality that is often painful and requires a different kind of psychic work, repetition and progressive symbolisation, rather than simply remembering the past, in order to master the cruelties of reality including inevitable abandonment, loss and traumatic experiences such as war. Rather than being insistent about the need to adapt to reality and give up infantile wishes, Freud presents a compassionate view of our struggle with reality, in which both the child and the adult needs to come to terms with reality as a cruel and demanding other. He is no longer describing the significance of reality as an objective experience, but his descriptions are a precursor to an intersubjective perspective on emotional experiences which can only be mastered through psychological work and the capacity to symbolise terrible experiences that reality presents. This paper (Freud, 1920) represented a revolution in Freud's thinking in which he moves past a previous simple view of reality and the dilemma of the neurosis as failure to adapt, into a contemporary perspective involving the necessity of creating personal meaning; understanding the insistence of the repetition compulsion which is independent of the pleasure principle and reality principle. Freud highlights the repeating experiences of unhappiness which we see in ourselves and our patients. In the following statement Freud inverts the relationship between the individual's unconscious wishes and reality to claim the central importance of psychic (subjective) reality over external, objective reality:

> Patients repeat all of these unwanted situations and painful emotions in the transference and revive them with the greatest ingenuity. They seek to bring about the interruption of the treatment while it is still incomplete; they contrive once more to feel themselves scorned, to oblige the physician to speak severely to them and treat them coldly; they discover appropriate objects for their jealousy; instead of the passionately desired baby of their childhood, they produce a plan or a promise of some grand present – which turns out as a rule to be no less unreal. None of these things can have produced pleasure in the past, and it might be supposed that they would cause less unpleasure today if they emerged as memories or dreams instead of taking the form of fresh experiences. They are of course the activities of instincts intended to lead to satisfaction; but no lesson has been learnt from the old experience of these activities having led instead only to unpleasure. In spite of that, they are repeated, under pressure of a compulsion.
>
> (p. 21)

Intersubjective reality: reality as consensual experience

The interpersonal school refocused our attention on the interpersonal field and reality as a culturally constructed human event which set the stage for the development of contemporary relational and intersubjective theories. Contemporary relational analysts (Mitchell, 1998; Aron, 1996) expanded the central focus of treatment beyond the patient's subjective experiences of reality and present the necessity that reality is constituted through enactments in the transference/countertransference relationship, a two-person process involving the analyst's and patient's unconscious and conscious participation in a dance-like experience of mutual creation. This concept of mutuality is critical to understanding the process, which like Freud's description of a patient repeating painful experiences in analysis, moves the concept of reality into the 'here and now' (Blass, 2011) experience of enactment as the new experience of intersubjective reality is presented in action.

The importance of these enactments within the evolving intersubjective reality are eloquently described by the Boston Change Process Study Group (BCPSG) as occurring within 'moments of meeting' in which reality becomes redefined as the repeating patterns of mutually created experiences in the analytic dyad which they describe as implicit relational schemas (Stern et al., 1998). The BCPSG describe different aspects of the temporal process of therapy (and life) as 'moving along' when suddenly a critical moment emerges, a 'now moment', in which the known, repetitive, implicit relational schema within the transference/countertransference relationship is challenged, opening the intersubjective system to potential change and growth. These 'now moments' occur when one person, usually the patient, asks a question of the analyst which disrupts the ongoing rules of the relationship, altering the expected or known reality. The BCPSG describe these 'now moments' in the following way:

> Now moments are not part of the set of characteristic present moments that make up the usual way of being together and moving along. They demand an intensified attention and some kind of choice of whether or not to remain in the established habitual framework. And if not, what to do? They force the therapist into some kind of 'action', be it an interpretation or a response that is novel relative to the habitual framework, or a silence. In this sense, now moments are like the ancient Greek concept of kairos, a unique moment of opportunity that must be seized, because your fate will turn on whether you seize it and how.
>
> (p. 911)

They continue giving the following examples of 'now moments':

- If an analytic patient stops the exchange and asks, 'Do you love me?'
- When the patient has succeeded in getting the therapist to do something out of the (therapeutic) ordinary, as when the patient says something very funny and both break into a sustained belly laugh.
- When by chance patient and therapist meet unexpectedly in a different context, such as in a queue at the theatre, and a novel interactive and intersubjective move is fashioned, or fails to be.
- When something momentous, good or bad, has happened in the real life of the patient (or therapist) that common decency demands it to be acknowledged and responded to somehow.

(p. 912)

These 'now moments' when met in a creative and oftentimes courageous way can lead to changes in implicit relational knowing, schemas of relationships which may be thought of as representing repetitive neurotic structures. The BCPSG utilises concepts of implicit process and procedural learning taken from cognitive neuropsychology, to discuss the patterns of relationship which other psychoanalysts describe as unconscious processes and the repetition of past neurotic (unproductive) patterns. From a relational perspective, Mitchell (1998) explains the difficulty of changing these repetitive relationship patterns describing the importance of the safety of the known from the risks involved in taking a chance which occurs in these 'now' moments.

Reality as a dream

Intersubjective and relational theories describe reality from a phenomenological perspective; both subjective (psychic) reality and the objective (external) reality are unmediated by cognitive processes. This is in contrast to Freud's and Klein's structural approach in which experiences of reality are mediated through primary and secondary thought or are represented within the concrete thought of the paranoid-schizoid and the symbolic thought of the depressive positions (Segal, 1957). The structural approaches focus on the process through which meaning is attributed to experience and see all experience as mediated by mental processes involved in conscious and unconscious thought. For example, this chapter is situated in contemporary, third-generation Kleinian thought (Grotstein, 2000; Ogden, 2010; Ferro, 2009; Lombardi, 2009; Newirth, 2018), which describes a transformational model of the mind, extending Bion's concepts of alpha function, the container-contained, reverie and waking dream thoughts, along with Winnicott's concept of transitional experience and psychoanalysis and psychotherapy as forms of play. In this transformational view, psychoanalysis and psychotherapy are conceptualised as developmental processes in which the analyst and patient struggle together to symbolise the patient's unarticulated and undeveloped unconscious fantasies which structure and organise their experiences of reality. The analyst becomes the container for the patient's evacuated and unthought 'not me' experiences and through his/her own capacity for reverie and symbolisation develops proto-symbolic transitional experiences, beginning to create affective meaning through reverie, enactment and play.

Ogden (2010), extending Bion's concept of waking dream thoughts, describes this process as dreaming oneself into existence. Ferro (2006) suggests that this activity reflects a change in the goal of psychoanalysis, stating that Bion's work shifted our attention from the contents of thought, the historical or narrative dimension, to the poetic or procedural dimension, the capacity to create meaning, to symbolise and dream. Ferro (2009) argues:

> The focus is no longer on a psychoanalysis that aims to remove the veil of repression or to integrate splittings, but on a psychoanalysis interested in the development of the tools that allow the development and creation of thought, that is the mental apparatus for dreaming, feeling and thinking.
> (p. 990)

In this model, reality and the nature of the external world is thought of as generated by the patient in either the paranoid-schizoid or the depressive modes of thought. Psychological and social reality are not things that exist independent of the observer but are created through the individual's capacity to make meaning in either the paranoid-schizoid or depressive modes of thought. We may live in either a paranoid world in which we find ourselves filled with persecutory anxiety or in a depressive world in which we must be on guard lest we injure the other and destroy the good in the world.

Beyond individual psychology: the Lacanian Real

Freudian, relational, intersubjective and Kleinian theories largely focus on the individual as both a unique subject and as an agent who adapts to, masters and moves beyond their subjective experiences of reality. Although psychoanalytic conceptions of reality have evolved from objective to subjective and finally to a constructivist perspective, each theoretical iteration stays true to the early psychoanalytic ideal of the individual's relationship to their reality, mastering the distortions of neurosis and ultimately living within a more benign version of reality. Within these theories it is difficult to understand experiences of the sublime, of awe; of a non-pathological experience of being unable to speak and even to think. As analysts we always try to have an explanation, an interpretation, and we are rarely left speechless. One exception is Bion's (1965) concept of 'O', which emphasises the unknowable aspects of experience which are beyond our capacity to symbolise. Grotstein (2000) has argued that Bion's concept of 'O' was an attempt to bring in the ineffable, mystical experiences of human life, expanding psychoanalytic theory into non-pathological areas of existence. In this sense, the concept of 'O' addresses similar issues as Lacan's concept of the Real.

However, Lacan (2007), like analysts influenced by the Frankfurt School, expanded our view of the individual subject and of reality to include the cultural, legal/social and economic structures which are determinative of the limits of conscious and unconscious experiences of self and the world. As a simple illustration of this perspective, Fromm (1994) argues that a serf living in the middle ages would have a very different experience of consciousness, of self and relationship with reality as contrasted to a twenty-first-century psychoanalyst or politician. Unlike the classical and other contemporary psychoanalytic perspectives which locate the individual within biology, Lacan (2007) located the individual within an anthropological and philosophical matrix in which psychological being is organised within the cultural, familial and linguistic dimensions within which the individual develops. How can we approach the experience of the sublime of the individual embedded in this matrix?

Lacan conceives of the individual as a function of three registers which generate conscious and unconscious experience: the Imaginary, the Symbolic and the Real. These registers are not thought of as pathological but rather as ways of organising the individual's experience with self, otherness and reality. The Imaginary is our experience and desire to be the most special, loved person who completes the (m)other and feels totally expansive and full, or when no longer the centre of attention (being looked at) feels deflated and empty. The Symbolic register involves the acquisition of language and becoming a subject of the rules of the family, community and culture. The Symbolic register differs from the Imaginary in the recognition that we are all subject to the same societal rules of who we are, including gender, kinship, and other implicit and explicit dimensions of the social contract and biological imperatives. Lacan's concept of the Real is an original idea, representing both existential and cultural limits that we are subject to such as lack, prejudice, disease and death, and which we have no control over.

Lacan (in Bailly, Lichtenstein and Bailly, 2018) continued to revise his theory of these three modes of generating conscious and unconscious thought, finally developing a topographic model of psychic experience which he described as the Borromean Knot. The Borromean Knot can be visualised as a Venn diagram in which these three registers of experience, the Symbolic, Imaginary and Real, are interlocking circles, braided together, as we articulate and generate conscious and unconscious experience. A contemporary Lacanian analyst, Burgoyne (in Bailly, Lichtenstein, and Bailly, 2018, p. 33) suggests that the Borromean Knot is also a way of conceptualising the progress of an analysis: 'At the start of the work the Imaginary is dominant over the Real … As the work proceeds, the Symbolic comes to dominate over the Imaginary … Finally, the Real comes to dominate over the Symbolic'.

These shifting intersubjective experiences of self, other and reality reflect the patient's expanding ability to know him/herself and to be less organised around the perception of the analyst's and the Other's desire. I believe that Lacan's concept of the Real is an often-ignored aspect of psychoanalytic experience as we focus on individual 'neurosis', or in a more contemporary language as the agentic qualities of the self. The Real represents the limits of our experience as subjects, as potentially active agents in the world, it suggests, not unlike Freud's early observation, that we are not masters in our own house, but we ultimately have little control over many aspects of our lives, our fate, and are subject to forces outside of our control. I believe that it is the Lacanian concept of the Real which allows us to begin to grasp the important experience of awe, of being unable to speak, as I was when confronted by my patient's experience of her daughter being diagnosed with a potentially fatal form of cancer. The Lacanian concept of the Real also allows us as psychoanalysts to address experiences of the sublime, of experiences of awe, in a non-reductive, non-pathologising way, by addressing both the limits of our capacity to understand and symbolise the transcendent qualities of nature, art, poetry and religion.

Experiencing the sublime through encounters with the Real

Lacan's concept of the Real, like much of his theory, brings an existential perspective to psychoanalysis broadening our concept of the individual and the development of subjectivity into questions of the nature of being with its inevitable confrontations with non-being (death) and thus with the sublime, which we may also think of as experiences which transcend our being. Lacan's concept of the Real allows us to approach these existential experiences, including the sublime, moments of unbidden, intense affective experience in which there is a loss of the self and an inability to know and to symbolise while simultaneously being subjected to an intense experience of pain and pleasure.

Two encounters with the Real

Several years ago, while on vacation in Argentina, my wife and I were on a tour of Lake Argentina. We were on a tour boat, with several hundred other tourists, all talking noisily in groups of family and friends. It was like many vacation experiences where people are in a good mood, drinking wine and beer, being uninhibited, joyful and loud. My wife and I were like the others on the boat simply enjoying this beautiful day on the water. Suddenly the boat entered the field of icebergs that we had all anticipated as the point of this journey. As we began to cruise between these huge, incredibly amazing icebergs, a sudden quiet came over the boat. My wife and I, like the others, came out on the deck and we're in a complete state of awe, speechless at this magnificent sight. These huge, beautiful icebergs dwarfed our sense of who we were. This was nature in its most magnificent form. This was truly an encounter with the Real. We were all speechless, literally unable to speak and in the grip of this experience. The quiet was incredible; it was as if we were in a church or temple having powerful religious experiences. This state of awe has stayed with me and I still cannot do anything other than describe the scene and my emotional experience of knowing that I am but a small part of the universe and that the universe is older, greater and ultimately indifferent to me. This experience can be thought of as transcendent, a recognition of the absolute beauty of nature, which also provides great comfort of being at one with nature, perhaps like Freud's (1930) oceanic feeling or modifying Searles (1966) idea suggesting that such moments of awe lift the burden of individuality which accompanies being a subject and being agentic. For me this was truly an encounter with the Real, an experience of the sublime, of awe, a recognition that I had seen the limits of my ability to affect the world around me and unlike my experience with my patient, I was part of this other form in an un-speakable moment of peace.

In my second example of an intense encounter with the Real that led to an experience of the sublime, I want to describe an experience of the erotic transference/countertransference that I believe did not fit the usual categories of resistance, enactment or the analyst's destructive behaviour. Psychoanalysis has struggled with the problems of the erotic transference/countertransference situation, from Freud's (1912) early warnings and Ferenczi's (Dupont, 1998) neo-cathartic experiments. This is an area of treatment that has been largely forbidden to engage in and on occasion to fantasise about. The erotic transference/countertransference has been seen as resistance, an enactment of past dissociated experience, and as the analyst's acting out in a highly destructive way. Khan (1974) describes a situation in which his patient has a sexual encounter with her previous analyst, which shattered her capacity for symbolic dialogue, undermining any possibility of the effectiveness of the analytic process. From a Lacanian perspective this represents a fundamental conflict between the analyst and the patient in which the erotic transference/countertransference relationship is in the Imaginary while the analyst's task is to stay within the Symbolic through interpretations and presenting the rules of analysis. It is as if the erotic transference/countertransference situation brings too much reality into the analytic relationship which requires either or both interpretation or limit setting if the analytic relationship is to survive.

I had been working with a female client for some time; a great deal had been worked out, and both the patient and the analyst had grown a great deal from their mutual experiences. Over a period of months, the atmosphere of the sessions had become more erotic, stimulating both romantic and sexual fantasies for both participants. This experience was becoming very troublesome, but the usual categories of understanding the erotic transference/countertransference did not seem to provide an analytic direction. After weeks, maybe months of struggling and feeling overwhelmed while we attempted to analyse the fantasies emerging from this erotic transference/countertransference situation, the Bob Dylan song 'Tangled Up In Blue' kept repeating itself in my mind. I finally realised that this song was a metaphor for our relationship. I told my patient about my reverie, my waking dream state, suggesting that those lyrics represented our relationship. In telling my patient about my experience of our relationship as this song, I was perhaps attempting to interpret it, to bring it into the realm of the Symbolic, of giving words to our experience so that it did not feel so overwhelming. However, from another perspective, I feel it was an attempt to move it into the Lacanian Real, to recognise that this sublime experience was greater than our ability to control or understand. In retrospect it was a way of recognising the limits of interpretation and to locate a place in which we could both continue to be in an experience of the sublime together. The lyrics of Dylan's song describe the complexity of impossible love relationships, the subjective and intersubjective fantasies that go well beyond the psychoanalytic categories of resistance, enactment and destructive acting out.

Dylan's song, like other forms of poetry and art, brings us to a place where we experience the sublime, and stand in a state of awe as we view something greater than ourselves. In a 1978 interview, Dylan (in Cott, 1978) explained this style of song writing:

> What's different about it is that there's a code in the lyrics, and there's also no sense of time. There's no respect for it. You've got yesterday, today, and tomorrow all in the same room, and there's very little you can't imagine not happening.

In this statement, Dylan puts his finger on the critical dimension of this erotic transference/countertransference moment and on experiences of the sublime; there was 'no respect for a sense of time'; past, present and future are all occurring at the same time, as if in a dream or a painting which leaves us awestruck. The patient and I were able to enter into this expanded version of our romantic and erotic fantasies, of ourselves in a timeless dreamscape. This description of the convergence of time captures aspects of the Real in psychoanalysis, the challenge of a 'now' moment which alters the implicit relational schema.

As I needed to further understand and symbolise this intense experience, which neither of us wanted to end while also knowing that we would not literally act on our feelings, that we were in a different realm, where we were experiencing the sublime, confronting the register of the Real, another set of images occurred to me from Keats's (1820) poem 'Ode to a Grecian Urn'. Keats' poem, like Dylan's song, is about love that is outside of time, that is either frozen in time or is ongoing, an eternal experience of truth, expressing the paradoxical relationship between the poem's world of the Real and the world of common reality and time.

These three experiences, the horror of the potential death of a patient's child, viewing the magnificence of nature, and experiencing the sublime in the erotic and romantic aspects of the transference/countertransference relationships, express moments of awe, which we as psychoanalysts have often had a hard time explaining and interpreting. I believe that Lacan's original concept of the Real allows us to take another step into understanding experiences of awe and the sublime. It involves the important recognition that there are limits to our ability to know and control our lives, that we are subjects to limitations and surprise. Lacan's concept of the Real, like Bion's concept of 'O', are attempts to expand psychoanalytic theory into both the transcendent, mysterious experiences of being one with the universe described in Eastern Religion and the sense of profound aloneness and alienation which is part of existential thought. Theirs are important unexplored similarities in these concepts and in other aspects of Lacan's and Bion's theories which are well beyond the scope of this chapter. However, it is important to recognise that these were two great theorists who were trying to expand psychoanalysis beyond the limits of its clinical focus. In this chapter, I have attempted to integrate or have a dialogue between concepts drawn from third-generation Kleinians and Lacan. Both theories focus on the possibilities of growth in psychoanalysis and not simply on psychoanalysis' possibility in the reduction of symptoms and unhappiness. Experiences of awe which we may situate in the Lacanian Real and in Bion's concept of 'O' allows us to grow in the recognition of inevitable limits and in the expansion of our connection to emotions that help us to transcend the limits of our self, our time and our culture.

References

Aron, L. (1996). *A Meeting of Minds: Mutuality in Psychoanalysis*. Hillsdale, NJ and London: Analytic Press.
Bailly, L., Lichtenstein, D. and Bailly, S. (Eds) (2018) *The Lacan Tradition*. New York, NY: Routledge.
Bion, W.R. (1965) *Transformations From Learning to Growth*. London: Tavistock.
Blass, R.B. (2011) 'On the Immediacy of Unconscious Truth: Understanding Betty Joseph's "here and now" Through Comparison with Alternative Views of it outside of and Within Kleinian Thinking'. *Int. J. Psycho-Anal.*, 92 (5), pp. 1137–1157.
Civitarese, G. (2014) 'Bion and the Sublime: The Origins of An Aesthetic Paradigm'. *Int. J. Psycho-Anal.*, 95 (6), pp. 1059–1086.
Cott, J. (1978) *Rolling Stone*. 16 November 1978.
Dupont, J. (1998) 'The Concept of Trauma According to Ferenczi and Its Effects on Subsequent Psychoanalytical Research'. *Int. Forum Psychoanal.*, 7 (4), pp. 235–240.
Ferro, A. (2006) 'Clinical Implications of Bion's Thought'. *Int. J. Psycho-Anal.*, 87 (4), pp. 989–1003.
Ferro, A. (2009) 'Transformations in Dreaming and Characters in the Psychoanalytic Field 1,2'. *Int. J. Psycho-Anal.*, 90 (2), pp. 209–230.
Freud, S. (1911a) 'Formulations on the Two Principles of Mental Functioning'. *The Standard Edition of the Complete Psychological Works of Sigmund Freud*, Vol. XII (1911–1913). London: Hogarth Press.
Freud, S. (1911b) 'Psychoanalytic Notes on an Autobiographical Account of Paranoia (Dementia Paranoides)'. *The Standard Edition of the Complete Psychological Works of Sigmund Freud*, Vol. XII (1911–1913). London: Hogarth Press, pp. 1–83.
Freud, S. (1912) 'Recommendations to Physicians Practising Psycho-Analysis'. *The Standard Edition of the Complete Psychological Works of Sigmund Freud*, Vol. XII (1911–1913), London: Hogarth Press, pp. 109–120.
Freud, S. (1920) 'Beyond the Pleasure Principle'. *The Standard Edition of the Complete Psychological Works of Sigmund Freud*, Vol. XVIII (1920–1922), London: Hogarth Press, pp. 1–64.
Freud, S. (1930) 'Civilisation and its Discontents'. *The Standard Edition of the Complete Psychological Works of Sigmund Freud*, Vol. XXI (1927–1931), London: Hogarth Press, pp. 57–146.
Fromm, E. (1994) *Escape from Freedom*. New York, NY: Macmillan.
Grotstein, J. S. (2000) *Who is the Dreamer who Dreams the Dreams?* Hillsdale, NJ: Analytic Press.
Keats, J. (1820) *The Complete Works of John Keats: Poems, Plays and Personal Letters*. Musaicum Books, OK Publishing, 2017.
Khan, M. M. R. (1974) *The Privacy of the Self*. London: Hogarth Press.
Lacan, J. (2007) *Ecrits*. Ed B. Fink. New York, NY: Norton.
Lombardi, R. (2009). 'Symmetric Frenzy and Catastrophic Change: A Consideration of Primitive Mental States in the Wake of Bion and Matte Blanco'. *Int. J. Psycho-Anal.*, 90, pp. 529–549.
Mitchell, S. A. (1998). 'The Analyst's Knowledge and Authority'. *Psychoanalytic Quarterly*, 67, pp. 1–31.
Newirth, J. (2018). *From Sign to Symbol: Transformational Processes in Psychoanalysis, Psychotherapy and Psychology*. New York, NY: Lexington Books.

Ogden, T. H. (2010). 'On Three Forms of Thinking: Magical Thinking, Dream Thinking, and Transformative Thinking'. *Psychoanalytic Quarterly*, 79, pp. 317–347.

Searles, H. F. (1966). 'Concerning the Development of an Identity'. *Psychoanalytic Review*, 53D (4), pp. 7–30.

Segal, H. (1957). 'Notes on Symbol Formation'. *Int. J. Psycho-Anal.*, 38, pp. 1–7.

Stern, D. N., Sander, L. W., Nahum, J. P., Harrison, A. M., Lyons-Ruth, K., Morgan, A. C., Bruschweilerstern, N. and Tronick, E. Z. (1998). 'Non-Interpretive Mechanisms in Psychoanalytic Therapy: The "Something More" Than Interpretation'. *Int. J. Psycho-Anal.*, 79, pp. 903–921.

Chapter 6

Wisdom through desire
When truth meets love as a sublime event

Anastasios Gaitanidis

Wisdom is not an enigma. People think they can achieve it by following one of two paths: the path of truth or the path of desire. The first is followed by lovers of truth and the second by true lovers. But wisdom that leads to an intimation of the sublime, ineffable and profound bond with another human being, could only be reached when the two paths are combined, when truth meets love and is realised through it.

The love of truth: the philosophers

But here's the problem: in our world, the two paths do not often meet. The lovers of truth (i.e. philosophers) feel the need to keep their distance and isolation from others in order to make sense of the facts of their existence, especially the fact of their own death. In this sense, relations to others are perceived as an obstacle to the attainment of this goal. Martin Heidegger (1927), for instance, was so preoccupied whilst he was writing *Being and Time* with how to transform the fact of his own death into his innermost truth and possibility, that he turned his back to love (apparently the word 'love' appears only once in all 500 pages of the book) and his beloved mistress, Hannah Arendt. In a letter, he tells her:

> I forgot you – not from indifference, not because external circumstances intruded between us, but because I had to forget and will forget you whenever I withdraw into the final stages of my most concentrated work ... And this 'withdrawal' from everything human and breaking off of all connections is, with regard to creative work, the most magnificent [sublime] human experience I know – [even though] with regard to concrete situations, it is the most repugnant thing one can encounter. In it one becomes fully aware that one's heart has been ripped from one's body ... Coming to terms with this in a positive way – not taking a position exclusively as a kind of escape – is what it means to exist as a philosopher.
>
> (quoted in Maier-Katkin, 2010, p. 68)

In a similar vein, 'to philosophise is to learn how to die' claims Socrates, the man who inaugurated Western philosophy by waxing lyrical in his (or rather Plato's) *Apology* (2017) about the political and moral necessity of his death without ever considering the pain this would cause to his wife, friends and followers.

The archetypal philosopher's fixation on *his own* death and consequent indifference towards his loved ones could be understood if one closely examines his views on love. For instance, in Plato's *Symposium* (1989), Socrates introduces (using Diotima as his mouthpiece) the idea of 'the ladder of love' which is a metaphor for the ascent a lover might make from pure attraction to something beautiful, such as a beautiful body, the lowest step of the ladder, to the appreciation of beautiful souls and the beauty of knowledge and, finally, to the actual contemplation of the Idea of Beauty itself which is portrayed as:

> an everlasting loveliness which neither comes nor goes, which neither flowers nor fades ... subsisting of itself and by itself in an eternal oneness.
> (Symposium, 1989, 211 a–b)

The description of this ascent can be regarded as an account of 'sublimation', the process of transmuting a 'lower' physical or sexual impulse into one that is viewed as 'higher' or more socially valued. In this instance, the lover's desire for a beautiful body is sublimated into a desire for insight and wisdom, thus becoming a *'philo-sopher'*, literally a *lover of wisdom*. Once s/he reaches the highest rung on the ladder and contemplates the Idea of Beauty, s/he does not need the ladder anymore and could let it go. In this respect, the particularity of the beloved and her/his beauty become irrelevant and could be disposed of.

One is reminded here of Søren Kierkegaard who broke off his engagement to Regine Olsen once he realised that his purpose was to go beyond his love for one particular person in order to reach the Christian love for 'man'. Kierkegaard (1847) insists that this love is not 'natural', but it is the love one feels for each human being for the sake of God and in a 'God-relationship'. The only element of 'this man' which is of interest to the Christian is 'the human', as revealed in this person. In love, the other person becomes a mere 'instance' of the more general and abstract love for 'man'. In other words, this love has no proper object as such: it is 'object-less'. In Kierkegaard's doctrine, Christian love is determined only by the subjective qualities of the loving one, such as disinterestedness, unlimited confidence, unobtrusiveness, mercifulness, self-denial and fidelity. It is not significant whether the beloved is loved. Thus, as Theodor Adorno (1939) puts it:

> It is unnecessary to point out how close this love comes to callousness. Perhaps one may most accurately summarize Kierkegaard's doctrine of

love by saying that he demands that love behave towards all men as if they were dead. Indeed, the book culminates in the speech *Wie wir in Liebe Verstorbener Gedenken* [How to think with love of those who passed away].

(p. 417)

In this sense, the beloved as a living, embodied person is not important and could be ignored or forgotten. What is important is the ability to experience love itself as the ultimate truth of subjective inwardness in a moment of sublime, ecstatic isolation.

The truth of love: the Romantic poets

Yet, if one wants to find love, one must be willing to abandon one's sublime (and sublimated) isolation in the pursuit of truth and take the risk of reaching out to the other by falling in love with her/him. One might think that this would be the case with the exemplary *true lovers*, the Romantic poets. Most Romantics, however, often fall in love only with their fantasy of the other and not with the other her/himself, that is to say, only with *what* the other represents to them – usually some-*thing* unattainable and dangerous – and not with *whom* the other is in her/his own right. This is problematic because when the Romantic poets' fantasy is challenged by the other's reality, they are usually unable to recognise (or be recognised by) her/him and they then abandon (or are abandoned by) her/him or destroy themselves and/or the other in the process.

This is beautifully illustrated by Alfred Lord Tennyson (1842), in his famous poem *The Lady of Shalott*. The Lady is portrayed as enjoying her contemplative seclusion by watching life unfold through the pale and shadowy reflections of reality observed in a medieval mirror and weaved by her into a tapestry. However, she is frustrated with the world of shadows whenever she glimpses a wedding or a funeral in the mirror (a clear indication of the subsequent association of love with death). '*I am half-sick of shadows*', she declares, whilst entertaining the idea of abandoning her shadowy isolation in order to come into the light and meet the other denizens of Camelot. What eventually pulls her out of the shadows though is that she falls in love with the seductive voice and mirror image of Sir Lancelot (and, one might say, with her fantasy of him) and feels compelled to see him and be seen by him. However, the moment the Lady of Shalott sets her tapestry aside to look upon Lancelot, a curse is unleashed upon her that leads to her untimely death. Yet, the greatest curse of all is that although she is compelled to see Lancelot, she dies without being able to truly see or be seen by him. The only remark Lancelot makes about her at the end of the poem is that 'she has a lovely face, God in her mercy lend her grace'. Having abandoned her shadowy, isolated existence, the Lady of Shalott comes into the light only to be plunged back into darkness by becoming herself a shadowy, ghost-like figure – not a living, breathing, beautiful woman-in-love, but merely a 'dead-pale' beauty.

As mentioned above, in order to find love, a purely contemplative position needs to be disturbed by confronting one's desire for the other which demands transcending one's isolation. One does not choose whom one falls in love with. There is an inevitability and fatefulness in this fall-ness. However, one can freely choose to say 'yes' to this fate and rejoice in what life has to give. For the Lady of Shalott, however (as she is represented by the Romantic poet), there is a compulsive quality to her desire that unavoidably 'drives' her to destruction. She is unable to celebrate her 'coming into light' and enjoy her love because she falls in love only with her fantasy of the other. This leads to the lack of connection with, and recognition by, the other and the return of the shadow of life's and love's negation. Death therefore becomes the only outcome of a love that cannot be sustained – and is inevitably eradicated – as she cannot willingly engage with her vulnerability that comes from exposing herself to the reality of the other's uniqueness and complexity.

When truth meets love: the poet-philosophers

Yet, unlike The Lady of Shallot, our love for the other does not have to die an inevitable death. As Stephen Mitchell (2003) argues in his book *Can Love Last?*, although the Romantic poets are right in proposing that love cannot be willed or forced, love can nevertheless be sustained by consciously committing to create with another, the beloved, a vessel into which new life and desire can be poured, contained and developed. Eros/Love is the 'great preserver' (Freud, 1920), claiming back in one's specific and unique sexual and emotional union with another a totality that is destined to become fragmented by the 'great destroyer', death and its emissary, time – only to be re-claimed again in a subsequent union.

This is succinctly captured by John Berger in his 1984 book, *And our Faces, my Heart, Brief as Photos*, in which he states that love functions as a container that constantly recovers the fragments of totality that time and death disperse (p. 41). For Berger, the inevitable tension between totality and fragmentation, infinity and finitude, permanence and transience, needs to be recognised in order to give form to 'that holding which is Being' (p. 41). Yet, this could only be achieved if one transcends the positions of the lover of truth and the true lover – i.e. philosopher and Romantic poet – so as to arrive at the combined position of the poet-philosopher where truth and love meet and become indistinguishable. If time is, as Goytisolo (2003) says, 'a blind rider nobody could unsaddle … ravaging all that seemed enduring … reducing dreams to ashes' (p. 32), the poet-philosopher's primary role is both to represent this truth and use words in order to wrestle scraps of existence out of time's inevitable destruction. For the poet-philosopher's genius works by offering us, through her/his poems, a glimpse of love as an imperishable, sublime event – not as an exposure to something 'extraordinary' that belongs to a 'beyond' (i.e. the metaphysical realm of Ideas), but as an experience of totality/eternity within our everyday, ordinary lives where everything is intertwined and relations with others are enjoined.

One cannot help but think here of Ezra Pound (1913) who began by writing a poem ('In a Station of the Metro') that was three-pages long only to spend a whole year trying to edit it down to two lines. By erasing all the elements in language that have become redundant in the attempt to capture the 'thing itself', by reducing a landscape overrun with words to two simple lines, Pound, like all poet-philosophers, asks us to take a leap of faith, to trust that, although at times words will fall in their struggle to represent the sublime, they will not fail us. They will ultimately deliver a vision of the sublime as an ordinary, everyday occurrence. This is an act of surrender: it requires us to give everything and expect very little, almost nothing, in return.

An exemplary poet-philosopher: Maggie Nelson

The wisdom of the poet-philosopher's work lies in her/his ability to imitate the path of philosophy without subscribing to its search for singular or ultimate truths. To paraphrase Adorno (1951), her/his 'art is [philosophy] delivered from the lie of being [the only] truth' (p. 222). This is the art of the American poet-philosopher-novelist Maggie Nelson. Her prose-poems are written in the form of short propositions in the style of Ludwig Wittgenstein. However, whilst the latter mistrusts words and believes that silence is the most appropriate response to our fundamental existential and ethical questions, including the question of love, Nelson trusts that, although words could not function as representations of ultimate reality and truth, they could still carry the truth of her love, pain and loss. As Anne Carson (1998) aptly puts it: 'Words, if you let them, will do what they want to do and what they have to do' (p. 120). The beautiful semblance they create is only illusory and seductive when it is not underscored by the existence of an authentic emotional core.

In her autobiographical/philosophical prose-poem *Bluets*, Nelson (2009) describes the various ways she is in love with the colour 'blue' (incidentally, Wittgenstein's (1977) last work was his *Remarks on Colour* which he wrote during the last 18 months of his life whilst he was dying of stomach cancer). Nelson takes us through a journey of 'blue' adventures and discoveries interspersed with her hatred for the colours green and yellow. Like a satin bowerbird, she collects and arranges blue objects, concepts, songs and instruments (i.e. *the cyanometer*) (p. 40), in order to create a kind of blue nest/bower. She hopes that by doing this she will find some kind of consolation, a dignity in her loneliness ('loneliness is solitude with a problem', p. 28) after her separation from the person she calls 'the prince of blue' who has now become a 'pain devil'.

However, 'blue' also represents her depression, the pain of experiencing intense love as a form of permanent affliction. She wonders whether one could actually know when and how to refuse or recover from this type of love. Falling in love with a powerful person, letting him/her inside you, could alter you irrevocably, in the same way that injecting or inhaling a powerful drug, like crack, could create such an 'unbelievable high that would live on in your system forever'. She believes this could be seen as a chronic condition she calls 'cyanosis' (literally, 'turning blue'), a sense of permanently feeling 'blue' due to the potency of the lover's addictive presence and the catastrophe ensued from his/her potential or actual permanent absence.

One is reminded of Gabriel Garcia Marquez's heroine Bernarda Carrera in his short novel *Of Love and Other Demons* (1994), the depraved wife of the Marquis, whose husband has given up on her. To escape from her own life and the intense longing she feels for her slave lover, Bernarda uses a type of 'magic chocolate' which induces in her a state of delirium and makes her spend most of her days lying naked on the bedroom floor. Yet, other characters in the novel (who do not consume magic chocolate) do not suffer a better fate. In their attempt to exorcise their demons, they fall prey to the worst demon of all, longing, and they are destroyed by it. In a Catholic universe dominated by the obsession with the sanctity of the soul and the sinful nature of bodily desire, longing for carnal connection is transformed into a demon that cannot be exorcised.

This form of longing seems to be at the basis of what Thomas Ogden (2012) calls 'addictive love' as a way of interpreting Ronald Fairbairn's (1944) account of the relationship between the 'libidinal ego' and 'the exciting object'. This relationship is best exemplified by the figure of Tantalus who was condemned to never being able to quench his thirst and satiate his hunger – water would always recede before he could drink a single drop, and the fruit of the nearby tree would forever elude his grasp. 'Tantalising' is therefore the term we use to describe this longing for a proximate but unreachable object: it is an interminably unsatisfying invitation to go through a door that is neither completely open nor closed, or more accurately it is a door that shuts when you come close to it and opens when you move away from it.

One might inaccurately assume that Nelson's description of her love as a tantalising affliction would enlist her in the camp of the Romantic poets who are addicted to the idea of love itself and the fantasy of an unattainable and dangerous other. However, she does not permanently occupy this tantalising state – as we shall see later on in the chapter, she finds the courage to face and begin to overcome her loss through her creative writing process, that is, through the process of expressing in words her continuous desire for her lover, naming the pain of their separation and gradually digesting the loss rather than remaining everlastingly addicted to it.

My work with S

I will attempt to illustrate this struggle – the work of facing and representing one's love and loss versus succumbing to the torture of tantalising longing – not through prose-poetry, like Nelson, but through the presentation of my therapeutic work with a patient. S was 32 when he first came to see me and stayed with me for almost three years before he decided to abruptly end his therapy. He said that he was a 'sex and love addict' and wanted to find a way to control this. He had a 'good' life and didn't want this 'affliction' to spoil it. He understood that his early experiences of loss and separation could partly explain this addiction: he and his twin sister were given up for adoption by their adolescent birth mother, but his sister didn't survive beyond the age of two. He didn't only lose a mother but a sister too – he was haunted by a 'peculiar sense of responsibility', blaming himself for these losses: 'I was 'too much' for them', he said, 'My mother had to give me up for adoption and my sister couldn't survive me'. 'There is 'badness' in me I can't exorcise'. It was more tolerable to see himself as 'bad'/'sinful' than to live with the 'badness'/'sins' of his birth mother's abandonment and his twin sister's death.

S was beautiful ... but his beauty was tainted by his icy, distant demeanour accentuated by the goth-like contrast between his dark hair and pale skin. I thought he looked like a 'male doll', externally 'cool' but empty inside.

S was terrified by the possibility that one might see him as 'ordinary' and tried really hard to present himself as 'special' by actively embodying his apparent 'contradictions'. He was an Irish 'lad' from a 'humble' background, but his closest friend was an English aristocrat. He was simultaneously a devout Catholic and an unrelenting agnostic. He would utter obscenities whilst listening to opera, reading Russian literature and admiring avant-garde art at Tate Modern.

He tried to excel at everything, even at things he was not supposed to excel at, like mathematics, which went against his artistic inclination. Pleasing his adoptive mother was his life's mission ('I had already lost one mother', he said, 'I couldn't bear losing another one'), an exciting but unforgiving woman, a lead nurse who was autocratic both at hospital and at home. Yet, what S was best at was acting. He thought that acting was his ticket out: he could perform his way out of his adoptive mother's tyranny and seductive manipulation by satisfying her greed for success and money.

Yet, after a brief stint as an actor on Broadway, he felt trapped by the excessive demands of his agent (another autocratic maternal figure) and, in order to escape, moved to London where he ended up marrying his childhood friend (a substitute for his deceased twin sister), who got pregnant and gave birth to a baby girl a year later. He carried out his duty as father and husband for eight years but did it begrudgingly and with great ambivalence – no wonder considering his history of maternal abandonment and oppression.

Although he loved his wife and daughter, he couldn't stand being a full-time husband and father. 'My "sinful" nature needed to come out', he said.

He decided to have an affair with a student he met at one of his acting classes. She was in her mid-20s, married with no kids. He was very attracted to her because she was unlike all his previous lovers who were mainly passive and docile. She knew she had the power to hurt him by abruptly cutting him off (she had already done this a couple of times during their affair). Yet, he also knew how to win her back by making himself tantalisingly proximate but unavailable: 'I'll have an affair with you but I'll never leave my wife! I don't confuse loyalty with fidelity. After all, I am a Catholic: I made a promise to her that I cannot break'.

S and his lover had very little time together, very little time to do anything apart from having 'ruthless sex'. 'Sex is so good … very good', he said, 'We know how to use our bodies so as to mess with our minds'. He described how they planned every move in advance, focusing more on the number of 'effects' than the quality of the experience and the complexity of the process. I saw it as a standardised 'tick-box' exercise that didn't take into account the false starts, breaks, difficulties of meeting that could only be overcome by the acceptance of each other's vulnerability.

I could see how sex was used as a defence against the desire to seek closeness and intimacy. Their sexual encounters were part of a care-less universe dominated by the tyranny of 'more' or 'less'. If he desired her more, then she wanted him less (and *vice versa*) … They needed to 'fuck' each other to bring things back to a relative equilibrium. Theirs was the triumph of exhibitionism – sexy lingerie, whips, belts, handcuffs – over the benign curiosity of erotic nakedness and care-free experimentation.

But then things started to change. His lover began to demand 'more' intimacy from him. She didn't want to only have sex; she also wanted to get to know him, to find out how he felt. This was dangerous for S: as long as their affair was restricted to sex, everything was under control; but feelings … feelings were uncontrollable. He entertained her desire for intimacy for a long time but when she finally insisted that they should both leave their spouses and get married, 'I gave her up the same way my birth mother gave me up for adoption … without looking back'. He continued: 'Yet, I told her that her love doesn't need to end just because we won't see each other. And, who knows, perhaps one day we might meet again. I don't know why I said this … I suppose I still wanted her to love me'. 'Yes', I replied, 'you wanted to stop your suffering by giving her up the same way you would give up an addictive substance. But you didn't want her to forget you. You wanted her to long for you by keeping the hope of a future reunion alive'. 'After all', I said quoting Heidegger (1954), 'longing is the agony of the nearness of the distant' (p. 420).

Yet, not long after the end of the affair, his icy exterior began to crack and I could observe signs of sadness appearing on his face. I told him that cutting his lover off from his life was not the same as ending the relationship with her. This could only be achieved through the prolonged and arduous work of mourning. I also explained that his fear of truly allowing himself to 'know', and 'be known' by, his lover was intimately related to his fear of experiencing and sustaining his erotic desire towards someone he actually knew, his wife. I tried to convey this painful realisation as an attempt to form a deeper connection with S. And when I finally felt that we were 'getting closer' and he would be able to openly talk about his pain, he abruptly ended his therapy without an explanation. I repeatedly tried to contact him, but to no avail ... I felt as if I were a little child approaching mother with the hope of receiving a kind response only to be thoughtlessly and cruelly dismissed and abandoned – perhaps he might have felt similarly when he was given up for adoption or when he was dismissed by his adoptive mother.

I was left alone to carry S's pain as he couldn't carry it himself. I realised that this was the only ending he was able to have, the only ending he could afford to have. This was the only possibility that (in)animated him: by uprooting himself from the land of pain and loss, he was also cutting himself off from the source of life, love and pleasure. I felt an enormous wave of sadness washing over me: to expend such an enormous amount of energy trying to protect himself by cutting off any intimate connection with the other. One might think that loving the other would have been so much easier ... but love is not easy for the walking wounded, for those who are burdened by heavy legacies of loss and longing.

Returning to Nelson

In order to further understand the adverse effects of S's loss and longing and how best to process them, let us return to Nelson. Although she feels there is no special knowledge or status to be gained by the intensity of her heartbreak, she nonetheless creatively engages with the process of naming it and thus slowly decreasing it – something that S was unable to do by deciding to abruptly end his therapy that would have helped him name and thus process the pain associated with the loss of his relationship (and, of course, the loss of his previous ones too).

Nelson continues this process by teaching us to abandon the dichotomy between mind and body when it comes to love. Of course, this dichotomy lies at the heart of the problem with both the philosopher's and the Romantic poet's views of love. Our love for the other consists of the indissoluble unity of two seemingly contradictory substances: body and mind. When we love, we think and feel the other with our body and touch them with our mind. If we exalt the mind and scorn the body (according to the aforementioned philosophical, Platonic and Christian traditions), then we create a split that attempts to artificially control what should be one's wholesome and heartfelt/embodied surrender. Without carnal attraction, there is no erotic connection with the lover. And what is more, were it not for the attraction of the lover's body, we could not love the mind that animates it. For the desired body is the lover's mind that speaks through their skin.

However, in our era, we often also make the opposite mistake: we reject the mind and reduce love to a bodily function. Love then becomes the mere 'fantasy' of love, the Romantic poet's addictive attachment to the imaginary and seductive appearance and characteristics of another person. Without the belief in a mind inseparable from our body, without the courage to continually face, symbolise and overcome our fears of intimacy and closeness, love regresses to mere erotic fantasy, or even worse, to bare 'fucking'. Like my patient S, we end up using our bodies to fuck our minds out of existence. 'There is a colour inside of the fucking and it is not blue' (p. 19) since 'fucking leaves everything exactly as it is' (p. 8), says Nelson.

Nelson then proceeds to use the example of an injured, quadriplegic friend so as to compare and contrast her love affliction to her friend. Nelson portrays her friend as acknowledging 'her intense grief for all she has lost, a grief she describes as bottomless' (p. 91) but she also recognises her friend's disability as conferring her special status and knowledge, akin to the blind seer Tiresias in Sophocles' *Oedipus Rex*, i.e. the quality of an oracle. Wisdom as the ability to see truth seems to only be attained once the desiring and desirous body is somehow disabled. For Nelson, loving her friend means keeping in mind and witnessing her friend's physical paralysis and suffering rather than succumbing to the temptation of perceiving her only as a disembodied, wise woman.

At the end of *Bluets*, Nelson also realises that her love for the colour blue is a poor substitute for the loss of her lover and provides no consolation:

> I want you to know, if you ever read this, there was a time when I would rather have had you … than all the blue in the world.
>
> (p. 94)

And then she goes even further by deconstructing the idea of love itself as a form of disembodied consolation:

> Simone Weil warned otherwise. 'Love is not consolation', she wrote. 'It is light'.
>
> (p. 96)

This is where Nelson's philosophy of life meets her poetic imagination, where the absence of the lover's body does violence to her mind. All divisions have been undone; all dichotomies have been undermined. Truth and love, wisdom and desire are brought together when she finally proclaims:

All right then, let me try to rephrase. When I was alive, I aimed to be a student not of longing but of light.

(p. 96)

One can see how Nelson begins to come 'back to light', whilst S was unable to do so. It is her ability to use her prose-poetry to represent her pain and process her loss that reminds her how to be a student of light again, whilst S's inability to process love and loss in therapy (or by using any other creative means available to him) reduces him into a permanent student of longing.

Conclusion

The ending of Nelson's *Bluets* signifies the beginning of a new process, the process of mourning the end of her relationship with her lover, by acknowledging the pain of her loss and refusing to be consoled by any disembodied, abstract substitutes, including her love for the colour 'blue'. Her *Bluets* reminds us, as she herself remembers by writing it, that love is 'light', a sublime event, the truth of which we can neither ignore nor isolate ourselves from without destroying our vitality and openness to the surprises and wonders of everyday, ordinary existence with others. The loss of love might plunge us into temporary darkness but engaging with the process of mourning can allow us to discern 'the light' again.

Of course, it is not easy to be a 'student of light' (i.e. a poet-philosopher): it takes courage to engage with the process of constantly having to empty out our fears, longings and preconceptions so as to allow ourselves to become in body and mind truly receptive of, and responsive to, the love of the other. Yet, when we try to control this process by cutting ourselves off from the source of light and substituting it with shadowy, disembodied forms and ideals (as many philosophers do) or by mindlessly adhering to our narcissistic erotic fantasies of the other which promote an addictive pattern of relating and prohibit our close connection with her/him (as many Romantic poets do), we contribute to the perpetuation of our tantalising longing and suffering.

References

Adorno, T.W. (1939) 'On Kierkegaard's Doctrine of Love'. *Zeitschrift fur Sozialforschung / Studies in Philosophy and Social Science*, 8 (3), pp. 413–429.

Adorno, T.W. (1951) *Minima Moralia*. London: Verso, 2005.

Berger, J. (1984) *And our Faces, my Heart, Brief as Photos*. London: Bloomsbury, 2005.

Carson, A. (1998) *Autobiography of Red: A Novel in Verse*. New York, NY: Alfred A. Knopf.

Fairbairn, W.R.D. (1944) 'Endopsychic Structure Considered in Terms of Object-Relationships'. In *Psychoanalytic Studies of the Personality*. London: Kegan Paul, 1952, pp. 82–132.
Freud, S. (1920) 'Beyond the Pleasure Principle'. *The Standard Edition of the Complete Psychological Works of Sigmund Freud*, Vol. XVIII. London: Hogarth Press.
Goytisolo, J. (2003) *The Blind Rider*. Trans Peter Bush. London: Serpent's Tail, 2005.
Heidegger, M. (1927) *Being and Time*. Trans Joan Stambaugh, revised by Dennis J. Schmidt. Albany, NY: SUNY Press.
Heidegger, M (1954) 'Who is Nietzsche's Zarathustra?' Trans Bernd Magnus. *The Review of Metaphysics*, 20 (3), pp. 411–431, 1967.
Kierkegaard, S. (1847) *Kierkegaard's Writings, XVI: Works of Love*. Ed Hong Howard V. and Hong Edna H. Princeton, NJ: Princeton University Press, 2017.
Maier-Katkin, D. (2010) *Stranger from Abroad: Hannah Arendt, Martin Heidegger, Friendship and Forgiveness*. New York, NY: W.W. Norton.
Marquez, G. C. (1994) *Of Love and Other Demons*. Trans Edith Grossman. London: Penguin Books, 1996.
Mitchell, S. A. (2003) *Can Love Last?: The Fate of Romance over Time*. New York, NY: W.W. Norton.
Nelson, M. (2009) *Bluets*. London: Jonathan Cape.
Ogden, T. H. (2012) *Creative Readings: Essays on Seminal Analytic Works*. London and New York, NY: Routledge.
Plato (1989) *The Symposium*. Greek text with trans. by Tom Griffith. Berkeley, CA: University of California Press.
Plato (2017)*Euthyphro, Apology, Crito, Phaedo*. Greek with Trans by Chris Emlyn-Jones and William Preddy. Loeb Classical Library 36. Cambridge, MA: Harvard University Press,
Pound, E. (1913) 'In a Station of the Metro'. *In Selected Poems*. Ed T.S. Eliot. London: Faber and Faber, 1928, p. 113.
Tennyson, A. L. (1842) *The Lady of Shalott*. London: Lulu, 2011.
Wittgenstein, L. (1977) *Remarks on Colour*. Ed G. E. M. Anscombe and Trans Linda Schättle. Oxford: Blackwell.

Chapter 7

'How extraordinary that you should exist'

On playing and experience of truth

Polona Curk

In the biographical film about physicist Stephen Hawking, *The Theory of Everything* (McCarten, 2013, p. 73),[1] there is a segment in the story where Hawking's indomitable spirit seems broken, resigned, as though he has lost the will to fight his disease. It refers to the period directly after his tracheotomy, and he seems weighed down by the realisation that no words will ever come out from his mouth again. He is offered to use the E-Tran board (a spelling board) to communicate, but he rejects it – as if the expectation that the disease will imminently win has suffocated his boundless curiosity to learn and motivation to engage in anything. It almost seems this is the end, if not of Hawking's life, then of his energy and spirit.

But in the memorable scene that follows, a shift occurs. Elaine, a new nurse, makes another attempt at introducing the spelling board. Whilst uncomplicated, the method is slow and tedious, and as before Stephen seems downcast and does not want to engage. Elaine notices his dispiritedness but nonetheless proceeds to explain again how the board is supposed to work: when she calls out the colour of the group of the letters, he should blink to indicate which one he wants to choose. Stephen looks at her for a second; then his eyes flick from group to group without blinking. Nevertheless, Elaine, following his eye movements across the board, is able to identify what he wants: tea. There is a trace of surprise on Stephen's face. Elaine then puts the board down and challenges him:

> You've memorised the board. Of course you have. What kind of tea? Blink when I say the group that has the letter you want. Green, Yellow, Blue, White, Black, Red ... I haven't got all day ... (He blinks).
> (McCarten, 2013, pp. 75–76)

Elaine's challenge is an invitation to *play*. Crucially, this immediately redefines the identity and position of the 'players': in the moment of recognition that both have memorised the board, they are not anymore a nurse and a severely disabled patient rather, '[t]hey are both EXPERT ...' (ibid.) – partners in a play. The moment turns out to be a breakthrough – Stephen's spirit is back: 'He grins. She smiles. She goes to get him some tea' (ibid.).

In this short scene, something that was until then an enormous exhausting and discouraging effort at overcoming a disability, has become *enjoyable*, a way to play with another. And with this, the whole course of events ensues. By not blinking, Stephen refused to comply with what was asked of him: with the rules of the board, with Elaine's requirements, and symbolically, with the ever-increasing demands placed on him by his condition. His non-compliance was a symbolic rebellion and protest against how things are, however unchangeable, and an assertion of his own, however minute, terms and conditions to his situation. His challenge to Elaine was also a request for understanding. Elaine accepted the challenge and responded to it. Instead of re-asserting the board's rules – the given reality rules – she was open to Stephen setting new rules and playing by his rules, as it were.

In this chapter, I first look at playing as belonging to the area of what has been called ethical or sublime experiences, and I explore what this might mean. Second, I look at the experience of the sublime in playing with another as a source of (self-)knowledge of a particular kind. I argue that there are parts of the self that can only be discovered through play with another, which makes the ability to play essential for the self in relationships. For these reasons, playing can be considered an ethical engagement: a sublime dimension of everyday life.

Playing: sublime and ethical

Freud saw love and work as the twofold foundations of communal human life (1930), and it has been argued that he understood the psychoanalytic aim to be rendering a person healthy in the sense of capable of 'love and work' (Forrester and Cameron, 1999, p. 934). But Donald Winnicott installed the ability to play as both the third aim of psychoanalysis and a sign of health; indeed, as what facilitates healing. It is play, Winnicott contends,

> *that is the universal*, and that belongs to health ... psychoanalysis has been developed as a highly specialised form of playing in the service of communication with oneself and others.
>
> (Winnicott, 2005, p. 56)

Playing is, in other words, the original, the natural thing, of which psychoanalysis is just 'the highly sophisticated twentieth-century phenomenon' (ibid.). Winnicott understands playing as the act of bridging the inner and the outer world in the third area – his famous transitional space; an outward activity of 'a simple and enjoyable dramatisation of inner world life' (Abram, 2007, p. 247). It is also not something to be outgrown with the domain of childhood – although focused on work with children, Winnicott unequivocally states: 'Whatever I saw about children playing really applies to adults as well ...' (Winnicott, 2005, p. 54). He stresses endlessly throughout his writings that playing is a source of aliveness, of creativity, of meaning, of the sense of feeling real: it facilitates health and supports group relationships, it is a special form of communication. Playing is, in this sense, an ethical experience.

Psychoanalytic profession's focus on neutrality und non-judgemental stance has often meant little explicit theorising about the ethical. There is a certain acknowledgement that psychoanalysis essentially strives to offer a relationship where one person tries to help another, through producing something that at least by its expressed intention is 'good' (Schafer, 2002), and that 'good' is something that might emerge in certain moments between the analyst and the analysand. But whatever it is that emerges remains forever tentative, known only by the emotional effects it has had on both parties. When psychoanalysts have tried to conceptualise these (potentially ethical) moments, they have thus often leaned on philosophy. Wittgenstein's work has been one of such sources for them, due to the shared concern with the indescribable and unspeakable in language (for example, Davoine and Gaudilliere, 2004; Clapham, 1997). In his 1930 *Lecture on Ethics* (Wittgenstein, 1965), Wittgenstein discusses the experience of sublime moments, something which psychoanalyst Miles Clapham deploys to think about ethical moments in therapy sessions. Clapham identifies such moments as marked by a wish that 'everything could remain as it is in this moment forever' (Clapham, 1997, p. 507). For both authors, the question revolves around how to express a certain absoluteness, out-of-ordinary-temporality, of such moments.

Wittgenstein uses an example of the experience of absolute safety – 'I am safe whatever happens' (Wittgenstein, 1965, p. 9) – to convey the specific paradox denoting such moments. For such absolute safety to be 'true', it would have to imply a physical impossibility that anything bad could happen to me. This is nonsensical in an ordinary understanding, but it feels real as an experience. Yet, Wittgenstein seems to suggest more than just a false or mistaken feeling. Rather, for certain experiences, an attempt to explain them would be nonsensical; indeed, it would even destroy them. Wittgenstein sets up his whole *Lecture* as an attempt to say something about ethics in a different way, for he argues that it is not possible to speak about it *in* language. He points out that when we use expressions – such as 'good' – we do so in two senses: the trivial (relative) sense, which judges something as 'good' relative to a certain predetermined standard and is thus merely a statement of facts; and the absolute sense, which expresses an absolute judgement of value (Wittgenstein, 1965, p. 6). It is only in the second sense that these expressions might refer to ethical experiences. The ethical is understood as the sublime, the supernatural; thus, using certain words in the first sense cannot express it: 'There are no propositions which, in any absolute sense, are sublime ...', thus, it seems obvious to him '[t]hat we cannot write a scientific book, the subject matter of which could be intrinsically sublime and above all other subject matters' (Wittgenstein, 1965, pp. 6–7). An ethical moment falls outside the ordinary way words convey sense.

Clapham similarly denotes ethical moments as experiences where 'our understanding falters' (Clapham, 1997, p. 508). How do we convey them? Whilst we cannot describe them *in* language, Wittgenstein proposes they can be expressed *by the existence of language itself*. When trying to express something about the 'absolute good' (Wittgenstein, 1965, p. 7), Wittgenstein proposes one can describe one's experience, with a hope *to invoke* a similar experience in the other, which might create 'common ground' to then proceed with a joint investigation. The experience Wittgenstein has in mind seems affective, too. He calls it a state of wonder: '[H]ow *extraordinary* that the world should exist' (ibid., p. 8, emphasis added).

Three important points seem to mark this kind of communication. First, the change seems to be in one's comportment: in the way we look at certain experiences. Should we look at them with scientific eyes (have them 'vivisected', as he puts it), the magic disappears: 'The truth is that the scientific way of looking at a fact *is not the way* to look at it as a miracle' (ibid., p. 11, emphasis added). There are experiences that are (potentially) miracles, and we need to find the right way to look at them in order not to destroy them. Second, for Wittgenstein, the sublime absolute value of such moments is particular *to a person* – to those that have experienced them. Finally, the experiences are facts at the same time as they have an absolute value: 'It is the paradox that an experience, a fact, should seem to have supernatural value' (ibid., p. 10).

This certainly sounds close to the psychoanalytic process: invoking experiences for a joint exploration with another, of their emotional moves and effects. Wittgenstein's proposed way to convey such moments has parallels to characteristics of Winnicott's moments in a transitional space. Winnicott would agree that attempting to describe what is going on in such moments would break the magic of the wonder, the illusion deployed in this space: it would 'destroy the moment in its momentousness' (Clapham, 1997, p. 507). The experiences in transitional space, crucially, involve a paradox in Winnicott's theory, too: they are personal and subjective, whilst also being shareable, real. Transitional space is a space where the ontological status of illusion is not challenged by other (in other words, not to be questioned about whether it belongs to inner or shared reality) as long as claims of its objectivity are not made on others (Winnicott, 2005, pp. 18, 19). Whatever the meanings one makes of one's experiences, they are at the same time both subjective and real – wonders and facts, as Wittgenstein may put it.

Playing happens in this transitional space, not as an escape into imagination devoid of reality – if an adult made a claim on others of objectivity of his subjective phenomena it would suggest madness (Winnicott, 2005, p. 18). It is, for Winnicott, a space including both illusion and reality. But a particular kind of comportment is required that we might describe as 'accepting nonsensicality' at the core of the experience of the space where creativity, playing and meaning making happen, just like Wittgenstein suggests that if the most absolute and *meaningful*, even miraculous experiences, continually compel us to describe them in certain words as ethical or absolute, we have to conclude that 'their nonsensicality was their very essence' (1965, p. 11). Perhaps, then, the comportment required to look at such experiences consists of an awareness that there is something 'nonsensical' – if by sense we should mean rational, scientific, describable – at the core of the very ethical moments that are referring to the 'sense' of life. By implication, if what we understand as rational, scientific, describable, cannot actually ultimately capture such 'sense', it must in some sense be nonsensical, too, and the division breaks down.

Wittgenstein discusses ethical moments through the idea of wondering, but psychoanalysts have understood ethical moments more widely, as any moving moments – that is, moments that produce affective *shifts* – even profoundly difficult moments in therapy. In the section below I come back to the idea of shifts and movements. Here, I want to suggest that playing, in particular playing with another, is a sub-group of ethical moments that goes further than wondering. A state of wonder is passive; engaging in playing with someone, on the contrary, is both passive and active, both losing oneself in the play, and actively participating. It involves engaging in a way that allows for a state of wonder about something that feels miraculous, whilst at the same time co-producing this 'miracle'. It's a particular kind of communication that is creative, but not creative (solely) on the basis of effort or work but through enjoyment in each other.

Playing, in Winnicott's sense, provides the spark, the creativity, the sense of being alive and communicating with another in a particular way as illustrated in the vignette at the beginning. The magic of play, its excitement and joy, *produces* psychic energy. This is important when we try to move from, in Wittgenstein's words, 'the desire to say something about the ultimate meaning of life, the absolute good, the absolute valuable' (1965, p. 12), to the desire to *create* or *do* 'good' in the ethical (and perhaps psychoanalytic) sense. The motivation for it can spring from one's values and identities, one's sense of belonging, one's sense of duty and responsibility. But often these reflect also how one would like to see oneself and what one thinks one 'should' be doing; something that, on its own, can use and exhaust one's mental energy resources, become superficial or self-righteous, or lead to giving up. My argument here is that playing is an activity that is a source, which continuously and sustainably also produces mental energy for such motivation to do 'good'. It enables a particular kind of connection to another human being which is ethics as creation, including of knowledge about the self and the other, but also, importantly, of the energy to go on, make an effort, believe. It is an encounter with, and a comportment towards, an other that can produce a wonder in a Wittgensteinian sense: 'How *extraordinary* that you should exist!'

Sublime as source of (self-)knowledge: mastery vs emancipation

Wittgenstein does not say much about how ethical moments, moments of wondering, could be used beyond noting their importance and his deep respect for this tendency of the human mind – indeed, he emphasises that what ethics says does not add to our knowledge. Here, the psychoanalytic conception of knowledge is very different: it refers precisely to something gained from sublime moments like that. For Winnicott, playing in particular can be understood as a kind of 'ethical' knowledge, a synergy-producing knowledge about each other: it is *only* through playing that 'the self can be discovered and strengthened' *and* a relationship can become a friendship (Abram, 2007, p. 264, also 252). Playing 'serves the function of self-revelation' *and* 'provides an organization for the initiation of emotional relationships, and so enables social contacts to develop' (Winnicott, 1987, pp. 144–146). If sublime moments, such as being immersed in play with another, are the basis for ethical engagement with others – in that they hold the potential to promote social contacts, emotional relationships, friendships – then they are *exactly* the basis for knowledge.

The knowledge of facts and propositions is an attempt of possessing knowledge (and, consequently, being able to use it in social relationships as a possession). Moments of sublime experience, on the other hand, can be understood as meaning-*creating*. This includes being open to becoming overwhelmed by something rather than just (consciously) understand. For example, Wittgenstein argues that wondering is not about the world being in a particular way (like the sky being blue, which you could describe, explain) but about it being '*whatever it is*' (Wittgenstein, 1965, p. 9). This brings to mind another psychoanalyst, Bion's concept of 'O', of being in awe (Civitarese, 2014, p. 1067). 'O', for Bion, is a different procedure from 'K', which is abstract knowledge based on the process of binding, of the language of logic. In particular, it is important that 'O' denotes a procedure of *becoming*, and 'becoming O … means knowing something emotionally' (p. 1067). In this process, then, despite failing to grasp something, I am endowed with a particular knowledge; whilst I am not in *possession* of this knowledge, my exposure to it is making me become something (else): it is transformational. It is, so to speak, knowledge that becomes me or is about me, rather than 'I' being in possession of it.

> To lie on the sofa with the person you love can be a sublime moment in itself. It seems less important to remember the content of conversations thus happening, for their content is less important than their existence. In one of these moments, I suddenly find myself being tickled. I curl up and try to defend myself but at the same time before my consciousness can come up with an objecting reaction, a most excited laughter comes out of me, as I might have sounded as a child when discovered in a hide and seek game. It surprises me. It's not that I have never been tickled before,

of course, but it feels different. It feels like a part of a long-buried child-like part of me whose existence I barely remember, has suddenly been seen by another human being; a part that was able to play with a certain spontaneity that the adult me has lost. My reaction surprises my partner, too; he stops and there is a moment of silence. The exchange that happens through the eyes suggests more than just curiosity about what is underneath my normal everyday composure, or satisfaction of 'out-playing' my will. There seems to be, on his face, a happiness, almost relief, about discovering this spontaneous part of me: as if what he has just discovered is also what he had been looking for. In me, despite the 'involuntariness' of it all, there is a certain relief, too, that this part that I could not have intentionally shown (indeed, might scold myself for childishness if I did), has, as it were, shared itself with him. Perhaps this is what moves him. 'I love you', he says and this, too, feels like it has burst out of him on its own.

A moment of awe, an experience of the sublime that is transformational and produces (self-) knowledge, can be an everyday, minute moment, like the one described in this vignette. Playing, like wondering, removes the boundaries and limits with which the self-conscious mind rules over itself and the body and sometimes releases an energy dam and a full flow of laughter ensues. This requires a certain space of trust and safety: one does not wonder nor play when one is scared or mistrustful. But playing is also creative of trust. In this sense it is paradoxical in the way that Winnicott would like: it has to be on your own terms (otherwise an attempt to play will just stiffen you up and you won't be able to relax enough to play) even whilst it is precisely that in play some of these terms will be loosened up or removed. My experience was pleasant because, even if involuntary, it was borne by the underlying 'voluntary' openness, trust and connection to this person. It would not have worked with another person, and it works (or doesn't) with each person differently, depending on one's relationship to them. After all, you can only be pleasantly surprised if you like surprises, if you 'agree', as it were, to be surprised, and so expect it and not expect it at the same time. Such playing also seems to involve a certain courage to let go of attempts at conscious, rational mastery of time, space, and self, in the presence of an other. In this letting go, playing, like wondering, is a psychosomatic experience; it even, in some sense, gives control over to your body over your mind, or at least we can say that a different kind of awareness is involved – being absorbed by something.

The vignette above points to three qualities of the sublime: it is a sensory, kinaesthetic, bodily experience; it is marked by an openness to surprise and a deviation from the expected, the repetition, the customary, the norm; and finally, it induces a form of knowledge through awe, wondering, in relation to what is perceived as 'sublime', which induces a strong attraction: a combination of desire (will) *and* powerlessness of will; a drive to understand (that is, to master, control) *and* to surrender. I look at these three 'aesthetic' qualities of the sublime next.

Both Wittgenstein (1965, p. 4). and psychoanalysts who have written on the sublime include elements of aesthetics into their understanding of it. Above we have seen the sublime described as moving moments – that is, moments that produce affective *shifts*. Psychoanalysis has of course focused on the psychosomatic, bodily, non-verbal and affective layers since Freud.[2] However, Sebastian Leikert argues that often these descriptions of psychic functioning as pre-verbal and non-verbal, even affective, still reveals a relationship to the hegemonic place of language. He wants to find an area where language does not hold this central place, and proposes the focus on perception, which he understands as changes in bodily tension that refer to the immediate. 'Perception' in this sense is in fact more about temporality and transformation than about form; indeed, perhaps 'experience' would capture it better. Leikert says as much himself, when he argues that the sublime experience is, technically speaking, *not* about form as such (as both language and beauty are, and both might be involved), but about *a particular temporal execution* of it. Thus, such 'perception' requires presence; more than that, it requires a commitment to joint temporality of the involved subjects. Similar to how for Winnicott the overlap of transitional areas of two people can strengthen their selves, for Leikert, the sublime in the form of an encounter of two bodies affects transformation and growth: the 'precise temporal coordination is a first component of the immediacy of the experience of psychic growth' (Leikert, 2017, p. 666). Invoking Freud, Leikert argues that such growth involves a 'willingness to be "moved by a thing without knowing why I am thus affected and what it is that affects me"' (p. 664). This willingness is 'demanded' for the experience. It is a moment when only *now* and *here* matters; a moment that connects the external experience with internal kinetic experience – being moved.

Nonetheless, one could argue we are still in the domain of affective exchanges and the well-known psychoanalytic ideas of transformation they invoke (Bollas, 1987). What Leikert goes on to add is another important element: the experience of the sublime is underlined by surprise and creation. Surprise and creation, he points out, are based on deviation: from tradition, from rhythm, from repetition, from the expected. This is where the sublime differs from the traditional beauty encompassing harmony, symmetry, control. Indeed, the sublime pertains exactly to the boundless, indeterminate, infinite, unconscious, uncertain (Civitarese, 2014, p. 1062). Suddenly, something changes; one is confronted by something different, unexpected. Under the condition that the collision between the two subjects is unguarded rather than 'analytic', this element of surprise can elevate an ordinary experience to 'the dignity of the Thing' (Leikert, 2017, p. 670) for someone, because it can evoke their desire. In this moment, of (creative) deviation, the encounter transforms into a seduction (Leikert, 2017, pp. 662–663); indeed, a *play*.

In the movie vignette above, Stephen did not comply with the rules of the board; he changed them. Elaine responded – she did not continue as expected; she put the board down and challenged them both to work from memory. In my personal vignette the conversation was suddenly interrupted by tickling.

Leikert argues, following Lacan, that creativity and desire are both directed at a certain reality beyond language (ibid., p. 669). It is desire's particular role to touch this reality – indeed, for Leikert this role is retained even in one's neurotic demand for love: the role is no less than one's emancipation. But what kind of emancipation is 'at play'? We saw that it is thought to emerge through animation of one's kinetic structure by the aesthetic environment that involves another, through a deviation that surprises, engages, perhaps seduces into play. It cannot be one that is a result of knowledge as mastery, least of all mastery through reason. Shoshana Felman has argued that we are talking, instead, about emancipation from the need to control, from the Enlightenment vision of human affairs, from the science that does not accept the uncertainty principle of the reality: from the rule of the Ego (Felman, 1987). Civitarese similarly views emancipation in relation to what he sees as the usual barren and dry 'Enlightenment vision of human affairs' (Civitarese, 2014, p. 1081), as seeking a less powerful Ego that can 'elevate itself to the level of the unconscious and its mythopoeic and "diagnostic" capacity' (ibid., p. 1077). Returning to Bion, Civitarese sees emancipation made possible by a sublime encounter as one that increases one's tolerance for 'being in uncertainties, mysteries, doubts, without any irritable reaching after fact and reason' (ibid, p. 1073). This expansion of perspective is, perhaps, what the sublime as an experience of the three 'aesthetic' qualities can sometimes achieve.

One does not reach such knowledge only through playing, of course. In fact, it has been more usual to connect it to tragedy. For example, when Clapham appropriates the Wittgensteinian idea of 'ethical moments', he is in fact referring to moments in therapy when the traumatic past is remembered, moments so difficult that they require only to be heard in silence, gathered in another's mind, not to be replied to or attempted to be understood. This is perhaps a different kind of 'wonder' – a bewilderment in the sight of someone's immense pain. Similarly, Paul Allan Miller discusses Antigone's choice as ethical in that it 'shake[s] us to our very core' and cannot be assimilated to a 'pre-existing set of critical categories' (Miller, 2007, p. 2), because it transcends the realm of any rational discourse and collective norms. Hers is an ethical and sublime choice in that it is a 'choice of a Good beyond all recognized goods' (p. 1); it makes her 'a model for an *ethics of creation* as opposed to conformity' (p. 1, emphasis added). Antigone, Miller also argues, defends the archaic view of 'friend' as representing 'an essential oneness, in which legal and Symbolic identity is secondary to the primal oneness of Being' (p. 10). What is ethical in this tragedy is an uncompromising commitment to desire beyond the pleasure and reality principles (p. 11), being true to 'its indeterminacies and contradictions, its self-transcendence, its awesome foolishness' (p. 12). Antigone's, too, then, in all its seriousness and tragedy, is not a rational, but a creative, even foolish, move; engaged with and giving over her whole self to *whatever* happens.

But the sublime as an ethical comportment does not emerge only in relation to tragic and painful events. Playing is special and worth discussing as a particular kind of the sublime because it has the potential to heal, grow, strengthen; to create self- and other-knowledge, emotional links and friendships. Marie Lenormand reflects on the spontaneity of play as opening a space where all various parts of personality (including erotic or aggressive ones) can be brought to: it is the ability to do that – to be oneself in the presence of somebody – that is healing (Lenormand, 2018, p. 87). Playing is creative not in the sense of producing an artwork of any kind (so not strictly speaking belonging to *poiesis*) but in the sense of being 'satisfactory because of its being creative or original to that human being' (Winnicott, 2005, p. 68). In other words, what is therapeutic in playing is its not being a means to achieve something else but rather an end in itself. Playing provides space for the parts of each self being whatever they are in the presence of another.

We can perhaps accept that such experiences are emancipatory in the sense that they support self-discovery and create social and relational bonds. But can such emancipation really have any effect on restrictions of external reality, whether personal, or even social or political? For example, clearly, the reality of Hawking's illness did not change, could not be changed. However, his perspective on the meaning of life, his spirit, was affected enough for him to re-engage with life in that moment. And that did, indeed, enable him to go on, which paradoxically, in turn, changed the course of external reality of his life from what might otherwise happen. Playing enables a particular kind of connection to another that has real physiological, bodily effects, which we can then deploy for other activities. It is transformative of reality not through effort but by emotional resources we realise through enjoyment in each other.

From the discussion above, playing emerges as a creative space that can shift, entice and even seduce one into a different state, by engaging surprise and deviation from the norms and rules. The final section looks at its relation to morality and producing experience of truth.

Playing: the non-compliant morality, the truth-producing myth

Discussing laughter in fairy tales, those cousins of playing similarly based on make-believe, Marina Warner positions laughter explicitly in the framework of seduction and non-compliance. Indeed, we could argue the stories she describes depict seduction *into* laughter, where laughter is a tool that breaks through (and therefore heals) a character's particular difficulty, for example, sadness, sorrow, depression, inability to speak, smile or do something. It can, like playing, shift one out of a state, make one 'forget to mourn for a moment' (Warner, 1995, p. 151). Indeed, such tales exist 'to excite responses, to bring life, to assert vulgar rude health against pale misery and defeat, to stir laughter or wonder or tears or hope' (p. 150).

As Warner points out, fairy tales do this through dynamics of elements related to 'delicate' matters: 'erotic, transgressive, personal, intimate' (ibid., p. 148). By engaging in such matters, they sanction a momentary transgression against social norms of behaviour, by flaunting something that would normally be considered socially inappropriate, even shameful, for example for being sexual, childish, or foolish. Like playing, they release one from self-censorship in relation to these norms, of how one thinks one needs to be. Laughter heals through enabling and enacting such transgression in these tales. Invoking Freud's thought about humour as a state of not being resigned but rebellious, Warner speaks about laughter as the expression of freedom, resistance to oppression and facing of fear; as a disruption of order, as change. It (if momentarily) defies authority, negates hierarchy and asserts equality, freedom, joy (p. 153).

Winnicott might be sympathetic to this view, for playing for him required a certain condition of non-compliance, a condition understood by him as at the basis of (true) morality. He thought it essential that one's self is negotiated in a way that does not require compliance with the environment, both as the basis of one's own health and aliveness, as well as, relatedly, of one's relationship to others. In terms of the former, Winnicott states no less than: 'Compliance is illness, and non-compliance is health' (Newman, 1995, p. 98). Giving oneself over to certain experiences that enable creativity produces a sense of life as meaningful; 'compliance', on the other hand, 'carries with it a sense of futility for the individual and is associated with the idea that nothing matters and that life is not worth living' (Winnicott, 2005, p. 87). In terms of one's relationship to others, for Winnicott, the very idea of morality depends on non-compliance. For Freud (1930), unavoidable civilisational discontents resulted from the fundamental conflict he saw between human being's instinctual nature and its socially required renouncements – repression or at best sublimation. Melanie Klein's (1935) view required acceptance of the depressive position as effectively admitting guilt for one's own destructive and envious nature. In opposition to both these views, for Winnicott any real moral code is personal and not based on repression, guilt or duty. Rather, it is a form of one's understanding of oneself as related to others that emerges from the individual herself within a supportive and facilitating environment. Instead of implanting a particular moral code into the child's psyche, in Winnicott's view, a natural process can be supported by which the child comes to a sense of right and wrong that runs deeper than the behaviour of the individual; one based in deep feelings of the self that relates to others through a wanting to contribute, to the other, or to the wider social community; from wanting to love (back). It is not related to 'fitting into our parents' version of us' (Newman, 1995, p. 103), nor, we might add, the civilisation's version of how a human being should be. It is related to how this human being wants to relate to others. Like Antigone's, Winnicott's is a *morality of creation* as opposed to morality of conformity.

Winnicott's understanding of morality as not based on compliance means it is not based on inducing a sense of guilt when one fails. Instead, it is based on a particular view of regulation and expression of aggressive impulses, which engages one's creativity.. The infant feels anxious about his destructive instinctual experiences but is gradually able to tolerate them when he comes to understand 'that there are opportunities for being sad and *creating* (not just repairing)' (Newman, 1995, p. 105). By accepting these creative contributions, the parents help the infant balance his impulses. As Winnicott has theorised elsewhere, this helps the infant develop a confidence that opportunities to contribute will occur, which in turn develops his capacity for concern (Winnicott, 1990, p. 77). This perspective suggests one does not abstain from behaving in certain ways because it is wrong or for the fear of punishment, but because one feels the hurt of others. To be able to feel concerned rather than guilty means to be able to take responsibility for one's instinctual impulses but also to accept the functions that belong to them: 'This', Winnicott concludes, 'provides one of the fundamental constructive elements of play and work' (ibid.).

Playing involves one's right not to be compliant with pre-existing structures but to engage in discovering yourself in relation to your environment. To do this, a level of letting go, carelessness, even ruthlessness, must be tolerated by the environment and the playing partner(s) without the return of hate or violence. In this way, an element of aggressive feelings, 'if they are expressed in more or less acceptable form' (Abram, 2007, p. 249), can be conveyed in playing, such as, for example, holding someone down when tickling, play-wrestling, teasing; or indeed, throwing a particular challenge back. For if Elaine, in response to Stephen's disengagement, just retreated instead of engaging him in a challenge, the space for play could not develop. The acceptable form of such elements in playing exists in their being against the background of safety and familiarity with the other. There is a delicate balance to be established, reflecting that despite one's role in the play, one, as well as the other, are still also their vulnerable selves. The cover of a fairy-tale on the other hand, as Warner shows, allows for a larger irreverence and rudeness of jokes.

The communication in the space of playing, where units and identities are evanescent and malleable, might appear unserious and insignificant, but it nonetheless effects the truth experience of the participants in play as well as their selves. To put two psychic universes into such communication so as to invoke the sublime, Civitarese believes, requires a 'poetic and oratorical' language (2014, p. 1064). Such language is like the one of psychoanalysis, which derives its effectiveness 'not from its truth value but from its truth encounter with the other' (Felman, 1987, p. 153). The truth emerging from this encounter is different from one based on facts: facts are found, whilst 'the psychoanalytic myth, in resonating in the Other, produce[s] a *truthful structure*' (ibid.). Civitarese suggests that the sublime is in fact a theory of unison with another: a search for an encounter that would allow for going out of oneself through the other and coming back to itself 'enriched by its temporary merging with the other' (Civitarese, 2014, p. 1069). Playing would seem to fall well with this description of sublime. The temporary unison, such as in a play of tickling, ever so brief, can bring out parts long-forgotten at the bottom of one's sea of experiences; to break out, they had to come on the wave of laughter from tickling that could only ever be induced by another person (Phillips, 1993), for 'I' might have precisely blocked this part.

Felman understands psychoanalysis as mediated by myth. Mythology is, of course, as Derrida theorised it, a language without a central authority reference point; more than that, it sits at the origin of language, exposing a requirement for such a centre itself as mythological, that is, a 'historical illusion' (Derrida, 1978, p. 282). A myth, then, can both produce a truthful structure and uncover an illusion of what we thought were certain 'factual truths'. The problem is perhaps that we like to keep the two sides of the 'truth' coin, the comportment of the scientific language and the miracle as Wittgenstein saw them, the perspective of the rabbi and the poet as Derrida describes them, separate. Perhaps we feel, as Marion Milner put it, that the moments when the poet in ourselves could still create the world for us are better kept as secret memories; 'because they were too much like visitations of the gods to be mixed with everyday thinking' (Milner, 1957, quoted in Newman, 1995, p. 333). As adults, we don't anymore think of playing as part of the serious, everyday 'reality': it is something to keep quite separate, if at all, as something perhaps slightly inappropriate, childish. But the perspectives discussed above in relation to playing point to the paradox of the sublime, the meaningful, and the life-affirming: it joins illusion with reality, facts with wonders and supernatural values. Perhaps, as Derrida seems to suggest, the two sides are not to be seen as a question of choosing, but sharing 'the field which we call, in such a problematic fashion, the human sciences' (Derrida, 1978, p. 294). In other words, human sciences need mythology, too. For it summarises human desire to find un-foreclosed ways to know each other, the emotional attunement and guesswork about what there is to be discovered in the moment that it is created, the chances and contingencies of various signs and expressions that can be tried on in playing.

How extraordinary that you should exist

The movement of playing as a category of the ethical and the sublime is described with terms of joint temporality of two selves in moments of loosening up the analytic, the logical, the rational and the struggle to master, and to accept the uncertainty, deviation and difference in the ordinary rhythms and views. It is both an active engagement of creativity and a passive openness to self-transformation, such that desire, seduction and the unexpected can emerge. Under these conditions, truth is something which 'is no longer communicated unilaterally but discovered in the sharing of emotion' (Civitarese, 2014, p. 1072). This 'flash of insight' (Clapham, 1997) invokes a certain knowledge, but not one that is in possession of something, even itself, since it always needs the other to re-discover itself. It is 'not a cognitive possession, it is an event ...' (Felman, 1987, p. 12): a myth, a drama even – a play.

What we think in truth can often not be said rationally. The sublime is an experience of the unspeakable, the ineffable: sometimes wonder and sometimes, like in the vignette at the beginning or traumatic moments in therapy, an overwhelming sadness. But sometimes at least, hopelessness can be broken with playing, when a comportment of another can produce a shift in oneself. Even if perhaps not monumental, but rather small and with an everyday character, these moments are invaluable. In passing through the other, they are creative of one's own story, one's own myth, one's own truth.

If one can only understand oneself through the other, then one must owe the other a comportment where they can freely discover and understand themselves, too: it becomes one's purpose, a kind of (Winnicottian) ethics of letting oneself be used in this way. Yet, it is a distinctive, perhaps we could say paradoxical, kind of owing or responsibility, for of course there cannot be a duty, demand or 'indebtedness' to play. In this sense, playing is a substance much like love – which, too, is the realm of the sublime.

Perhaps, instead, one could start with re-thinking how one has learned in this society to be a serious person. That what is important is to ana-lyse, evaluate and calculate, be factual and able to prove, produce a sophisticated argument with the confidence as if it is the only right one. One learns that one should master this comportment and people will take what one says to be the truth and for this confidence to be the truth about that someone. One will often believe that one knows all there is about oneself.

Often so do I. Except when somebody I love tickles me. And then all kind of other things come out.

Notes

1 All references are to the scene and the story as represented in the script of *The Theory of Everything*. No link to the actual relationships or events between real people on which the script and film were based is assumed.
2 See, for example, Andre Green's (1977) work.

References

Abram, J. (2007) *The Language of Winnicott: a Dictionary of Winnicott's Use of Words*. 2nd Edition. London: Karnac, 1996.
Bollas, C. (1987) *The Shadow of the Object*. London: Free Association Books.
Civitarese, G. (2014) 'Bion and the Sublime: The Origins of an Aesthetic Paradigm'. *International Journal of Psychoanalysis*, 95, pp. 1059–1086.
Clapham, M. S. (1997) 'Ethical Moments in Psychotherapy: Interpretation, Seduction or …?' *British Journal of Psychotherapy*, 13 (4), pp. 506–514.
Davoine, F. and Gaudilliere, J.-M. (2004) *History Beyond Trauma*. New York, NY: Other Press.
Derrida, J. (1978) 'Structure, Sign and Play in the Discourse of the Human Sciences'. In: *Writing and Difference*. Chicago, IL: University of Chicago Press, pp. 278–294.
Felman, S. (1987) *Jacques Lacan and the Adventure of Insight. Psychoanalysis in Contemporary Culture*. Cambridge, MA: Harvard University Press.
Forrester, J. and Cameron, L. (1999) 'Cure with Defect'. *The International Journal of Psychoanalysis*, 80, pp. 929–942.
Freud, S. (1930) 'Civilisation and its Discontents'. In J. Strachey (Ed.), *The Standard Edition of the Complete Psychological Works of Sigmund Freud*, Vol. XXI (1927–1931). London: The Hogarth Press and the Institute of Psycho-Analysis, 1961.
Green, A. (1977) 'Conceptions of Affect'. *International Journal of Psychoanalysis*, 58, pp. 129–156.
Klein, M. (1935) 'A Contribution to the Psychogenesis of Manic Depressive States'. In M. Klein (Ed.), *Love, Guilt, and Reparation, and Other Works, 1921–1945*. London: Karnac Books and the Institute of Psychoanalysis.
Leikert, S. (2017) '"For Beauty is Nothing but the Barely Endurable Onset of Terror": Outline of a General Psychoanalytic Aesthetics'. *The International Journal of Psychoanalysis*, 98 (3), pp. 657–681.
Lenormand, M.N. (2018) 'Winnicott's Theory of playing: A Reconsideration'. *The International Journal of Psychoanalysis*, 99 (1), pp. 82–102.
McCarten, A. (2013) *The Theory of Everything, Shooting script*. [Online] Available at: https://www.raindance.org/scripts/theory-of-everything.pdf [accessed December 2019].
Miller, P. A. (2007) 'Lacan's Antigone: The Sublime Object and the Ethics of Interpretation'. *Phoenix*, 61 (1/2), pp. 1–14.
Newman, A. (1995) *Non-Compliance in Winnicott's Words: Companion to the Writings and Work of D.W. Winnicott*. London: Free Association Books.
Phillips, A. (1993) *On Kissing, Tickling, and Being Bored: Psychoanalytic Essays on the Unexamined Life*. London: Faber and Faber.
Schafer, R. (2002) 'Defenses Against Goodness'. *Psychoanalytic Quarterly*, 71, pp. 5–19.
Warner, M. (1995) *From The Beast To The Blonde: On Fairy Tales and Their Tellers*. London: Vintage.
Winnicott, D. (1987) *The Child, the Family and the Outside World*. Harmondsworth: Penguin, c1964.
Winnicott, D. W. (1990) *The Maturational Processes and the Facilitating Environment. Studies in the Theory of Emotional Development*. London: Karnac, c1965.
Winnicott, D. W. (2005) *Playing and Reality*. New York, NY: Routledge, c1971.
Wittgenstein, L. (1965) 'A Lecture on Ethics'. *The Philosophical Review*, 74 (1), pp. 3–12.

Chapter 8

The sublime and the feminine *jouissance*
A Fantastic Woman, The Untamed and St Teresa

Agnieszka Piotrowska

There is a scene in the Oscar-winning film *A Fantastic Woman* (dir. Sebastián Lelio, 2017) in which the transgender woman Marina, the main character of this film, visits her elderly music teacher. In the scene Marina is in pain, but her old teacher tells her something that changes the final message of the film and delivers beauty despite the ugliness and the prejudice – it delivers the sublime. In another Mexican film, *The Untamed* (dir. Amat Escalante, 2016), the sublimation of this nature is impossible: the ugly and the everyday push the characters of the film into a space that appears to be a sublimation to begin with and indeed is sublime, but then ends up as a destructive and disastrous conclusion.

This chapter attempts to combine different ideas about the sublime and ask some questions about its connections to the body. In particular, I will discuss two films in which the everyday is presented as a difficult construct which can stand for a reductive space in which there is hate and discrimination. The scope for the sublime in these films only takes place when one steps out of the repetitive ordinary and allows for openings of different kinds, including encounters of the trans-gender, trans-cultural, trans-species and trans-disciplinary kind. However, it is the everyday that does present a possibility of the sublime if one looks for it. One could also venture that the two films represent the sublime as achieved through very different means: one deals with the mourning of love and the loss of love, including a physical love, and the other deals with despair and an escape into pure physical *jouissance* without the tampering influence of the spiritual. To what extent can thus one say that the sublime and the sublimation are always connected to the spiritual and perhaps also to the divine and to love? I will also briefly present another solution to the issue of the sublime through Kristeva's presentation of St Teresa, which is to do with auto-eroticism, God and a profound fantasy of the Other.

Before I get to the films, it is worth briefly evoking definitions of the sublime.

Sublimation and the sublime?

Sublimation and the sublime are not the same thing, but they are linked. The *Oxford Dictionary* suggests that the sublime can mean something beautiful, producing a sense of awe.¹ One can argue further that the sublime, including the sublime beauty, can be the result of sublimation. That psychoanalysis always involves a translation of sexual desire in a creative way – as opposed to a repressed desire which is always destructive. Very briefly I will revisit here some reading of the psychoanalytical notion of the sublimation.

Simon Critchley (2007) in his discussion of Lacan's notion of sublimation in *Seminar VII* makes two points: the first one is in relation to one's desire which instead of being repressed is sublimated – that is, it gives a rise to an artistic creation of sorts. The second point is to do with beauty, which is inherent in the sublimation of desire – at least in *Seminar VII*. In connection with this, Critchley also reflects on the aim of (Lacanian) psychoanalysis:

> What is the moral goal of psychoanalysis? 'the moral goal of psychoanalysis consists in putting the subject in relation to its unconscious desire'. This is why the sublimation is so important, for it is the realisation of such desire.
>
> (Critchley, 2007, p. 73)

In *Seminar VII*, the person who sublimates her trauma through an act which is both beautiful and ethical is Antigone. However, as we know, she also perishes in her achievement. One could take issue with Critchley: the sublimation of her anger and her complicated love for the dead brother is indeed beautiful: sublime, but then it becomes destructive – to herself and the others. It is possible that the price is too high for the beauty of the gesture.

Lacan in *Seminar XI* again comes back to the idea of sublimation but in rather more prosaic terms, stressing the issue of the language of sorts: the sexual desire can be sublimated through a metaphorisation, through a way of representing that desire, that is outside the body. First, he reminds us of Freud's position: sublimation is a creative activity which satisfies libidinal drive. It is a substitute, but it gathers the energy of the drive and channels it into something different than a bodily sexual activity:

> Freud tells us repeatedly that sublimation is also satisfaction of the drive, whereas it is *zielgehemmt*, inhibited as to its aim – it does not attain it. Sublimation is nonetheless satisfaction of the drive, without repression.
>
> In other words – for the moment, I am not fucking, I am talking to you. Well! I can have exactly the same satisfaction as if I were fucking. That's what it means.
>
> (Lacan, 1998, pp. 165–166)

Antigone's stubbornness in 'not giving up on her desire' is an ethical act which stems from love, and is defined by the Greek 'ate' – the destiny (Lacan, 1992 [1959–1960], p. 321), that is to say there are limits imposed on her, and on anyone, simply by the circumstances of the moment in time and place anybody finds themselves in. I have written about this extensively elsewhere (Piotrowska, 2014, 2017, 2019) but in this chapter I look too at the (un-sublimated) feminine *jouissance* through a different prism, focusing more on the (auto)erotic ecstasy and fantasy as portrayed in the famous Bernini's sculpture St Teresa also mentioned by Lacan – and forming the basis for Kristeva's creative non-fiction (2008) to which I will return later in this chapter. Somehow the notion of love hovers around even when it is not spelt out, and often it is spelt out, for example, when Lacan warns his students that in talking about love, 'one always descends into imbecility' (1999, p. 17) simply because one becomes a pawn of strong unconscious drives as well as narcissistic desires. He stresses that love is always a fantasy; that it is autoerotic and has a fundamentally narcissistic structure (Lacan, 1998, p. 193). Elsewhere, he adds, 'it's one's own ego that one loves in love' (Lacan, 1991, p. 142) and 'as a specular image, love is essentially deception' (Lacan, 1998, p. 268). Indeed, romantic love which connects to sexual desire features extensively in Lacan's life work. One could argue that love is a form of the sublime, so let's see how it, the sublime – and love – is presented in these two films and indeed in Kristeva's essay novel about St Teresa.

It is in this context that I am now returning to the Oscar-winning film *A Fantastic Woman* to contrast it briefly with another award-winning film, *The Untamed*. One of the films deals with love and music, the other deals with a non-sublimation, an extreme deadly pursuit of *jouissance* with no limits. One could argue that despite its apparent similarities to the sublimation and indeed the sublime, it is the very opposite of the sublime. In *A Fantastic Woman*, the escape from the ugliness of discrimination and prejudice of everyday life comes from music and the moment of utter submersion in it. Conversely, *The Untamed* shows how the lack of the sublime in everyday life can lead to a search for the sublime through a sexual fulfilment in ways, which can be destructive. Love of sorts is also at the heart of the two films. I will discuss the ways in which the narratives of the work deals with some of the philosophical notions linked to the sublime.

A Fantastic Woman

A Fantastic Woman has been described in a review in *The Guardian* as the 'sublime study of love, loss and the trans-experience'.[2] In the scene which takes place in about the middle of the narrative, the transgender woman Marina visits her elderly music teacher, clearly after a long time. He asks her why she has visited him. By this point the narrative of the film has taken the viewer through a range of emotions: from Marina losing her partner, through the humiliations she has suffered at the hands of her late lover's family, to a physical violence she has suffered and the moment of magical realism that help her come to terms with her loss. The everyday in this film is a site of mundane and ugly, prejudice and small-mindedness, which is not conducive to any moments of the sublime. But then the sublime does happen.

One of the most important of the many themes that this film touches upon is the body. The difficulties that Marina has with her deceased partner's family are to do with her own body: the body which is perceived as that of being male despite her desire and presumable some efforts to make it more feminine. Marina, played by a real-life transgender woman Daniela Vega, does not completely succeed in 'passing' for a woman. In truth, she appears less convincing than many others seen on the streets of London but also in cinema, including, for example, a male actor Eddie Redmayne playing a transgender artist Einar Wegener in the movie *The Danish Girl* (2015). In real life Redmayne is a man, but somehow his transformation from male to female appears very successful. Marina, on the other hand, is 'read' straight away, which causes issues on every level: when the police ask about her name there is an immediate air of suspicion, before even any discussion about her ID takes place. Later in the film, she walks into the male changing room with no difficulties, displaying her tiny breasts, not even real breasts but perhaps a suggestion of a breast, like in an adolescent girl. Marina is tall, her body is slim but has a heavy frame, her face is quite square, and somehow not feminine, although why that is, is hard to define. There are of course very many biological women who look quite masculine, but Marina's body becomes a crucial point in her life and the story world of the film: this body of hers is forever the object of examination, both her own and those by others – until, eventually, in the moment of total sublimation, this problematic body does not matter anymore. It is not clear whether in some way she chooses to be a non-binary person, and it seems that this is not quite the case. She is known by a female name 'Marina', she wears mostly very feminine clothes and her lover also used to treat her as a woman. On the other hand, her own endless fascination with her own body and her retention of the masculine characteristics (very small breasts clearly not enhanced by surgery) might suggest that she chooses to occupy the liminal space in between the binary divisions. It is also possible to argue that even for her the acceptance of her difference as a trans-identity is not quite what she desires. This is never discussed in the film directly. We witness the ugly prejudice and even violence – directly precipitated by her embodiment. It is only finally, through her performance of music, through her public sharing of the beauty, that the sublime happens and wipes out the problem of/with the body.

It is worthwhile to reflect more on the everyday that is presented in this film, and how Marina's body seems to be challenging it. Marina's late lover's family treat her body and her as an abomination. It is possible that his ex-wife (who, we learn in due course, is not the mother of the grown-up son who Marina has disputations with) would have been very hurt on meeting her former husband's young lover in any event, without the complication of the sex change. But in the restrictive bourgeois everyday of the world which we observe (presumably Catholic Chile, although it is not spelt out), this complication becomes an unbearable burden, a slight, an offence, a catastrophe which cannot be repaired: Marina is the repulsive Other who cannot be forgiven or shown any empathy precisely because she is perceived as offensive to the very foundations of the Symbolic order on which this society is built. In this order, gender and sex roles are prescribed and rigid, as is class. Her late lover was a-well-to do businessman. She is a struggling singer, working in her sister's café to earn a living. Marina is seen as crossing all of these boundaries. She is a trans-woman and a person who desires and lives a different life to the one prescribed for her.

The film's construction and its narration are mostly realistic, except for the moments of the magic realism in which curious things to do with her pain happen. Marina's pain is overwhelming and real. Indeed, the film is very much about the pain of mourning but without being allowed to do so openly and using the accepted rituals: she is the hated and shamed outsider precisely because she took a decision to change her body – presumably many years ago, in order to have a different gender identity. The film does not give us a back story regarding this decision, nor do we know anything about her lover's desire and his decision to live with Marina, the decision which clearly is perceived as very different from his previous life. The film does not tell us about any of that; it just focuses on bodies and their desires, on their fragility and their importance despite our continuous drive to disregard their ephemeral nature. The director of the film makes sure we understand that Orlando and Marina had a passionate intimate life; when we meet them at the beginning of the film, it is her birthday and he is planning to take her on an expensive holiday to one of the seven wonders of the world to Iguazú Falls. Importantly, their life together is not exactly secret but it is on the peripheries of society: both the restaurant they have their celebration at and the club where she performs popular songs, are placed in subterranean spaces, under the surface of the city, on the borderlines of the acceptable.

The sublime in *A Fantastic Woman*

The film is relentless in its painful representation of the discrimination and humiliation Marina suffers until we come to the aforementioned scene of her visit to the elderly music teacher. The scene is shot in a traditional way consisting of a static camera shots, reverse shot, wide shots and mid shots. The camera emphasises the *ordinariness* of the conversation. It could be an ordinary television drama. Its simple conversation is a crucial part of it precisely because out of this ordinary and everyday encounter something special emerges. It is very clear that the music teacher is expecting her and that it has been a whilst since she has been to see him.

He tells her that she looks 'terrible' (and repeats it in case she missed it) and then interrogates her further: 'Did you come here to work on your technique or hide from the world?' Marina hesitates and says 'both'. The music teacher is unimpressed but affectionate. He tells her off kindly. He reminds her he is her mentor and her professor – for classical music. She adds as if this had been a conversation they had had before: 'and you are not a psychologist and you are not my father'. And he nods. So she muses – why did she come at all? 'To sing I hope' says the music teacher. But Marina does not agree yet – 'or maybe to look for some love' she says. There is a simple warmth in this exchange, a dialogue which presents a deep connection that might be similar to love between a father and a daughter.

Again, referring to previous conversation or conversations, she says she doesn't want to talk about St Francis, but her teacher insists. In this crucial moment, he reminds her that St Francis did not pray for gifts to God, asking for things for himself. Instead, he asked 'make me an instrument of your love, make me a channel of your peace'. This is where the secret message of the film is revealed, where the sublime can come and when you shift your attitude to giving instead of taking. Here the sublime is akin to getting close to the love of God, something that in Christian tradition might be called a state of Grace. One can appreciate this message of the film whether one is a believer or not, for it transcends religion. The sublime here is presented as available to all through beauty – here the beauty of music, but clearly it could be read as the beauty of that which rises above the ugly and limiting prejudice.

In the next shot Marina goes up to the old man and puts her arms around him as he is sitting down by his piano. There is a moment of stillness and then the old teacher says: 'Sing a little for me'. The following scene is a simple wide shot which features the music teacher by his grand piano and Marina. He begins. It is an 18th-century aria which Marina sings in her angelic mezzo-soprano, a song about a spurned wife Sposa Son Disprezzata: 'A shadow has never been as tall and wide as this tree's shadow. Thank you for sheltering me'. As soon as Marina starts singing, the film cuts to a tracking shot of her walking against a strong wind. It seems that all the debris in the world is blown against her but somehow she is not falling. The shot becomes unrealistic and very beautiful with her leaning against the wind but not falling. This is crucial. This song creates a paradigmatic transition to a different mode in the narrative of the film in which the sublime is possible. Throughout the tracking shot the aria sung by Marina is heard creating, as Amy Herzog (2009) would say, a 'musical moment' in which the music takes over and becomes a crucial moment in the film. As the experience is outside language, it touches the viewer in the Lacanian register of the Real, through the body. The beauty of the images and the knowledge of the lyrics of the song later bring it back to the Symbolic via the Imaginary, but the first reaction is to the beauty of the music which also brings home the suffering of Marina.

I will come back to the final scene of the film which is a reprise of the moment of sublimation through music but is even more significant. Before then I want to pause and reflect on the moment of a translation of the pain to language to music – it is a classic psychoanalytical 'metaphorisation'.

Bodies and language

A relationship between bodily experience and the speech was of course crucial at the outset of psychoanalysis. In *Autobiographics in Freud and Derrida* (1990), Jane Marie Todd makes a connection between a bodily symptom and an autobiographical statement: 'The hysterical body is a text, in fact, an autobiographical text. Every symptom tells a story about the patient's life, or rather several stories' (Todd, 1990, p. 5). Todd further points out that the work of a psychoanalyst is really that of a 'translator', a translator of symptoms:

> It is the task of the psychoanalyst to work with the patient, to collaborate on a *translation* of this secret and motivated language of the body into the conventional language of the words.
>
> (ibid., p. 5, my emphasis)

Freud calls this collaboration, this task of translation, 'an analysis'. Todd further glosses that 'analysis' is the name given to 'an autobiographical practice whose principal purpose is neither to testify nor to confess (one's sins or one's devotion), though both modes may be part of an analysis. The work of analysis is autobiographics as *cure*' (ibid., pp. 5–6).

One could take issue with the above – or many issues – one of these being Freud's at times patriarchal attitude to females which I have discussed elsewhere (Piotrowska, 2019). I am putting a marker here but bracketing the discussion in order to focus on another question: is translating one's experience into words always therapeutic? It is interesting to note that the moment of 'translation' from bodily experience to language which, psychoanalysts believe, has a curative effect, could in addition have other effects if that 'translation' enters a public space: psychoanalysis names (artistic) sublimation as a way of channelling (indeed translating) one's frustrated sexual energy into a creative activity.

Lacan famously took away the 'frustrated' element and suggested that there is enjoyment (*jouissance*) in talking and writing which is equal to sexual satisfaction. In the introduction to her recent book on sex, Alenka Zupancic argues: 'The point that Lacanian psychoanalysis makes, however, is more paradoxical: the activity is different, yet the satisfaction in talking is itself "sexual"' (2017, p. 1), meaning further that it needs not have roots in its 'sexual origin', that is to say, the talking itself can be a sublimation without the content being in any way sexual. This is crucial to note as it connects directly to my discussion of sublimation and the sublime: to put it bluntly, sublimation is not the repression of sexual desire, it is at times its fulfilment, just as successful as an actual physical encounter. Zupancic says further that it is narrating the experience that makes it special and not the other way around: 'The satisfaction in talking contains a key to sexual satisfaction (and not the other way around)' (ibid. p. 1).

Freud and those who followed certainly wanted to relieve the symptoms of their suffering patients, but the main objective of psychoanalysis has been for more than a century the project of gaining knowledge: both in terms of self-knowledge on the part of the patient/analysand but also the knowledge which can then be shared with others *through language* in order to advance our collective knowledge – or non-knowledge – of who we are, as humanity or perhaps as merely Western civilisation. Psychoanalysis in its clinical psychotherapeutic guises has often had normative aspirations: that is to say to make the patient fit into society and culture more easily. But that was emphatically not Lacan's idea, not at the moment of enunciation and even less so towards the end of his life. The 'not giving up' on one's desire can be a controversial proposition: what if the desire is not ethical? For that reason, Alain Badiou, for example, attempted to present a reformulation of the idea to make the 'desire' somehow always ethical – but the category is troublesome and slippery and needs further interrogations. Zupancic and other members of the Slovenian school of psychoanalysis and philosophy have emphasised the profound links between psychoanalysis and philosophy, the inherent contradictions notwithstanding (ibid., p. 2). Jacques Lacan (1998), of course, by pronouncing that 'the unconscious has a structure of language' did in some way inadvertently confuse the issue as the phrase was promoted by structuralist thinkers (including structuralist film theorists), who focused on languages as a system of signs, ignoring the body and its experience.

The importance of the body and embodiment notwithstanding, there is much we can learn from linguistics and from semioticians. Umberto Eco's *Experiences in Translation* (2001) reminds us that in order to translate anything from one system of meaning to another there must be at least some points of convergence, some meta-system of meanings that is accessible by all despite different ways of expressing it. He therefore makes the following point:

> If, in order to translate a text α, expressed in a language A, into a text β, expressed in a language B (and to say that β is a correct translation of α, and is similar in meaning to α), one must pass through the metalanguage X, then one is obliged first of all to decide in which way α and β are similar in meaning to a text γ in X and, to decide this, one requires a new metalanguage Y, and so on *ad infinitum*.
>
> (Eco, 2001, p. 12)

Roman Jakobson identified the type of translation that Eco discusses as interlingual translation ('an interpretation of verbal signs by means of some other language' (1971, p. 261)), which he distinguished from intralingual translation ('rewording ... of verbal signs by means of other signs of the same language') and intersemiotic translation ('an interpretation of verbal signs by means of signs of nonverbal sign systems' (ibid.) – in which we can include the translation of experience into language).

The terms 'intralingual', 'interlingual', and 'intersemiotic' might be useful in a discussion of a translation of a desire for love to a desire to create something full of love – the sublime. A belief in the divine might be helpful in the moment of the attainment of the sublime for some, for those who have faith.

St Teresa – *jouissance* through language

A conversation about Grace, about the body and pain, and body and sublimation, often becomes a conversation about God it seems, which brings me to the psychoanalyst and philosopher Julia Kristeva's peculiar novel *Teresa my Love, an Imagined Life of the Saint of Avila* (2008). Kristeva's main notion is that St Teresa's complicated life, her suspected epilepsy, her mental health issues, her problematic relationships with others in her daily life and, finally, her deep pain and pleasure, her *jouissance* (as Lacan described it in *Seminar XX*) and her sublimation of her libidinal drives, comes only because of her writing and through it. She becomes the sublime because of the writing. Her everyday experience is secondary – the writing is primary. The sublime can only come through writing, through the naming – it is the sublime of Marina's teacher: 'Let me be the instrument of your love'. You cannot be anybody's instrument without a direct action of some sort, which will also involve a public space, even if it begins as a very private moment. In *A Fantastic Woman* the direct action is singing: singing, as the teacher tells Marina, 'in a lyrical way'. 'Lyrical' here also means classical, nonetheless the word 'lyrical' having links to the Greek 'lura', is significant. 'Lura' is linked to the word 'lure' – which can also mean 'to tempt', or 'to attract with a promise of reward' – but here the temptation is away from the everyday non-sublime and into the beauty of the promise of the divine love – both in the film and in the story of St Teresa.

Nonetheless, there is also something else that brings the experience back into the everyday rather than remaining an isolated God/individual relation: the issue of *sharing* the joy with the other people, translating the sublime into something that can last and live and can be shared in the Symbolic, with the other. Without the description, the interpretation, the creation of the narratives, not only would Teresa of Avila have been totally forgotten *after* her lifetime, but also, and importantly here, she would have lost this precious subliminal *jouissance* in her lifetime. Her experience alone was not enough to make her happy or make sense of her life; it was the writing, the description of the experience, which made it become real at all. Kristeva's argument, and her thesis is very clear: the process of writing translates the individual experience, including a bodily euphoria or suffering, into something which can become a work shared by others, and therefore can perhaps become the sublime. Here is what Kristeva says:

> And so I arrived at this conclusion: Teresa's ecstasy is no more or less than a writerly effect! Spinning-weaving the fiction of these ecstasies to transmute her ill-being into a new being-in-the-world, Teresa seeks to 'convey', to 'give to understand' the link with the Other-Being as one between two living entities: a tactile link, about contact and touching, by which the divine gifts itself to the sensitive soul of a woman, rather than to the metaphysical mind of a theologian or philosopher. To sense the sense, to render meaning sensible: in Castilian, *Teresa's writing and her ecstasy overlap.*
>
> (Kristeva, 2008, 105, my emphasis)

Teresa of Avila in her writings, which she began to carry out only on behest of her male confessors, in order to help her soften her pain and improve her health, describes a variety of *places* she visits during her ecstasies and which she perceives as actual and not imaginary. The writing helps her develop the embodied notion of the sublime – of her own body but also that of her place in the patriarchal hierarchy of the Church, so it is also a translation of a kind. But what is crucial to understand here is that St Teresa was waging a war – against her own limitations but also for *her right to create the sublime* in the system which did not allow for such curious women to exist. The times of St Teresa's life were brutal. This is 16th century Spain with the accusations enunciated by Luther and the Reformation against the Catholic Church on the one hand, and the threat of the Illuminati on the other. According to Kristeva, Teresa of Avila was lucky in so far as she had the protection of her priestly father confessors, as it happens mostly Jesuit, like the famous philosopher of the everyday Michel de Certeau, in the political climate forbidding certain forms of mysticism. Those could even be seen as heresy and lead to severe repercussions. On the other hand, the Roman Catholic Church at the time did need something different and attractive to hold on to the congregations shaken by the Reformation. The sublime that Teresa was developing was an important instrument for the divine loves, yes, but also for her own place in the system. In the misfortune of her bad health, Teresa was therefore very lucky to have met some people (male philosophers) who would support her, and it was very lucky indeed that she was able to write. In other words, she was in a position to intersemiotically *translate* her bodily and spiritual experience into words that others were able to receive.

The Holy Inquisition took some interest in her visions but her writing, interpreted by the father confessors, convinced them she was no Illuminati after all: that Teresa was a legitimate visionary who could document her experiences in her writing to the benefit of the Church. This was a good enough solution for the times, and it did save her life, but I wonder whether the truth was somewhat different: Teresa translated her deep *autoerotic* enjoyment, her *jouissance* into the divine sublime words and that saved her. Her writing saved her. Kristeva sees this process of translation as crucial:

> Hunting for the *mots justes*, for an exact image of the touching-touched body thrown open to the plenitude of Other-Being, Teresa adds to the water fiction of the Life and later works of fiction of *overlapping dwelling places inside a castle*: heaped, penetrable, ostensibly numbering seven but consisting of a host of doorless rooms and cellars, porous spaces separated as if by the stretches of translucent film.
> (ibid., p. 106, emphasis in the original)

It is here that we can ponder the connection between Kristeva's St. Teresa's writing as the expression of the sublime and Marina's singing – the everyday is difficult and ugly for both women. The translation of the pain into the sublime ecstasy, which is shareable, offers the beauty and the salvation – in the moment and for eternity. It would be an error and an oversimplification to imagine that Marina's loss, and the pain of the prejudice she suffers in addition to her bereavement, is simply alleviated by the singing. It is rather that her ability to shift the focus from her pain to the beauty of the music she can perform for others to enjoy moves her out of her singular suffering and closer to the sublime, to the state of spiritual Grace. Similarly, St Theresa's ability to write and create stories is both her personal salvation but also a way into the sublime which is clearly and importantly outside the normative ways of thinking about the world. There would be a way – within some psychoanalytical canons certainly – to view these two characters as pathological. This is not my view. What is interesting to me is these people's ability to create beauty out of their desire – the desire could be singular and peculiar to some people's minds, but the outcome can be seen as sublime and spiritual.

I now turn briefly to a film which presents an alternative to the search of the sublime in the everyday: the unbridled *jouissance* without a spiritual engagement.

The failure of the sublimation – *The Untamed*

The setting of the narrative and the story world of *The Untamed*, just as in *A Fantastic Woman*, is a hostile urban space of a large city. The everyday here does not offer any chance of the sublime: it is thwarted by the convention and the tradition. It is a hostile environment of stifling, limiting encounters, full of misogynist abuse and homophobic pressures which fuel vague longings on the part of its inhabitants for escape. These longings, if unmet, can be corrupted into crime and violence. It is a life in which desire, including sexual desire is prohibited, a situation that leads to dysfunctional, violent and ultimately destructive relationships. The physical closeness appears to offer a rare escape. The sublime in the film lives just outside the everyday – and as such it might be interpreted as a metaphor. The sublime lives in the forest, close to nature, and a brief contact with it will make the recipient transported out of the ordinary encounter. However, this film, as opposed to *A Fantastic Woman*, does not offer a way out of the (harsh) ordinary. Instead it offers a warning about our greed for an embodied sensuous experience, which, if totally unchecked will be the opposite of the sublime.

The Untamed occupies a space between the horror movie, science fiction and a gritty urban realism. In a forest, just outside the city, in a house guarded by an elderly couple there is an extra-terrestrial creature, which, it is revealed in the course of the movie, is a huge octopus-like being which can and does give an otherworldly sexual pleasure to anybody who *chooses* to enter its space. The choosing is important. This is not a predatory being; this is not the scenario of Jonathan Glazer's *Under the Skin* where the alien embodied by Scarlet Johansson prowls the city looking for lonely men. Their sexual longing is exploited in *Under the Skin* but there is no physical gratification – or any other gratification for that matter as the seduced men disappear into an oblivion of blackness, never to be seen again, their internal organs dissolved. The turning point in the narrative of *Under the Skin* comes when the woman in her ploy to seduce a disabled man, invites him to *touch* her face and hands as she drives him to her alien lair (Piotrowska and Jenner, 2019). Apparently because of the touch, she is unable to destroy him and instead we see her own desire emerge. It is worth pausing briefly here to reflect on the importance of touch, as a sexual encounter is but an extension of that. The philosopher Jacques Derrida in his discussion of Jean-Luc Nancy's book *Corpus* (2008), reminds us that to touch means 'to tamper with, to change, to displace, to call into question; thus it is invariably a setting in motion, a kinetic experience' (Derrida, 2005 [2000], p. 25). The touching, therefore, is a harbinger of change – it can be a good change, or bad, but it is a movement, and it can become explosive and revolutionary.

In *The Untamed*, as opposed to *Under the Skin*, there is no element of seduction coming from the Other. The creature is no prowler or predator. The desire comes from the subject who seeks out the creature's abode, succumbing to her or his longing to experience the all-embracing pleasure and a fusion with the non-gendered Other. Once a person decides to enter the house where the octopus-like large alien resides (and when I say 'large' I mean elephant-like large) she or he is first treated to a mind-altering experience, before entering into a voluntary sexual encounter with the alien creature. People turn up in the lair usually encouraged by stories of the experience – the creature's fame spreads by word of mouth. The nature of the pleasure is consummate and connects to the subject's innermost sexual fantasies and desires.

The danger of the encounter appears to come from a sense of merging. To put it differently, those who experience the physical euphoria with the alien, often lose all sense of drawing a boundary between them and IT. It seems – but is not made clear – that only if you can pull yourself back in time, no harm will come to you – but the issue is the ability to pull back, when all you want is more – and more. The encounter therefore has the structure and dynamic of addiction.

The film opens with a frame of a young woman, Veronica, touching her bleeding abdomen. We see a suggestion of a shape as it moves away. We hear of the voices of the couple outside, the creature's guardians. They order the young woman who is now on her own, to leave. She does not want to move despite being hurt. 'Let me stay a little longer' she pleads with them. But the moment is gone, the creature pulls back – for now. Through the young woman's visit to the hospital to have her wound treated, we are drawn into a gritty and grim depiction of urban relationships in the unnamed city in Mexico. In *The Untamed*, Veronica, the woman we meet at the beginning of the film, draws us into the urban space after her accident with the creature. She befriends the male nurse, Fabian, who we learn is having a homosexual affair with a man married to his sister, Ale. Ale and her rough husband Angel have two young children too, suggesting a trans-generational passing on of the restrictions, limitations and abuse. In addition to his adultery with his brother in law, Angel appears to be arrogant, violent and a bad father. After a series of revelations told in a slow low-key realistic mode, almost stifling the viewer, the betrayed wife is led to the house in the forest by Veronica. A move away from the city to a forest where the creature lives is significant for its move away from the urban. One of the guardians of the creature tells Ale that in the first instance her mind will be transported – presumably by the powers of the alien, before the pleasure is entered into. The pleasure is indeed sublime – otherworldly, freed from emotional ties to another human. It is in a different league.

The first encounter is very successful. The wife feels liberated through her pleasure, through the all-subsuming encounter that, as she explains to her friend, leaves her feeling happy 'when all resentment and hate are gone'. When her violent husband seeks reconciliation, she rejects it saying that she feels well for the first time in her life and begins dragging him through the forest to the creature so that he too can experience the liberating euphoria. However, it becomes clear when they get there, that further deaths have taken place, as the *jouissance* which dissolved all boundaries, has destroyed the lives of new subjects. This is the other side of the sublime euphoria – precisely because it is a direct unmediated experience, not a translation of that experience.

It is not that the creature is inherently evil, as opposed to the inexplicably predatory femme fatale of *Under the Skin* – where for the record, no sex actually takes place between the alien woman and the annihilated men: the promise of sex is a pure ploy to destroy. In *The Untamed*, on the other hand, the desire comes from the longing subject and is realised beyond any imagination on the part of the recipient who, perhaps because of it, cannot keep it within reasonable boundaries.

This is indeed the territory of the Death Drive, first mentioned by Freud in his groundbreaking and still controversial publication *Three Essays on Human Sexuality* (1905) and developed in the *Beyond the Pleasure Principle* (1920). In the preface to the fourth edition *The Three Essays on the Theory of Sexuality*, Freud links his notion of sexuality to that of destruction and danger. In this context, he mentions Plato's *Symposium*, a treatise in which the Greek philosopher Socrates and his guests talk about physical love:

> what psychoanalysis calls sexuality was by no means identical with the impulsion towards a union of the two sexes or towards producing a pleasurable sensation in the genitals; it had far more resemblance to the all-inclusive and all-embracing love of Plato's *Symposium*.
>
> (Freud, 1925, p. 218)

In Plato's *Symposium*, the female priestess Diotima explains to the young Socrates what the older Socrates will explain to his dinner companions and to us: namely, that Eros is neither a god nor a mortal, but a *daemon*, an intermediary and hybrid who unites and binds together all separate spheres. This as an idea holds a promise and a threat – the 'binding' heralds a change, a submission to the Other, a union which can have catastrophic consequences as well as exhilarating ones – for if we are to be bound to another being, we lose our separateness, our comfort zone, in fact, we lose who we are, our identity.

It is this ancient idea of a *daemon* of physical desire, which whilst having a quality of the sublime is in fact not sublimated and therefore cannot be controlled, which is both life-giving and also potentially fatal, that we observe in *The Untamed*.

The final scene of *A Fantastic Woman*

The moment where her elderly music teacher tells Marina about St Francis, about his prayer not to receive things from God but to be given an enlightenment as to how to share the divine love – and the suggestion is that for Marina this will be through her signing – becomes the crucial turning point of the film. The narrative continues with many humiliations still to come, but it is clear that Marina will find her way to the sublime.

The very final scene of the film begins with her feeding the dog which was the only thing she asked for and clearly finally got from her late lover's family. Now we see Marina on her way to a concert. She changes to a simple black trouser outfit, with her hair tied back, with careful make up, looking beautiful and androgynous. This is the first and only time in the film that we see her wearing trousers. One could interpret this as her own final acceptance too of her trans-identity, of her non-binary presence in the world, as mostly her identity is that of an artist, of a singer, gender aside.

She comes out onto the stage where her music teacher is already seated by the piano and begins to sing another 18th-century aria. The scene is profoundly moving. Marina sings so beautifully that her singing indeed transcends the discussion of her body, which is present throughout the film. She is the body but she is so much more than that. The moment is sublime because we understand that the prejudicial and discriminatory audience listening to her performance will be transported out of their ugliness, that Marina indeed has found or re-found the sublime instrument of the divine love and is bringing it to the everyday of the urban life, and that it will be taking place through a sublime *jouissance* of a pain translated into a public beauty through her singing. It is in that moment that the issues with her body – such as they were – cease to exist, cease to matter, because the only thing that matters is her singing and her letting herself be the sublime instrument of love. This is indeed the moment when the sublime becomes Grace, regardless of our actual belief in God.

Notes

1 https://en.oxforddictionaries.com/ [accessed 10 May 2019]
2 https://www.theguardian.com/film/2017/feb/14/a-fantastic-woman-review-sebastian-lelio-daniela-vega [accessed 8 May 2019]
https://www.theatlantic.com/entertainment/archive/2018/02/a-fantastic-woman-is-a-powerful-portrait-of-grief-and-prejudice/552116/ [accessed 7 May 2019]

References

Cohen, K. (1979) *Film and Fiction: The Dynamics of Exchange*. New Haven, CO: Yale University Press.
Critchley, S. (2007). *Infinitely Demanding: Ethics of Commitment, Politics of Resistance*. London: Verso.
Derrida, J. (2005 [2000]) *On Touching – Jean-Luc Nancy*. Trans C. Irizarry. Stanford, CA: Stanford University Press.
Eco, U. (2001) *Experiences in Translation*. Trans Alastair McEwen. Toronto: University of Toronto Press.
Freud, S. (1905 [1920]) 'Three Essays on the Theory of Sexuality'. In *Standard Edition of the Complete Works of Sigmund Freud*. Vol. VII. Trans J. Strachey. London: Hogarth Press and the Institute of Psychoanalysis, pp. 125–245.
Freud, S. (1925) 'The Resistances to Psycho-Analysis'. In *Standard Edition of the Complete Works of Sigmund Freud*. Vol. XIX. Trans. J. Strachey. London: Hogarth Press and the Institute of Psychoanalysis, pp. 211–224.
Herzog, A. (2009) *Dreams of Difference, Songs of the Same: The Musical Moment in Film*. Minneapolis, MN: University of Minnesota Press.

Jakobson, R. (1971) 'Word and Language'. In Ed Stephen Rudy. *Selected Writings Vol. II (1971–1985)*. The Hague and Paris: Mouton Publishers.
Kristeva, J. (2008) *Teresa my Love, an Imagined Life of the Saint of Avila*. Trans L. Scott Fox. New York, NY: Columbia University Press.
Lacan, J. (1991) *The Seminar of Jacques Lacan: Freud's Papers on Technique (Book I)*. Ed Jacques Alain-Miller, Trans John Forrester. New York, NY: Norton.
Lacan, J. (1992). *The Seminar of Jacques Lacan: The Ethics of Psychoanalysis (Book VII)*. Ed Jacques-Alain Miller, Trans Dennis Porter. New York, NY: Norton.
Lacan, J. (1998). *The Seminar of Jacques Lacan: The Four Fundamental Concepts of Psychoanalysis (Book XI)*. Ed Jacques-Alain Miller, Trans Alan Sheridan. New York, NY: Norton.
Lacan, J. (1999 [1975]). *Seminar XX. On Feminine Sexuality, the Limits of Love and Knowledge*. Ed Jacques-Alain Miller, Trans B. Fink. London and New York, NY: Norton.
Lacan, J. (2006 [2002, 1999, 1971, 1970, 1966]). *Écrits*. Trans B. Fink. New York, NY: Norton.
Nancy, J. L. (2008) *Corpus*. Trans R. Rand. New York, NY: Fordham University Press.
Piotrowska, A. (2014). '*Zero Dark Thirty* – "War Autism" or a Lacanian Ethical Act?' *New Review of Film and Television Studies*, 12 (2): 143–155.
Piotrowska, A. (2017). *Black and White: Cinema, Politics and the Arts in Zimbabwe*. London: Routledge.
Piotrowska, A. (2019). *The Nasty Woman and the Neo Femme Fatale in Contemporary Cinema*. London: Routledge.
Piotrowska, A. and Jenner, J. D. (2019). 'Desire, Commitment and the Transformative Power of Touch: The Posthuman femme fatale in Under the Skin'. In Eds A. Piotrowska and B. Tyrer, *Femininity and Psychoanalysis: Cinema, Culture, Theory*. London: Routledge.
Plato (1997) *Symposium and The Death of Socrates*. Trans T. Griffith. Ware: Wordsworth Editions Limited.
Todd, J. M. (1990) *Autobiographics in Freud and Derrida*. New York, NY: Garland.
Zupancic, A. (2017) *What is Sex?* Cambridge, MA: The MIT Press.

Filmography

A Fantastic Woman (2017) *dir.* Sebastián Lelio.
The Untamed (2016) *dir.* Amat Escalante.
Under the Skin (2014) *dir.* Jonathan Glazer.

Chapter 9

The lure of humiliation
Sublime aspects to success in the school mathematics classroom

Girish Jivaji

The 'sublime' is, in many ways, a daunting concept. It is variously used to denote instability, the transcendental, contradiction and the combination of opposites: of pleasure and pain, of dissolution and formation. It is both the promise of something perfect, whole, and a marker of its impossibility. The breadth of its use and the depth of its theorisation both attest to a concept that resists circumscription (Shaw, 2007). A key thread in this theorisation is the experiencing subject in a relation to language, where the sublime seems to reside within the nexus of experience and representation.

Feminist approaches to this relationship of the subject, language and the sublime, have suggested a model of the subject in relation to categories through which they come to exist or are constituted. In this frame, the sublime is both the fantasy of completion and that which interrupts or disturbs the boundaries of this constitution; a kind of unavoidable failure of this necessary productive relation of representation and the subject (e.g. Freeman, 1995). Therefore, in such approaches, we have an analytic frame of the subject constituted by socio-historical categories but always in a relationship of uncertainty or failure. Importantly, moments of failure become a means to access elements of the subject's relation to such categories that may not be readily apparent.

In this chapter, I use this analytic frame to read ethnographic data produced in a school mathematics classroom; where I attempt to situate the sublime as a continuous presence in the intimate moments of seemingly routine social processes. To this end, I use the concept of the 'sublime' in two ways: first, to think of the ideal subject of this space as a 'sublime object'. Then, second, to open up what happens on the boundaries of this sublime object, how moments of excess or interruption, of failure, fleetingly make hitherto veiled subject processes and categories visible.

In what follows, first, I discuss the 'sublime' as a concept in order to situate my use of it. I then consider the school mathematics classroom as a socio-historically constituted space that makes specific demands of its subject. After some thoughts on method, I present ethnographic work read through this analytic frame.

The sublime

The sublime as indicative simultaneously of something ideal and its impossibility is theorised in various ways. One approach is to posit the sublime as transcendental; a really existing thing that representation tries and always fails to reach. An alternative approach questions the internal coherence of representation, to situate this failure *within* the field of representation itself; such that it is necessary for the production of meaning (an intimation of something ideal) and simultaneously generates the sense that this meaning missed what it sought. Here the sublime is not transcendental but contained within the very act of representation; representation's always present and necessary missing element. In this sense, the sublime is brought back from the transcendental into the everyday, an essential aspect of the relation of a subject to the categories that constitute them.

One theoretical approach that attempts to work this nexus of the subject and a philosophy of representation that is founded on necessary failure is that of Jacques Lacan (2013a), one that I will make use of in this chapter. Lacan provides a rich theoretical frame that focuses precisely on this intersection of the subject, the socio-historical categories that constitute it and the inherent instability of such categories as productive of a felt excess or a missing 'thing'. He founds this instability on his subversion of the coupling of the signifier and the signified, where the signified is conjured, alluded to, through the interplay of signifiers. This makes the signified fragile, something the subject desperately clings to as its essence, but in a necessarily precarious way (2013b).

There are two consequences of this position that bear specifically on notions of the sublime. First, the sense of what is missing is productive of the inferred 'Thing', that which fills what is constitutively missing, what Žižek terms as 'absolute negativity' (1989). Here the inferred 'Thing' or 'sublime object' is a means for making thinkable what is felt to be missing at the core of subjectivity. It is a continual conjecture on the part of the subject with respect to what it is they are supposed to be, what a particular relation or space demands of them; and, therefore, productive of their positive attributes. However, this subject necessarily fails to be the ideal that concepts seem to demand. In a Lacanian frame, 'the subject is nothing but the impossibility of its own signifying representation' (Žižek, 1989, p. 208); that is, the subject is precisely the constant struggle to connect with an imagined 'sublime' whole, a coherent, integrated image promised by words, concepts, categories but impossible to make material in their ideal sense.

This impossibility or intolerable dissension leads to a second consequence with respect to the sublime. The subject, formed through unstable categories, is in a continual relation to boundaries. For example, if the category of 'cleverness' is unstable, seeking certainty but continuously leaking into and requiring the support of other categories, then the 'clever' subject is incessantly obliged to reiterate a constellation of mutually signifying behaviours that allude to an essence. One may think of the subject of schooling, caught in an axis of competition–cleverness–success, compelled to a continual reiteration of eloquence, exam success, extra-curricular accomplishments, analytical thinking and so on; a constant shoring up of the boundaries of cleverness. It is the continual relation of the subject to boundaries that, in turn, brings into view the work of constitutive, productive but tacit categories within moments of failure. I consider the productivity of one such category, that of shame, in the next section.

Therefore, for the subject within the frame of the socio-historical categories that form them, the sublime is *both* the inferred, whole object *and* their relation to capricious boundaries as a constant reminder of potential dissolution. In a Lacanian frame, this double aspect of the sublime follows from the foundational uncertainty of the signifier.

Categories are not transcendental, but are specific to the socio-historical context in which the subject is constituted. The subject of this chapter is that of the school mathematics classroom; therefore, in the next section, I shall look at some properties of the socio-historically specific assembly of this space.

The school mathematics classroom

The school classroom has become a seemingly naturalised dimension of modern childhood; where, ostensibly, it fulfils the role of preparing the child for society through the diffusion of knowledge by means of pedagogy. A seam of literature that questions the surface rationale of the school classroom has sought to analyse its assembly within the specific socio-historical circumstances in which it came to hold its predominant position (e.g. Hunter, 1994; Allen, 2013). A key assertion in this literature is the central role that the 'formation of moral character' holds as the frame in which this assembly takes place at the turn of the 19th century. Here, this focus on 'moral character' is situated in the imperative to deal with hitherto unknown numbers of the urban poor congregating around concentrations of new modes of factory production. Consequently, the very design of the classroom is structured by the imperative to develop moral character, where the contemporary arrangement of an adult teacher in relation to a 'batch' of children within an enclosed classroom only comes to predominate toward the end of the 19th century as a suitable solution from various alternatives (Hamilton, 1989; Markus, 1993).

Therefore, to understand the demand that the contemporary classroom makes of its pupil subject, it is helpful to examine the socio-spatial arrangement of teacher–classroom–batch of children (TCB) as a design with specific properties. The TCB system establishes the presence of an adult teacher who represents the self-governing ideal required of the successfully schooled; in addition, through increasing familiarity, they are positioned as knowing something that is internal, intimate about individual pupils within the frame of a stable group (Jones, 1990). The enclosed classroom was a development from the open halls of previous 'monitorial' arrangements where the whole school was gathered through the day. This enclosed classroom allowed for an adult teacher to focus on one batch of children through simultaneous instruction; that is, by holding the attention of the batch of children simultaneously even though they may address one pupil. The segregated batch of children therefore acts as a constant, watching group of the similar; witnesses to those instances that the adult authority decides should be the focus of simultaneous attention (Hamilton, 1989).

In this 'social technology' (Lawn, 1999), a key element of the interaction between an adult authority, a watching batch of children and an individual pupil, momentarily the point of focus, is the constantly circulating possibility of shame through public scrutiny. This circulation functions at two levels; first, as conferred on or implied with respect to an individual momentarily made visible as the focus of attention within the gaze of the group; and, second, as a continual possibility, and, therefore, a source of anxiety, for all members of the group. In this way, shame positions the individual as intersubjectively constituted, within the gaze of the group (Scheff, 2014). Public scrutiny, and its attendant possibility of shame, is therefore used to police the imposition of norms that the adult authority decides is the focus of this system. In this sense, the content of the norm, such as 'cleverness' or 'kindness' or 'thoughtfulness' or 'competitiveness', is independent of the work of this 'technology' or socio-spatial arrangement that functions to police its mandate.

In addition to the general demand for the development of 'moral character', whose norms are culturally and temporally specific, the school classroom is also the forum for the diffusion of knowledge. To this end, knowledge is compartmentalised into subject areas, which are then internally organised into 'curricula' such that their ideas are arranged in a hierarchy. Pupils are then placed along this hierarchy through internal and external assessment; in this way, pupils may be put into relations of competition. Each subject area then demands specific attributes both in terms of knowledge of content and its thinking processes, often in relations of competition.

For the purposes of this chapter, I will concentrate on three aspects of the specific demands made by a mathematics classroom. First, the public spectacle of 'being good at maths' is to take a position with respect to a 'marked category'; that is, 'being good at maths' has cultural signification as possessing specific attributes, such as knowing mastery of processes and ideas, to which the majority of people cannot aspire (e.g. Damarin, 2000). Second, the practice of mathematics contributes to this status in the way the messy, haphazard nature of its development is hidden when its results are publicly presented (e.g. Livingston, 1999). Following on from this, third, its transformation and subsequent presentation in school as a set of easily assessable, disconnected processes is the source of considerable, and continual, debate and critique (e.g. Popkewitz, 2004; Boaler, 2016).

Therefore, the subject of the school mathematics classroom, as a necessary aspect of being its successful product, is required to understand and conform to its general moral demands as well as the more specific demand of knowing the capricious processes of school mathematics, often in relations of competition and further policed by continual public scrutiny. In the context of this chapter, within a Lacanian frame, these demands are inflected by their constitutive uncertainty, where its inferred ideal subject may be thought of as a sublime object. In the next section, I consider how this theoretical frame may be used with ethnographic data before I look at how one student negotiates a path through the multiple, ambiguous but exacting demands made of him in this space.

Ethnography and theory

The ethnographic data that I use in this chapter was produced during a year-long placement in a 'top-set' mathematics classroom in London with students preparing for their GCSE exams at the end of year 11 and expecting to get the top grades. The students were either 15 or 16 years old and ethnically mixed, with a large proportion of Indian or Pakistani background. The teacher, Karen, was in her late 20s, white and from a self-professed working-class background. She had been there for a number of years and was well established and respected in the school. I worked as a learning support assistant in the class and made my notes outside of class time. In addition to these notes, I also interviewed Karen and some pupils. These interviews are parsed using an oblique (/) to indicate separate spoken phrases.

The notes were made without any theoretical framework in mind; but, during the year-long study, I would use theory to open up my thinking about what I considered was happening. This theoretical work then entered into my notes as I used them to open up or test what I felt this theoretical work was alluding to. My ethnographic notes have three layers, an initial attempt to describe a moment, a commentary of thoughts (presented here in italics), and later thoughts that arose with respect to these acts of representation (presented here in italics and square brackets). This division of representation is never wholly clear but seemed to help with my note-making at the time and I present them here as they were composed.

Balwinder

In this section, I present data that bears on three aspects of Balwinder's relation to the mathematics classroom. First, his (self)-positioning as the material counterpart to the inferred thing, the sublime object of this particular mathematics classroom. Second, the discord present in this positioning. Finally, his unease with this positioning as manifested with respect to the play of shame within this TCB system.

Balwinder's presence in class is one that is commented upon in the ethnographic notes on numerous occasions. For example, when the seating plan may be relaxed, Balwinder takes on a central position around whom there is a vying for seats in socially secure groups or the way conversations and explanations come to involve him as a focal presence. This presence that Balwinder has, wherever he is sat, appears to be a function of a confidence that he seems to have with regard to how he can be with fellow pupils, together with his familiar and knowing relationship to Karen, the class teacher.

One may ask what it is that drives this desire to have a 'presence' in whole class terms. In some way, it seems to be an active stance to take, but he seemed to accomplish it without any ostentatious attention-grabbing tactic. There may be myriad means for gaining attention in the local economy of the classroom, one which he knows intimately and therefore can think of the right thing to say or do at any time such that he establishes a presence in people's minds.

Balwinder and competition

In the following excerpt, the head of department, Matthew, enters the classroom after the Christmas break. The whole year group had sat their 'mock' exams before the break and were now discussing the results and also the paper that they had sat.

> **Thursday 10th January**
> Matthew came into the classroom and addressing the whole class asked who had got the highest mark for their mocks. Jilan shouts out that that would be him, Karen points at Balwinder, saying 'it's probably him'; Balwinder seems slightly embarrassed/pleased? Matthew then asks what the highest mark was and upon being informed, he states that a 'freshie' in set 3 got 92% on paper 3. Having shared this information with the whole class, he less loudly but still publicly suggests to Karen that she will have to make some room in this class for this new boy from India as he will have to do coursework designed to allow pupils to get an A*. He leaves the class reeling from his presence. As Karen attempts to gather her thoughts to continue her way through the paper, Matthew pops into another room and is quickly back asking very publicly whether anyone had managed an overall mark above 150, again Karen suggests that it was probably 'him' indicating Balwinder. Balwinder thinks for a moment in this public spot and says yes he had, while Matthew was explaining that the new boy had only managed to get 50 odd on paper 4. Matthew waited for effect as people in the class digested this in a somewhat

startled fashion. After this pause, Matthew says naah only joking he got 94 on paper 4 and leaves. Karen makes a face at me and I smile at her. Slightly flustered she continues with her exposition.

How will this new boy change the dynamic of this class? Those who react to him are likely to be boys, most especially those who harbour thoughts of occupying the position of the top student in the class. Balwinder seemed to be working hard to contain the thoughts that may have been coursing through his mind during this whole episode. Both as he was suddenly the focus of overt public attention, not a position he covets it seems, and also that he would no longer be the unassuming star of the class as soon as this new boy from India would be making his appearance.

Both times that Karen referred to Balwinder she said 'it's probably him' and she said it in a surprising (for me) way as if she didn't want to give him the recognition publicly that she thought he may have been angling for, as someone who keeps a cheery, nonchalant front in class getting the top mark. It is as if she knows the real work that he puts in to making this combination work. Perhaps I'm wrong; however, perhaps there is a deep understanding between them after five years of teacher–pupil and tutor–tutee relationship that allows for this way of talking to mean something other than its surface tone.

Within this economy of competition and success, Balwinder is publicly positioned as not only one of the winners but 'the' winner; it seems an almost public capture of Balwinder in this role. In some way, the position of 'winner' has to be filled in this class and Balwinder is placed there whether he likes it or not. This position seems to fulfil functions that exceed simply coming top of an exam. An excess that may be located in the public spectacle that marks success, within which this moment takes place; an unspoken knowledge in the class that already knew who had come top and the quality of ambivalence in Karen's reaction. In this way, perhaps this excess marks the necessary presence of a material counterpart to an inferred 'sublime object' of the classroom, where pupils are constantly asking: 'what does this space want of me?'

The work involved in being Balwinder

In the following excerpt, Karen, positioned as an adult exemplar of this space with intimate knowledge of the processes involved in being its successful product and also of individual pupils, shares some aspects of her ambivalent reaction to Balwinder during an interview after this episode.

K: erm Balwinder in the class is very fervent / although he doesn't show it
[This also seems like a means to put me to rights about any impression I may have formed about Balwinder in class where he is seemingly laid back and confident]

G: really?
K: but now
G: it's funny yeah
K: but now he really used to./ He used to be very very nervy
G: right
K: where he / just got this sudden shot of confidence
G: I know he really is isn't he yeah?
K: erm yeah I think he's got a girlfriend [laughs] *[Says this quietly as if this is a secret shared, a kind of explanation that should not be given but is nevertheless believed to be the true reason]*
G: oh, I see ... is that what it is?
K: he's turned a little beatboxer as well / and he's discovered other talents
G: oh right
K: and now he's y'know ... suddenly class comedian or y'know
G: yeah ... God, he's so laid back and confident isn't he
K: yeah whereas in year 7 / he was almost a nervous wreck at times
G: really?
K: erm
G: did he get an A* as well?
K: yep he did yeah and *[a change of tone now to a more serious appraisal of Balwinder]* he's such A student as well / who if he got an A / he would've been crushed... he would've been /
G: oh really
K: he's got an elder sister who / burst into tears / when she got some of her GCSE results/because they weren't A*s
G: really?
K: because of how their ... the parents want A*s / y'know it's ridiculous / some of the pressures that they're under / that aren't y'know luckily for them
G: did you meet his parents?
K: erm it was always his mum that comes at parents' evening
G: right
K: but it's always his dad that puts ... / ... exerts the most pressure and talk ... / talking about from what I know about the family / he and his sister both days at weekends / sometimes do FIVE hours of school work
G: right

Perhaps what is most striking in this excerpt is the language Karen uses to describe the nature of this particular family–school relation; where words such as 'crushed', 'ridiculous', 'nervous wreck' or 'bursting into tears' provide a sense of the investments and emotions that run through them. In addition, the means by which Karen questions the public persona that Balwinder presents in class, of being effortlessly successful, both socially and academically, is important with respect to a sense of discord between this public persona, an approximation of being this classroom's 'sublime object', and the hidden processes at work in its maintenance. We get some sense of these hidden processes in his relation to mathematics in the following excerpt from earlier in the same interview:

K: erm – so Balwinder yeah he's another

G: yeah

K: another funny one. *[This 'funniness' seems to be for Karen a mixture of anxiety, ambition and its public display but mixed in, in Balwinder's case at least, with a burgeoning sense of confidence]* / He is definitely somebody who / erm ... completely over complicates things / so he doesn't actually realise sometimes / erm maybe it's just ...the fact that when he does tests / they're obviously not ... erm ... you can't get a sense of what grade the question is / like you can in a paper because / y'know once they do the paper they ... they realise like the first few questions are

G: right

K: C's and B's and then the A's and the A*'s / so often the question that would've been for say 5 or 6 in their paper / are really not that hard

G: hmmm

K: he would just do / something absolutely ridiculous *[Said with real feeling: as if this is something Karen really struggles hard to understand – maybe for her it's another manifestation of an almost overwhelming ambition to succeed that means he can't just think through the question in front of him on its own terms. This seems to be something that she alluded to in Narinder and seems to be something Karen finds troublesome to accept.]*

G: so why's that do you think?

K: and to try and solve it / and I don't know whether he's just got this because sometimes he finds the classwork hard / maybe it's then hard – hard to then to shift back to a question in the exam that's actually not

G: hmmm hmmm

K: not that bad at all/and just tries to make y'know much more of it. / There...there's something missing that doesn't tell him / this can't be as hard as I'm making it / *[What is this missing thing – a kind of awareness or ability to occupy the moment or particular question without an anxiety to succeed in a more global sense.]* so a classic question that catches them *[So at some level she's talking about more pupils in the class than just Balwinder]* out is to do s ... er – a question that I've given out is one that came up in a paper a few years ago / where he got something like $(x + y)^2$ then they'd ask you to prove that that's $x^2 + 2xy$

G: right

K: $+ y^2$ and then use that to solve

G: yeah yeah

The lure of humiliation 131

K: $(3.47 + 1.53)^2$ / and not a lot of them to be honest / do spot that Oh hang on a sec… if I make that A and that B and that's 5 and then I square 5 erm / but they'll leave it / but Balwinder will be doing it on the paper
G: right
K: 3.47 x 1.53 d … d … d …
G: I've seen that
K: doing it
G: [laughs]
K: it's a ridiculous amount of working

One might make sense of Balwinder's tendency to over-complicate answers unnecessarily as a function of his capture by the demand to be the ideal subject of the school mathematics classroom. Within this capture, he feels a compulsion to guarantee reaching 'correct answers' by any means necessary, despite experiencing school mathematics as a set of opaque, capricious processes. In his overwhelming anxiety to be successful and to appear successful, he is unable to enter into a mathematical idea or problem in an open, questioning way; where failure to understand is a necessary and unthreatening step. Given this relation to mathematics as constitutively enigmatic, one can only surmise the processes that Balwinder goes through to maintain his public positioning of effortless success within this class.

Below is an instance in which there seems to be a slight perturbation in the smooth means by which Balwinder's public, social presence is established.

Friday 11th January
A moment at the start as the pupils start to file in comes to mind, Balwinder is assailed by three girls: Jade, Joanne and Teresa, as some incident from a previous lesson is continued into this. The moment comes back to me since the girls seemed to have a particular quality of enjoyment or delight in this moment of focus on Balwinder. I couldn't hear the details except for Balwinder plaintively countering 'I was only joking'.

My only thought in relation to this moment was that somehow the girls sensed some vulnerability in Balwinder's almost impenetrable shield of someone who is universally popular because of his ability to be involving in a generous way toward others. This moment of breach therefore perhaps tells us something about Balwinder and perhaps something of how this popularity is experienced by others.

About Balwinder, perhaps we learn that this popularity or presence in this group of pupils is a carefully cultivated position. That is, not in some Machiavellian sense of politicking but rather in a sense of always being beyond reproach, that nothing negative can ever be said about him. He is sensitive and involving, he doesn't say things that can then in the way of groups and mores of 'he said' or 'she said' come back to him as gossip that he initiated. He is careful to say things that can only be construed as pleasant, positive, involving but at the same time funny.

[*This is conjecture based on two points; first, my experience of him in this class; second the particular quality of these girls' enjoyment that this perfection may have been breached.*]

How others experience this popularity seems to be manifested in this reaction to a potential breach of his generous self. The girls' enjoyment at chiding him about something he said seems to suggest some sense of their experience of his position as active, rather than something innate or essential of being a generous, good-humoured person. That is, that he works at maintaining this position of having no flaws or saying something that can be in some sense mocked or ridiculed or can be the subject of banter. To keep up such a position in a group where talk is constantly flowing through the day and across many weeks, where what is said is continuously circulated and re-circulated, requires constant vigilance and monitoring of the situation, of what people are thinking, how they will react and so on.

This moment of 'breach', the day after Balwinder had been publicly positioned as 'the winner', the girls' reaction to it, and Balwinder's seemingly intense engagement with defending his position, may provide a sense of the work 'normally' involved in maintaining a social/academic position that is beyond reproach. Perhaps one aspect of the troublesome properties of Balwinder's positioning may be in the shared but unspoken knowledge that the class has of this discord between effortless occupation of the ideal subject of this classroom and the actual work required to be this thing.

Having come top of the Christmas mock exam, after his very public positioning during the 10th January episode, Balwinder seems to develop a more ambivalent persona in class, one that asks to be somehow released from this public gaze through minor acts of self-subversion. I can only infer this from the number of public instances of disturbing how he thought he was perceived by the class that I recorded in my notes of this time. It would seem from these minor acts of self-subversion that although doing well at exams is welcome, the consequences of this in the classroom system in which the public position of winner should be occupied, had a level of discord that he found troublesome.

Thus far, we have an impression of Balwinder as socially popular and publicly positioned as good at maths in ways that mark him as the 'one', a kind of material counterpart to the inferred ideal subject of the school mathematics classroom. The sense of effortlessness that inflects this position is, however, questioned both by fellow pupils and the class teacher as well as instances of self-subversion by Balwinder. In the next section, I look at two moments which provide some sense of the strain involved for Balwinder in maintaining the public position of effortlessly ideal subject of the school mathematics classroom, when its demands are felt to be enigmatic, uncertain, continually to be worked at.

The lure of humiliation

In this section, I present two episodes that go beyond minor acts of self-subversion; they suggest a more fundamental unease with his (self)-positioning. It is in the context of the preceding cumulative sense of Balwinder that these two moments of the fantasy of escape may be thought through. The first episode is before the mock exams, and it therefore suggests an ongoing anxiety about his position prior to its troubling/satisfying confirmation on 10th January:

Thursday 29th November
During this period of exposition, Karen went through a trial and improvement question based on something like $x^2 + x^3$, and she tried the two given values between which the solution would lie. She made a subtle point here, which seemed lost in the speed of her running through these questions, that having tried 5 and 6, the information gleaned should be used to make a reasoned first trial. She put up $6^2 + 6^3 = 252$, in this moment she seemed to have many things running through her mind and seemed unsure as to whether this was indeed the answer, Balwinder shouted out that this was indeed the answer. As soon he had though he pulled a face as if he had just shouted out on a whim as he hadn't actually attempted the question, he took his calculator and tried to work it out quickly, he then shouted out that he was sorry and that the answer was actually 278, Karen changed the answer on the board without seeming to get annoyed or making a comment, after a few moments, others intervened to say (perhaps those who had actually done the question) that the first answer had in fact been correct. At this Karen quickly did the sum in her head and realised that this was so, she didn't say anything to Balwinder who became embarrassed, Jatinder looked around at him to which he (Balwinder) replied 'killed it'.

Why did Balwinder intervene in this manner if he hadn't done the question? It seemed like a moment of whimsy. Can it be said that this whimsy stemmed from a defensive reaction to the lesson as a whole? The lesson seemed to be anxiety-provoking, the mock exam is about a week away, pupils know they will be judged on their grades, yet this paper that they have been asked to do seemed too difficult for them to do without going through a hard slog at home, putting a lot of mental energy into coming to understand what is asked of them and the procedures that they need to know. Perhaps in the context of these worries which were made concrete during this lesson Balwinder momentarily let things go and opened himself up to being embarrassed.

> Normally Balwinder is immune to being picked on for ridicule as he seems so confident and self-contained. *[Perhaps 'ridicule' is too strong a word, the moment happened through looks and smiles, many of which I suspect I missed, but more than that, the reaction seemed to be in Balwinder's mind in front of some imaginary audience?]* He seems so careful with his public interventions. He has a light-hearted and smiling countenance that seems impervious to the ongoing minor skirmishes of classroom relationships.
>
> Why once he intervened, did he get it wrong on the calculator? It seems that this intervention perhaps then produced a moment of overwhelming panic or anxiety that was contained on the surface. One can only surmise how the keys of the calculator became difficult to discern or that the screen somehow became opaque. This is an easy calculation that Balwinder is well capable of, but this moment of intervention if found out as pure whimsy would be ridiculed and furthermore would invite anger from Karen. Yet despite his wanting to check it and get it right, he ended up getting it wrong, can we go further and say over and above anxiety, he somehow knew or deliberately got it wrong (a moment of jouissance?); a case of repetition of an earlier experience of ridicule or anxiety in a classroom; which child hasn't suffered that through their long careers of being educated in front of others looking on?

This moment, when thought of as a momentary escape from the demand to be the ideal subject, can illuminate some of the less easily discernible subject processes at work in the classroom, specifically at the continual potential of shame, or public ridicule, structured into moments of simultaneous attention led by an adult authority.

The next excerpt also occurs during a time when Karen is addressing the whole class; it is the first lesson after the end of coursework, Karen gives out paper to those who hadn't bought their books in the hope of carrying on their coursework:

> **Thursday, 31st January**
> When the paper is given out, Balwinder has two pieces, on one he immediately starts to draw a large graffiti or tag, he doesn't try to hide what he is doing, and eventually he covers the whole paper. He is sat on the side row next to Ravinder and therefore easily visible to Karen. She doesn't seem to notice what he is up to. At the time, I didn't think too much of it. However, after a period of work, into the meat of the lesson, Balwinder asked for some more paper, he had covered up the graffiti with a scarf. Having the scarf on the table was ostentatious. Karen didn't respond straightforwardly by giving him paper as she picked up a strangeness to the request perhaps from the way Ravinder was looking, his customary smiling way of looking that seemed to say that there is more to this than meets the eye and there will be some fun to be had. Karen

sensed this and the interchange began to involve Ravinder in to saying that 'he already has paper'. Balwinder eventually picked up his paper with graffiti on it, turned it over and showed it to Karen saying, 'it's ok I've found some'.

Balwinder in this ostentatious act of drawing graffiti seemed to be performing a public act. He had a very serious countenance, not something that I associate with him. I would say that this moment was an acting out or a moment in which he was asking to be noticed as someone who is troubled in some way.

One can conjecture at what is troubling him; it may be that he is ceasing to be enthralled by his sense of himself as personable, good-humoured, successful and therefore he wants a public moment of recognition that he is someone who can transgress the norms or the rules, as if this will be an actual material moment of experience that will stand for whatever seems to be troubling him.

How sensitive Karen was to the possibility of playing the dupe, she sensed something awry behind this moment of asking for paper; perhaps it was Ravinder's look or perhaps something in Michael or perhaps something in Balwinder, the kind of unspoken knowledge that one reacts from within a relation of deep familiarity.

Balwinder played along for awhile, wanting this public mock telling off; the scarf seemed to be saying please look underneath me, but once it went on too long, once it seemed that Karen was wary of playing her assigned role in this play as she didn't completely understand the circumstances, Balwinder called the whole thing off by holding up the reverse side of the graffiti paper. In this moment where he seems so troubled, he is wary himself of being thought of as inviting attention by the onlooking class, which would be a real judgement not the play telling off he was seeking from Karen. [This reading of the outside, of the scarf acting as a means for hiding the paper so ostentatiously, perhaps may be read in another way. Perhaps it may be conjectured that it stands for something more in this moment in relation to how Balwinder is feeling. The very ostentation of the act that Balwinder is involved in seems to be mirrored by the ostentation of the scarf as a means to hide graffiti.]

The effort required to occupy and to be occupied by his public (self)-positioning seems overwhelming in two senses: first, the continual, relentless nature of this exertion; and, second, the constant sense of being a fraud, of being an unworthy material counterpart to a flawless ideal object. Therefore, Balwinder seems to exist in a state of ambivalence with respect to his public position. He has both a sense of satisfaction gained from it but also a sense of persecution or compulsion to keep on working at it that he seeks to free himself from in some way.

What seems important in the two moments described above is the public spectacle that Balwinder invites; each moment has a similar structure, where Karen is holding the attention of the whole class. Therefore, each moment is a dalliance with a kind of humiliation or ridicule, an extreme version of shame; a public moment, which seems to accord with the very public image/position that Balwinder occupies in this classroom. The subversion of this public position should therefore come in terms of the structure in which it makes sense. Since public scrutiny, and its possibility of shame, is the frame of intelligibility within which he both wishes and feels obliged to continue to be this 'thing', he chooses shame, or its potential, as the forum in which to experience the possibility of escape, or perhaps as a reminder of the consequences of escape.

A key aspect of both these moments is that Balwinder withdraws from the edge. In this way, Balwinder's relation to the sublime is incorporated into the everyday; it is a continual exercise in dealing with the constitutive discord of being the subject of ideal, socio-historically specific norms policed by the socio-spatial technology that is the school classroom. In this sense, perhaps this sublime relationship with boundaries is a continual flirtation, an acknowledgement of liminal space/processes as a constant presence even within seemingly secure social positioning. That is, the subject is precisely the lived 'impossibility of its own signifying representation'.

Conclusion

The subject of the classroom, placed in a space whose demands are exacting but never quite made clear, is continually in a state of questioning: '*what is it that is required of me here?*' The answers range from effortlessness, charm, public confidence, 'beat-boxing', dividing fractions, curiosity, winning ... the list goes on and constantly changes; these inferred properties are those of the continually supposed sublime object, the thing that this capricious, demanding space must want. At various times, in different ways, those who traverse this space come into relation with this fantastical, ideal thing that one supposes is demanded by it. The properties that are thus demanded are then policed by a continual public scrutiny structured into the TCB system.

I have used this chapter to look at the usefulness of this theoretical frame to make sense of the classroom experience from the perspective of a participant-observer. Perhaps this frame's main attribute is in the theoretical traction it provides for thinking about the discord that is continuously present, woven into, what seems to be an effortless occupation of the key positive qualities demanded by this space. Positive occupation of these qualities is accompanied by efforts at self-subversion; effortlessness is accompanied by hidden exertion; insouciance by fervour; public confidence by a past of paralysing shyness. These seemingly necessarily bound contradictions are contained in the discord of being the material counterpart to the inferred ideal that this space wants. In addition, this discord, and the interruptions it brings, serves to make visible/tangible the potential of shame through continual public scrutiny that is structured into this space, a policing emotion that is immanent and implied.

Perhaps what an exercise in thinking ethnographic data with this theoretical frame brings to the theory is to root seemingly transcendental, abstract concepts such as the 'sublime' in very specific, socio-historically constituted, spaces. The play of the sublime may only be discerned by familiarity with such spaces, both personal and with its socio-historical constitution. The subtle movements of relations between individual subjects; the implicit, intimate knowledges that they have of one another; their relations with teaching, learning and mathematics; the hidden moments of discord and contradiction may only be glimpsed within relations of committed familiarity. Perhaps it is in these moments that the sublime comes to inflect the everyday; as a continuous, discordant presence, rooted in a constitutive absence.

References

Allen, A. (2013) 'The Examined Life: On the Formation of Souls and Schooling'. *American Educational Research Journal*, 50 (2), pp. 216–250.
Boaler, J. (2016) 'Designing Mathematics Classes to Promote Equity and Engagement'. *Journal of Mathematical Behavior*, 41, pp. 172–178.
Damarin, S. K. (2000) 'The Mathematically Able as a Marked Category'. *Gender and Education*, 12 (1), pp. 69–85.
Freeman, B. C. (1995) *The Feminine Sublime: Gender and Excess in Women's Fiction*. Berkeley, CA: University of California Press.
Hamilton, D. (1989) *Towards a Theory of Schooling*. London: Routledge.
Hunter, I. (1994) *Rethinking the School: Subjectivity, Bureaucracy, Criticism*. London: Allen & Unwin.
Jones, D. (1990) 'The Genealogy of the Urban Schoolteacher'. In Ed Stephen Ball, *Foucault and Education: Disciplines and Knowledge*. London: Routledge.
Lacan, J. (2013a)*The Ethics of Psychoanalysis 1959–1960: The Seminar of Jacques Lacan*. London: Routledge.
Lacan, J. (2013b)*The Psychoses 1955–1956: The Seminar of Jacques Lacan*. London: Routledge.
Lawn, M. (1999) 'Designing Teaching: the Classroom as a Technology'. In Eds I. Grosvenor, M. Lawn. and K. Rousmanier, *Silences & Images; The Social History of the Classroom*. London: Peter Lang.
Livingston, E. (1999) 'Cultures of proving'. *Social Studies of Science*, 29 (6), pp. 867–888.
Markus, T. A. (1993) *Buildings and Power: Freedom and Control in the Origin of Modern Building Types*. London: Routledge.
Popkewitz, T. (2004) 'The Alchemy of the Mathematics Curriculum: Inscriptions and the Fabrication of the Child'. *American Educational Research Journal*, 41 (1), pp. 3–34.
Scheff, T. (2014) 'The Ubiquity of Hidden Shame in Modernity'. *Cultural Sociology*, 8 (2), pp. 129–141.
Shaw, P. (2007) *The Sublime*. London: Routledge.
Žižek, S. (1989) *The Sublime Object of Ideology*. London: Verso.

Chapter 10

The sublime in *Catch-22* as bridge between post-modern literature and psychoanalysis

Chris Vlachopoulos

The sublime is a notion as difficult to adequately define as any in psychoanalysis. For the purposes of this chapter, I will attempt to loosely define the sublime as an internal experience that involves some measure of extraordinary beauty. This encounter with the sublime can be intentional or not, and, generally speaking, its value is supplemented by its capacity to provide a substantial shift in perspective; that shift in perspective can be about the world, or the self, or both. An example of an encounter with the sublime can involve absorbing a painting, for example, whereby appreciating the colours within can lead to a newfound appreciation of nature and the self's relation to it. It can come through a breakthrough in science, some new discovery about the universe, or it can come through something as seemingly mundane and ordinary as the soft feeling of something as fleeting as a raindrop landing inside our hand.

This loose working definition comes with two important caveats. First, I propose that the value of experiencing the sublime is not totally dependent on the lessons it teaches us. That means that experiencing the sublime can be something completely ephemeral, and contained exclusively within a moment in time, or indeed it can last for the rest of our lives. That doesn't diminish the experience itself. What matters most about the sublime, this chapter argues, is *the moment of the experience itself; its own capacity for existing.* Second, that the essence of an encounter with the sublime itself can take infinitely many forms and is endlessly malleable. Therefore, communicating what an encounter with the sublime is like to anyone else is a significant challenge, since that experience can be subjective.

That doesn't mean, however, that conversation around an encounter with the sublime is without merit; far from it. This chapter argues that it is precisely these little gaps in communication that provide us with an excellent opportunity: the process of communicating to others what an encounter with the sublime means to us allows us to look at the same subjective experience through separate vantage points, thus enhancing our understanding of not only that experience (encountering the sublime), but also of our theoretical models too.

Two such models that I believe can mutually benefit from this form of cross-examination are psychoanalysis and post-modernist fiction. This chapter will attempt to look at some of their shared history, before using examples of encounters with the sublime from Joseph Heller's *Catch-22* to discuss some of the merits this interaction can bring forth.

Post-modernist fiction and psychoanalysis

Now that we have provided a working definition for the sublime, this chapter is going to examine just exactly why the sublime provides us such a good opportunity to talk about post-modernist fiction and psychoanalysis side by side. A good starting point would be to talk about their relationship up until this point.

For a significant portion of theoreticians today, post-modernism and psychoanalysis are not two branches of theory that have always had an easy co-existence. I would argue that this is also largely accurate when it comes to a significant portion of the people who put these theories into their respective practices as well, namely writers of post-modern fiction and psychoanalytic therapists. That is not to say, however, that literature as a whole hasn't profoundly influenced psychoanalytic thought, and vice versa (this chapter will mainly focus on the former). Freud distinctively went so far as to name a certain famous complex after a somewhat tragic protagonist from a cycle of Ancient Greek tragedies. By and large, psychoanalytic theory is teeming with references to works of literature from all over the world, from antiquity until today. This is anything but incidental, of course: it merely reflects the simple fact that for a very long time, the two were literally inseparable. One might even argue that, before the formulation of psychoanalytic theory itself, one of the multiple functions of literature *was* to serve as an early attempt at psychoanalytic theory. *One* function out of many, but a vital function nonetheless.

Therefore, I believe that it is important to remember that literature has always been a central part of psychoanalytic theory's DNA, an indispensable element of its origin story, namely the urge to understand the many facets of our human experience.

Indeed, perhaps as a reflection of this long period of symbiosis between literature and psychoanalysis, many important works of psychoanalysis would seem to be right at home when discussed within the context of post-modern literature – despite the limited interaction these two strands have had. In a critical essay named 'The Mirror Stage', Jacques Lacan (1977) protested against the prevailing trend of psychoanalysts in the late 1940s, which tended to look at the human mind outside of its social context and only in terms of consciousness and the unconscious. The mind, Lacan argued, strives to perceive itself as a coherent whole, or at least to give itself the illusion of wholeness, when in reality it struggles to balance out its component parts, such as the tides of unconscious activity, instincts and drives that characterise it a lot of the time. Lacan argued that in the midst of all that, the conscious mind cannot necessarily always know what is Real in a complex and interrelated web of realities.

This line of thinking is completely compatible with many arguments in post-modernist thought, namely that the mind is not a constant, but an ever-shifting web of relationships between its constituent parts (and the function of time) that remains ultimately unknowable. This type of argument wouldn't be out of place in a work of post-modernist fiction by Barthelme or Pynchon. For example, the topic that Pynchon toys with a lot in his monumental 1974 work *Gravity's Rainbow* in typically irreverent post-modern fashion: one of the many, overlapping, labyrinthine narratives follows a certain Lieutenant Tyrone Slothrop in London during the World War II. Slothrop has troubles. The locations of his sexual conquests around London seem to inexplicably, and very accurately, predict the sites at which German-launched V-2 Rockets will crash a few days later – every single time. What accounts for that? The novel draws us in on a spiralling odyssey in search of answers but at the same time seems to make a mockery out of our near-constant obsession with them. The imagery of locations of sexual conquests and launching rockets suggests further influence on the novel of the psychoanalytic ideas of libido.

Another alignment between post-modern fiction and psychoanalysis appears in Lacan's work with structuralist ideas that also showed a strong preoccupation with language in a way that would be right at home in post-modern thought: the idea that it is language that allows us to form a sense of self through the word *I*, something that according to Lacan doesn't happen before the acquisition of language, and what Lacan called the Symbolic Order of our culture. Again, post-modernism's core ideas here seem aligned with psychoanalytic thinking, ideas that are sceptical against concepts of total finality or strict resolutions.

Despite this alignment between psychoanalysis and post-modern fiction, it would seem that authors of post-modern fiction have not engaged much with psychoanalysis. There are of course writers whose work was famously influenced by psychoanalytic theory as well as a strand of the post-modern tradition, such as Samuel Beckett's *More Pricks Than Kicks* (1934), as well as his latter stellar trilogy of novels: *Molloy* (1951), *Malone Dies* (1958) and *The Unnameable* (1960). The latter books coming in a period a number of years after Beckett's crucial and formative process of undertaking therapy at the Tavistock Clinic with psychoanalyst Wilfred Bion in 1934. However, writers like that tend to be the exception rather than the rule. Perhaps there is something to be said about a Writer's Ego that possibly prohibits most writers from 'surrendering' to an authority higher than themselves and even attempting therapy in the first place. Writers are Creators, the highest possible authorities inside the Universes which they create, the pacesetters for everything that pulses through them, and so it might be somewhat difficult for writers generally to acknowledge that there are narratives they might not even be aware of, especially if those narratives inform some of their work. Not that therapy should be mandatory of course, though those willing to attempt it do show an inquisitive spirit and willingness to push boundaries further – something very evident in Beckett's work as well. But even without engaging in actual therapy, there does not seem to be much fruitful engagement by writers of post-modern fiction with psychoanalytic ideas.

A similar lack of engagement seems to occur the other way round, too. After a certain point in time, around the mid-1960s, direct references to works and writers of the post-modern tradition specifically within literature also seem to disappear from the cultural radars of the most important works of psychoanalysis. An exception might have occurred with one of the most important cultural exchanges between post-modern literature and psychoanalysis that seems to have influenced the way ideas are communicated between these two strands of theory: the posthumous publication of a 1975 seminar by Jacques Lacan on the work of James Joyce,[1] under the title *Le Sinthome* – an archaic, playful variation on the French word for *The Symptom*. Lacan is impressed by Joyce's wordplay and linguistic inventiveness, particularly the way the latter draws on religious imagery to enhance language and reinvent meaning; however, I would argue that, with regards to post-modern fiction, one of the most important contributions of that seminar was to link the idea of Joyce's possible psychopathology to the daring experimentalism and linguistic inventiveness that characterises so much of the latter's work, and extend that to many more works of post-modernist fiction. In *Le Sinthome* Lacan argues that Joyce's latent schizophrenia stayed dormant because James Joyce was able to find meaning and express himself through his work; that Joyce's uniquely creative excursions helped him maintain his lucidity, and thus his work can largely be seen as the canvas on which that battle for his sanity played out. Lacan has a lot of admiration for Joyce's daring, but those are the terms in which he largely deals with this body of work. Whether or not Joyce was truly schizophrenic is well beyond the scope of this chapter; but I hope there is some space for a constructive, creative debate with regards to the efficacy or intrinsic value of an indirect diagnosis made 30 years after the death of the author in question, and that that conversation can be allowed to continue (if one is indeed interested in that question at all).

I believe the problem with this seminar is not so much with making diagnoses itself but with the apparent symptomising and pathologising of Joyce's work. What the relationship between post-modernism and psychoanalysis translates to in practice is not so much that Joyce becomes pathologised, but that *the work itself* becomes pathologised. Our perceptions around post-modernist fiction are implicated because novels of extraordinary artistic value, like *Ulysses* or *Finnegans Wake*, become viewed as another expression of that same psychopathology. It is not like the work itself doesn't offer itself up for that view, at least initially, as the threads of its logic can so easily resemble a divided mind. Even the publication history of *Finnegans Wake* reflects its unique nature: originally published in 1942, it was finally restored in 2012 by Oxford University Press in an edition that seems reliably close to what Joyce intended, seemingly free of typographical errors. The reason it took so many years to even restore is that the novel is a highly experimental work of fiction completely unashamed of itself, with fractured, circular narratives, written almost exclusively in a made-up, jumbled, dream-like version of the English language that renders most of it unintelligible to a reader uninterested in issues such as the many functions of language, consciousness and representation. The very structure of the book invites multiple revisits: the last sentence of the book ends right where the first begins, so the work flows right back into itself, like a river in perpetual motion (indeed the sentence in question talks about the river Liffey). It is safe to say that *Finnegans Wake* anticipated many of the works of post-modernist literature that followed.

However, *Finnegans Wake* is a daring statement, work that takes absolutely nothing for granted, and one of the very few works of post-modernist fiction that dare ask the very question: *Should a piece of literature even be readable or intelligible?* I find that it is easy to jump at that question and be collectively outraged as readers that the answer might at any point be a *No* – but I think that the essence of that question ultimately points to other questions: *Does a work of art owe us at all times an explanation, a nicely packaged, deliverable raison d'etre? Or is it up to us to sometimes discover reasons for its existence? Is it okay not to have a raison d'etre, given our human mind's drive to draw meaning in everything? Could meaning sometimes be a trap in a cold, indifferent universe?* And, *Is it possible that by not being accessible, a work of literature can actually gift us the space to draw our own meanings and conclusions?* In true post-modern spirit, I believe that the real value of questions like these lies not so much in the answers we provide, but in the very process of asking them. Whatever else may be said about Joyce's work, I can only stand in awe before the type of work that dares ask these fundamental questions so bluntly, and so bravely forces me to ponder them, and in the process allows me to approach other works of fiction as a better reader. Yet, this is not something that psychoanalytic engagement with such fiction has brought out.

If post-modernist fiction sometimes resembles the work of a fragmented, or a divided mind, it is because the authors have intentionally presented us with a fragmented reality that it is up to us to put back together (if we so choose). Whether or not we choose to stitch it back together, it allows us to recognise the chasms between the many disparate realities which we find ourselves attempting to inhabit, and how hopelessly we are sometimes trying to reconcile them. In any case, in the process of doing so, we are presented with an opportunity to discover a little something about ourselves (our many, overlapping, ultimately unknowable selves, of course).

Jean-Francois Lyotard, in his work *The Post-Modern Condition* (1984), argued that what primarily defined post-modernism was, broadly speaking, a scepticism towards grand unifying narratives that aim to smooth out the conflictual nature of human experience. Metanarratives such as: technology is progress, industrialisation helps everyone achieve their dreams, the totality of the human mind is fixed and ultimately knowable; these propositions seek to sum everything nicely, but ultimately fall short. It could be argued that this makes post-modernism as a cultural phenomenon a constant shape-shifter opposed to any fixed identity and this makes its constructive dialogue with other disciplines difficult.

In post-modern fiction specifically, this quality of the wider post-modernist movement, namely its ironic detachment, has been identified by one of post-modern literature's last cultural exponents (as well as critic), the writer David Foster Wallace, as the main problem in post-modernism's long literary tradition. In an excellent 1993 essay titled 'E Unibus Pluram: Television and U.S. Fiction', Wallace argues that post-modernist fiction has used irony to expose the shortcomings of other narratives, but irony alone brings no redeeming qualities to the table itself. Post-modernist fiction turned into this caustic cultural commentator that ends up unable to sympathise with why people behave the way they do, only points out what's wrong at every turn. Perhaps that is why Wallace turned to works unrelated to post-modernist fiction, like the novels of Dostoyevsky: despite their bleakness, the Russian's novels often detail the journey to redemption (Max, 2012). Wallace acutely saw a hole within post-modern fiction, and tried to fill it with humanist values. Mary K. Holland went on to build upon this, and in her excellent study *Succeeding Postmodernism* (2014) she identifies different strands within post-modernist fiction, namely an obsession with opposition to metanarratives that ends up spreading an anti-humanist message. It is by a return to humanist values, Holland argues, that we will be able to look past post-modernist fiction with the lessons it sought out to teach us finally learnt.

Despite all the shortcomings, I strongly believe that post-modernist fiction has important lessons to teach us, lessons about subjectivity, representation, language, and – even – humanism. I seem to not be alone in this: in the introduction to the excellent *Understanding Experience: Psychotherapy and Post-modernism*, Roger Frie (2003) talks about the lessons psychotherapists can learn from post-modernism, and the fact that it can encourage therapists to have a more rounded, philosophical approach to their practice, something that Frie identifies as something of a gap in psychotherapeutic training. By keeping a philosophical approach to things, Frie argues, therapists can become better practitioners, and post-modernism can contribute to that. I also believe that fiction writers would benefit greatly from listening to the conversation around psychoanalytic theory more and would be better at using post-modern elements in their writings, since the narratives that psychoanalysis has to offer can be so illuminating in understanding our human experience.

One area where psychoanalysis and post-modern fiction can find common ground is the idea of the sublime, which I will explore in the remainder of this chapter. I believe the sublime offers us an opportunity to connect with the highest parts of ourselves by allowing us to process information in a different way. I will attempt to start this conversation off by talking about a particular work of post-modernist fiction: one that I find impeccably written; passionately presented; by turns irreverent, hilarious and tragic. A work that comforts and challenges the reader. A work of fiction that stresses the importance of something that I expect psychoanalysts to be at least partly familiar with: the importance of living life on your own terms, rather than blindly surrendering to an institution. A novel that serves as the perfect allegory for every institutional and bureaucratic opponent we've ever faced, real or imaginary, internal or external. The tale of an American bombardier caught in the closing stages of World War II. A man whose sole objective is to stay alive in the face of an absurdist nightmare. The legendary protagonist of Joseph Heller's *Catch-22*. Poor old Yossarian, whom everybody wants to kill.

Catch-22 and encounters with the sublime

The reason that I believe the sublime offers such a great opportunity to look at psychoanalysis and post-modernism side by side is that encountering the sublime tends to be such a strong moment that it contains the potential to erase all artificiality around it. Labels such as post-modernism and psychoanalysis become irrelevant on the face of a truly awe-inspiring moment. A novel that delivers a sublime moment isn't, at that moment, *just* a war novel, or a post-modernist novel, or a romantic novel. It is an encounter with the sublime.

Not that labels such as these become completely inconsequential: indeed, they are useful to keep in mind as a way of remembering the way artificial concepts surround us all the time. It is through an extraordinary experience like an encounter with the sublime that we can be fully aware of their artificiality. So, it is perhaps worth noting that *Catch-22* belongs in all three aforementioned subcategories. Some readers might have trouble finding the romanticism, but it's right there in the opening line: *It was love at first sight.* The second line then reads: *The first time Yossarian saw the chaplain he fell madly in love with him.* Yossarian is only interested in the chaplain in so far as the chaplain might find an explanation for all this absurdity of war. The joke would be completely lost if we didn't momentarily believe in the opening line's romanticism. In just two sentences we have witnessed the novel's modus operandi: it will invoke our highest ideals, and then contrast them with the reality of them crash-landing inside an experience as absurd as war. The chapter will go on to discuss how absurdism is utilised in the novel in more detail below, as well as how absurdism can be linked to the sublime within *Catch-22*.

The sublime is a moment of genuine connection with the highest parts of ourselves that the novel allows us to experience, by shaking us and forcing us to process the information in a different, more personal and profound way, perhaps bypassing some of our preconceptions. *Catch-22* is full of moments that I believe allow us to encounter the sublime, and in doing so constantly toys with our expectations. But first a few words about the novel itself.

Catch-22 was published in 1961 and became instantly popular. The plot is set mostly on the island of Pianosa, in northern Italy, and is detailing life in a fictional US Air Squadron of which, the novel's central character, Yossarian, is a part. *Catch-22* has all the essential post-modern pick-n-mix characteristics: it is deeply incredulous towards grand narratives (such as the American Way of Life, or unquestioning patriotism), it has a fractured, circular narrative that only allows episodes to become clear when viewed from multiple points of view, it is deeply absurdist. But, crucially, it isn't part of later post-modernism's anti-humanist trend that Mary K. Holland identified as problematic. *Catch-22* holds very clearly stated humanist values, it treasures and celebrates life-affirming moments (such as the sexual encounters of Yossarian with the nurses) and satirises with unrelenting force those of Yossarian's squadron that succumb to the narratives that require them to give their lives for the grand ideas they were sold back home. A defining moment comes when Yossarian, early in the book, is contrasted with Appleby, one of those serving alongside him in Pianosa. Appleby is presented to us as almost a model soldier: effortlessly good at everything he attempts, all the whilst holding on to traditional values dearly, values such as believing in God, in the nuclear family and the American Dream – presumably all things worth of dying for, right? Well – Yossarian certainly doesn't think so. Every time they interact, Yossarian gets so irritated by Appleby's gung-ho attitude that every encounter becomes an exercise in frustration for Yossarian and hilarity for the reader.

In typical post-modernist fashion, the inciting incident has occurred before the action starts, and the reader only finds out about it near the end of the novel. Yossarian has witnessed the slow, agonising death of Snowden, a crewmate of his, on a plane, during a mission, and that left him deeply in shock. Yossarian realised the absurdity of dying like this, and throughout the whole novel remains incredulous that nobody else is concerned that they are asked to give their lives for this war. The device which keeps everyone on board is the famous catch-22, a piece of winding logic that nobody can argue with to get out of flying more missions. Flying missions over the enemy is crazy, catch-22 states, and so it is rational for somebody to want to get out of it. But if one is sane enough to recognise that, that means that they are sane enough to fly their mission, and so they have to do them. There is no getting out of catch-22's devastating simplicity: if you have the capacity to be concerned for your own well-being, that automatically means that you also have the capacity to fly these suicidal missions, and any and all concern about your own self becomes null and void. I find it strangely fitting that Yossarian first hears about this obvious disregard for life from Doc Daneeka, the squadron's *doctor* out of all people – makes me wonder what sort of twisted Hippocratic Oath Heller would have made his characters take in the world of *Catch-22*.

I will attempt to describe a few ways in which I personally encountered the sublime in Catch-22. Of course this is highly subjective: as subjective and personal as an encounter with the sublime can be. Nonetheless, I will attempt to showcase a few aspects of the novel that I believe merit discussion.

To begin with, I find that the novel is brilliantly written and linguistically beautiful. The crystalline quality of its prose is always eloquent, in direct contrast to the bureaucratic hailstorm that it depicts. This is particularly acute because it showcases a particularly deep faith in the novel not just as an art-form, but also in *the novel as an institution* that deserves to be as polished as it can possibly get. This is in stark contrast with the unrelenting criticism other institutions receive, namely the armed forces, or blind patriotism.

The novel also allows for an encounter with the sublime through its very structure. It follows a non-chronological path because it always waits for a reason to reveal more. The novel only reveals crucial information when the characters, and we, the readers, are ready for it. For example, many of the novel's crucial catalysts, such as Michaela and Snowden's deaths, are only revealed when the impact they have on Yossarian is of particular importance. The novel also has an exquisitely disciplined pace, slowly building towards a dramatic crescendo, very slowly at first, almost at a glacial pace, but builds up so assuredly that when the dramatic events do pick up steam, the experience of reading *Catch-22* feels like a nightmare from which we don't want to wake up. The novel constantly subverts our expectations, linking tragic events with satire in a way that not only diminishes their impact, but helps the reader digest them and try to make sense of them. Here is a dimension in the jokes that follow a tragic event which seems to be comforting rather than dis-respectful or crass – lesser novels would keep a solemn tone throughout, but *Catch-22* refuses to stumble and recovers almost instantaneously, in a way that lets us process the events in a different light.

One such example that I believe showcases an encounter with the sublime in *Catch-22* really well is the part of the novel that deals with the events leading up to the 'death' of Doc Daneeka, the squadron's doctor. Most of the men in *Catch-22* are very young, just barely out of boyhood, and yet here they are, in a theatre of war, being asked to steer and command big steel monstrosities in the air. It is only natural that some of them deal with this as a sort of game, especially the pilots. One such pilot is McWatt, who at some point performs a training flight over the waves around Pianosa. He flies his aircraft dangerously low over the waves, and this results in the gruesome, horrible death of another character, Kid Sampson, who gets caught in the propeller whilst he's standing on a raft. Once McWatt realises what he's done he flies directly into a mountain, killing himself. The scene is gruelling. Heller keeps the perspective on the ground, and we hear the screams, we see Kid Sampson's lifeless body (or whatever's left of him) dangling in the air for a moment, we feel the hopelessness of the plane's erratic flying up to the moment it crashes on to the mountain, the panic of those jumping with parachutes out of the plane trying to save themselves, the finality of the plane crashing. It is as tragic as it is needless, more needless fatalities, young people dying for no good reason, one step further away from humanity. But then perspective shifts abruptly to Doc Daneeka, who is right there on the ground, only he was meant to be on that aircraft as well. Doc Daneeka has a well-established fear of flying, but, as all squadron members have to have a certain number of flight hours logged per month, Doc Daneeka's name was put on the register for the flight so that he can reach his quota without actually having to fly. Doc Daneeka is physically right there, on the tarmac, yet people say that they didn't see him jump out of the plane like the others; hence the only logical conclusion is that he must be dead. In the eyes of the institution, Doc Daneeka died on that plane crash. No amount of arguing or pleading can change the opinion of everyone involved. His job is given to others; he stops being able to draw his pay. He truly becomes a dead man, something he comes to accept by the end of the novel. His widow is devastated by the loss, but as the GI life insurance kicks in, and more donations start pouring in, she receives a 'heartfelt' note from the army, supposedly informing her of her husband's fate – but the note itself is hilariously vague in that it provides no actual details, only the fact that Daneeka is somehow nebulously incapacitated. That lack of closure, then, moves Doc Daneeka's widow into action and she decides to move, leaving no forwarding address behind. Doc Daneeka's death becomes final as his final link to the world of the living is severed, all due to the army's cruel, all-erasing inhumanity.

The sublime in this moment manifests in the way it forces us to reinterpret a tragic event through the lens of a bureaucratic institution: anything pertaining to the individual ceases to matter, and the institution finds ways to override family by 'bribing' them, and showering them with gifts. It virtually erases somebody out of existence, and it doesn't even matter *how*. The case could be made that, at times like these, the novel unapologetically slips into absurdist territory. How could absurdism be linked to experiencing the sublime? Indeed, that note is very far from how a 'normal' human being is supposed to behave, right? Nothing about it is remotely redeeming *in and of itself*, so how could this experience be linked to an encounter with the sublime? It is important to note, however, that absurdism isn't randomness. Rather, it points toward something. It is very obvious that behaviour such as sending a note such as this to a bereaved family wouldn't allow someone to get very far in the world, because it is so blatantly disregarding many of our core values, such as empathy, respect for life or just basic decency. But it is exactly because this type of absurdist behaviour evokes the rejection of so many of our core values that it ends up reaffirming them: after all, such behaviour wouldn't seem absurd if we didn't share those same values in the first place. So, very much like a photo negative can still reveal the features of a person, the absurd reaffirms our core values by pointing not to photo-realism, but to their negative. We know black is still black, even if it might appear momentarily as white. What we hold dear is 'activated' regardless. And when we experience the full engagement of our core values, of everything we hold dear, whether it be by affirming them or rejecting them, it is clear that this becomes a moment of 'recognition', of being able to hold our own against the seeming absurdity of life, and thus unlocks the potential for an encounter with the sublime. I would argue that any text or medium that manages to engage with our core beliefs in this way has the potential to unlock such an encounter, and *Catch-22* does this brilliantly throughout, always in fresh and unexpected ways.

Another episode that allows us to experience a range of emotions so wide and profound that affords an opportunity for an encounter with the sublime is the episode detailing Michaela's death. It happens near the end of the novel, in the infamous Eternal City chapter. Yossarian has left Pianosa without leave, disgusted by the situation in the Air Squadron, and is aimlessly wandering in Rome. Whilst walking around he sees the corpse of Michaela, a local maid that Yossarian is familiar with. Michaela has been thrown off a balcony from a building nearby, and Yossarian investigates. When he enters the building above he finds Aarfy, a crewmate of his. It is well established throughout the novel that Yossarian hates Aarfy with a burning passion because of the blind way he follows orders whilst in the air, endangering their lives – Yossarian can be heard many times throughout the novel yelling at Aarfy to get out of the way, as Yossarian always runs towards the plane's escape hatch. Yossarian hates Aarfy even more because he is always eerily calm during missions, and Aarfy shows the same disturbing lack of emotion here as he admits to raping and murdering Michaela. Yossarian is beyond words. Why would he do that? He tells Aarfy that he will be arrested, maybe even executed. He can't go around killing innocent women. Aarfy laughs this off, saying nobody would do that to 'good old Aarfy'. The lack of remorse Aarfy shows is astounding, and only showcases the effect institutions have, making individuals do the most horrible things and numbing them to basic human responses. Nonetheless, Yossarian tries his best, telling Aarfy that he killed another human being! Surely he understands that there have to be consequences for that, right?

But again, Aarfy's sociopathic lack of empathy is put on full display. He casually admits that he killed that woman because she would have been bad-mouthing the Americans after he raped her. Yossarian, half-demented by this point, proposes to Aarfy that he didn't have to kill her, or even rape her, because paying some other girl for sex is the easiest thing in the world. To which Aarfy casually replies that he would never do a thing like that – because he's never done such a lowly thing as pay for sex – so he would rather commit murder.

Yet there is still hope for justice. People start congregating around the fallen woman in the street, start murmuring, they throw accusatory glances up at them. Then, there is the sound of approaching sirens. Yossarian tells Aarfy that they are coming to arrest him. There will be consequences. He can't go around murdering people, and the Military Police are on their way. For the first time ever, Aarfy begins to lose his cool as he is about to deal with the consequences of his actions. Cars screech nearby. Voices can be heard from down below. People start to gather around. Yes, maybe there will be consequences for this murder after all. Aarfy really starts getting nervous as fists pound at the door, loudly, forcefully demanding entry. The door finally gives way and two tough MPs barge in, and both Yossarian and Aarfy immediately know that they are here to arrest someone, and yes, surely this is vindication, Yossarian thinks, vindication for the memory of the poor woman that was so cruelly murdered, this is what justice looks like, Yossarian allows himself to think, surely!

Only, as the reader already suspects, justice isn't served in the world of *Catch-22*. Not by the military, at least. Because the two MPs proceed to arrest Yossarian for some minor army-related transgression (being away without a pass), whilst at the same time they take the time to kindly apologise to Aarfy for their unwarranted intrusion in his room.

The notion that there can be any sort of justice in the middle of an institution as absurd as war is done away with for good. Yossarian needs little more to plan his escape afterwards, which he does. He steals a plane and escapes to neutral Sweden, away from the absurdity of all this. Yossarian never stops fighting for his life, for his sanity, and it is significant that Heller's faith in him is unwavering. Far from post-modernism's sometimes cruel, ironic worldview, the heart of *Catch-22* remains a funny novel that affirms our faith in humanity and in ourselves.

Conclusion

This chapter has argued that an encounter with the sublime is, ultimately, a highly subjective experience that is not only difficult to clearly define or quantify; it is also not easily placed within theoretical frameworks. In this sense, the sublime is like a high mountain peak that reaches way out into the Stratosphere and does not care what the weather is like beneath it. This chapter's central premise has been that it is by looking at how those frameworks at the base of the mountain try to conceptualise encounters with the sublime that teaches us about the way those frameworks operate.

We have examined a few encounters with the sublime within *Catch-22*: its brilliant use of absurdity in dealing with character's lives and deaths, its use of humour, the novel's structure and linguistic freshness. The novel also retains a generous, warm attitude towards its characters, far from most of post-modernist fiction's cold, indifferent, ironic worldview. It remains true to post-modernism's natural scepticism towards grand narratives whilst at the same time holding on to its core values, instead of blindly substituting them with ironic nihilism. In fact, one of the most fruitful encounters with the sublime in *Catch-22* involves the way characters, especially Yossarian, struggle to find a coherent sense of self within the institution of war. Indeed, from a psychoanalytic point of view, it is possible to read *Catch-22* as a crisis of the *I*: Yossarian is one of the very few people in the novel who seems to have a healthy definition of self: his sense of self does not include institutions, not continents, not wars. Most of the rest of the cast of characters, however, seem to define themselves as the shared space of the institution, and, crucially, *exclude their own bodies* from their own sense of self. All that matters is the institution, and what that dictates them to do, even at the cost of their own lives, or the lives of others. Their sense of self includes the space of the institution that includes everything *except* human bodies. Yossarian's sense of self, however, does include his connection to others who feel pain, even those who have perished, like Snowden. Snowden is much more alive and impactful in the novel than others who are alive and define themselves purely as part of the institution. It is significant that the enemy never appears in *Catch-22*. Germans are nowhere to be seen, never once make an appearance. For this novel, the only enemy resides inside us. Our twisted sense of self. It's not the whole truth, of course, but it doesn't need to be to have value. Yossarian will not compromise; he will not give up and surrender to the institution. There is a certain sublimity in that – in his refusal to play the game. Because we all play the game. Someone who is as determined as Yossarian is needed, as stubbornly in love with his right to choose the terms of his own life, someone who refuses to be a part of this endless cycle of destruction.

The way in which these ideas about the self are expressed in a post-modern novel such as *Catch-22* illustrates their value with regards to psychoanalysis. It shows us that serious psychoanalytic concepts can be effectively expressed in various forms, and at the same time, the novel's irreverence and playfulness (even on the face of tragedy) can show the value of looking at the absurdity of everyday situations with humour. The absurd, as already discussed, can be a wonderful teacher about ourselves. This is something that *Catch-22*, and post-modernist fiction in general, can teach us. The value of not taking ourselves too seriously, and at the same time to fight ferociously for what we believe in.

Ultimately though, I believe that the value of encountering the sublime in *Catch-22* is that it represents a step into deeply subjective and personal territory (the sublime) but – crucially – that same deeply personal and subjective territory is such a unique experience that it remains a reliable point of reference. Most crucially, that reliable point of reference might be dealt with outside of the language or ideas we might be comfortable using. And thus – miraculously – encountering the sublime in the everyday can be one of those very rare experiences that can be both highly subjective *and* a reliable frame of reference, both for persons and for disciplines. And yet, with different language, different ideas can come about, ideas that might not have come about without this wonderful process of cross-pollination.

Thus, we can encounter the sublime in unexpected ways – which is another way of saying, we can encounter *each other*.

Note

1 The work of James Joyce, particularly his magnum opus, *Ulysses*, is widely regarded as a milestone in modernist fiction, not post modernism. In so far as post modernism is a reaction against modernism, though, and as Joyce certainly reacted to how his own work was perceived in the years after Ulysses was published, *Finnegans Wake* is thought to exhibit post-modernist characteristics (Zangouei, 2013).

References

Beckett, S. (1934) *More Pricks Than Kicks*. London: Faber and Faber.
Beckett, S. (1951) *Molloy*. London: Faber and Faber.
Beckett, S. (1958) *Malone Dies*. London: Faber and Faber.
Beckett, S. (1960) *The Unnameable*. London: Faber and Faber.
Frie, R. (2003) *Understanding Experience: Psychotherapy and Postmodernism*. London: Routledge.
Heller, J. (1961) *Catch-22*. New York, NY: Simon and Schuster.
Holland, M.K. (2014) *Succeeding Postmodernism: Language and Humanism in Contemporary American Literature*. New York, NY: Bloomsbury.
Lacan, J. (1977) *Écrits, A Selection*. Trans A. Sheridan. New York, NY: W.W. Norton.
Lacan, J., and Miller, J.-A. (1975) *Le séminaire. Texte établi par Jacques-Alain Miller: Le sinthome 1975–1976*. Paris: Seuil.
Lyotard, S.F. (1984) *The Postmodern Condition*. Trans G. Bennington and B. Massumi. Manchester: Manchester University Press.
Max, D.T. (2012) *Every Love Story Is a Ghost Story: A Life of David Foster Wallace*. London: Granta.
Pynchon, T. (1974) *Gravity's Rainbow*. London: Vintage.
Wallace, D.F. (1993) 'E Unibus Pluram'. *Review of Contemporary Fiction*, 13 (2), pp. 151–195.
Zangouei, J. (2013). 'Backward Glance at James Joyce: Finnegans Wake's Postmodernist Devices'. *Studies in Literature and Language*, 7 (2), pp. 63–71.

Chapter 11

The Diogenes complex
Sublime living in irrational times

Daniel Rubinstein

In memory of Nily Mirsky

Introduction

There are two main ways by which the sublime has contributed to political theory, and possibly to the practice of politics itself. For brevity's sake, the first can be name-checked as the Kantian sublime, and the second as the postmodern sublime. In this chapter I will briefly outline these approaches before suggesting that both versions of the sublime cannot quite measure up to the experience of living in the first half of the 21st century. While it might be tempting to come up with a new sublime that is more fitting for our times, such as an ecological sublime or a corporate sublime, I would like to suggest that the renewed interest in the sublime risks to appear as old wine in new bottles, unless it is taking seriously the ending of liberal/neo-liberal ethics and finally breaks with the contemporary critical discourse that still moves within the Enlightenment paradigm. The problem, to put it succinctly, is that in the age of viral social media, our fascination with smartphones and other industries of instant gratification means that both political representation and aesthetic perception are managed through technologies of speed, 24/7 news channels, always-on immersive media and modes of expression that privilege instantaneity. To misquote Antonio Gramsci, the problem is that the old sublime is dead, but the new sublime is not born yet.

This chapter will elaborate an altogether different way of looking at the sublime, broadly defined as a leap from the sensible to the super-sensible, as that which happens when there is a 'glitch in the matrix' – when the symbolic order is breaking down, revealing the phantasmagorical abyss that is lurking beyond the ostensibly smooth surface of social normativity. It is the moment in *The Truman Show* when Truman (played by Jim Carrey) sails towards the horizon in a boat, until the boat strikes a wall, and he realises that the sea and the sky are not real, and that the world he lived in all his life is a fiction constructed in a television studio.

Because this sublime is a tear in the fabric of reality, it is simultaneously an ethical and an aesthetic event; it reveals reality as an ideology – something constructed and artificial, rather than the natural and organic entity it purports to be. Understood through the dual viewfinders of performativity and ideology, the sublime is an ethical stance because it exposes reality as a fiction, a cover-up so successful that we no longer see it as such. As Lacan is at pains to point out, the sublime is a revolt against the tyranny of the reality principle, because it refuses to accept the given as the only conceivable form of reality (Lacan, 2007). As I will go on to show, Diogenes the Cynic – a homeless drifter, wandering tramp and a philosopher of great renown – provides an alternative response to the perennial question, 'What is to be done?' Diogenes answer is that especially in moments of great danger it is important to remember that reality is not all that it purports to be, that an alternative, virtual reality is sometimes the only saving grace, for it announces that the real is also work in progress. The alternative reality principle here is not a form of escapism, but a reminder that the irrational cannot be overcome by rational means.

Categories of the sublime

There are three ways by which the sublime is defined as an ethical experience. First, Edmund Burke conceived of the sublime as a bodily and spiritual experience of horror that is being mitigated by the sense of one's safety. The sublime is what happens when the drive for self-preservation clashes with fear that results from encountering something mighty, confusing and threatening and is mitigated through the feeling of physical security.

Second, Immanuel Kant, in *Critique of Judgment* revisits the question of representation (*Vorstellung*) that was central to the *Critique of Pure Reason* as an activity of the mind, but he approaches it in terms of aesthetic judgement. The experience of the sublime reaffirms human nature as rational through its ability to conceive of immeasurable formlessness (Kant, 2007, pp. 75–96). The subject determines him/herself by clamming superiority over nature. In this way Kant attempts to bridge the gap between theoretical and practical reason by placing the aesthetic experience of the sublime as a mediating mechanism between the sensible and the analytical. Kant distinguishes between mathematically sublime and dynamically sublime but asserts that in both cases it is the power of reason as the super-sensible force that triumphs over nature (Kant, 2007, p. 145).

Third, in *The Post-Modern Condition: A Report on Knowledge*, Jean-Francois Lyotard (1984) identifies a shift between the modern, i.e. Kantian, and the post-modern sublime: in modernist aesthetics the sublime is explored at the level of content leaving the form of the artwork intact; while the content can be transgressive, the form is reassuringly traditional. In postmodernism, however, the denial of solace is precisely the political point of the sublime, as it is the identity – manifest through representation – that is being shattered through the operation of the post-modern image, putting forward 'the unpresentable in presentation itself' (Lyotard, 1984, p. 81).

Lyotard's view of postmodernity highlights the fractal nature of the unrepresentable experience that refuses to become part of a totalising system or be subjected to the operations of rational logic that establishes some kind of reciprocity between reason and experience. Lyotard seems to imagine a work of art that is constantly striving to expose the diagram of its own foundation and push through its limits by perpetually using the work against itself and by undermining its own mode of production. While the Kantian sublime still holds on to the certainty and clarity of form, it is this very clarity that is not self-evident and problematised in the post-modern discourse.

Lyotard draws a further distinction between the Kantian sublime and the post-modern sublime, whereby in Kant the sublime exposes the failure of representation to reach out to ideas that cannot be represented, such as 'the idea of the world' and 'the idea of a simple (that which cannot be brokendown and decomposed)' (Lyotard, 1984, p. 78), but the post-modern sublime goes further, exposing the structure of representation itself as the will to mastery over all things. This encounter with the immeasurable and the irrational is sublime not because of the magnitude of the experience but because it causes subjectivity to realise the error of subject/object relations. In the sublime, subjectivity is dissolved. Neither language nor visual representation can encompass these moments of total dissolution of identity, which for Lyotard makes the sublime into a political problem as it shows the desire to categorise, identify and classify as a form of political control.[1] For Lyotard the sublime is a tool of radical politics because it points to those aspects of social life that cannot be adequately accounted for through representational schemas that rely on rational logic. The sublime becomes the refuge of the misfit, the mentally ill, the deviant, the immigrant and the political radical.

For Lyotard, the 'post-modern sublime' is symptomatic to the sense of crisis that envelops both the contents and the structures of knowledge, i.e. an epistemological crisis caused by breakdown and loss of trust in the foundations of rational knowledge. In the sublime, reason is reaching its limit and entering a domain of the incomprehensible, the monstrous and colossal. In our own time, the crisis of knowledge in all its forms is manifest in the current dismantling of the institutions of liberal democracy, against the background of climate emergency.

What this leads to is a need for a way of thinking, questioning and doing that does not rely on the same values that feed the industrial-entertainment complex otherwise known as life. Naming this modality of being 'Diogenes complex' I want to draw attention to what Foucault called 'the aesthetics of existence' – a sublime moment in which the ethical and the aesthetic are one and the same, where truth is equated not with the rational or the real but with the beautiful, the striking and the memorable (Foucault, 2011, p. 163).

Getting to this remarkable place requires a tripartite move. First, it will be shown how postmodernism tried and failed to provide an alternative to the logical-rational foundations of Western civilisation. In the second, it is necessary to show how the principle of identity plays out in the field of politics and what are the consequences of mistaking it for the real. In the third part Diogenes the Cynic is shown to find a way of truth-telling (*parrhēsia*) that does not rely on logical reason and the correspondence of ideas with reality. In so doing Diogenes might be proposing a way of life of radical and political activism, that is itself sublime.

The lament over postmodernism

It is strange to live at a time when political liberalism and democracy are seeking new and more imaginative ways of damaging and even destroying themselves. Key preoccupations of liberalism are being employed specifically to undermine and discredit cultural pluralism and to advance new forms of nationalism and racism aimed at repressing the very 'other' that is the focus and the concern of progressive politics. One by one all of the staples of liberalism – such as class, gender, sexuality, race, faith, the body, diversity and identity – are being weaponised not to advance inclusion and communitarianism but in order to promote intolerance, bigotry and racism through insisting on the right for self-determination of specific groups, whether these are white supremacists, misogynistic gamers, autocratic nationalists or pro-life activists. In this hall of mirrors, the 'other' is no longer the LGBTQI, the black, or the woman; rather it is the defender of white masculinity, the protester against the demolition of confederate statues, and the born-again Evangelical Christian.

What is even more worrying, is that a number of people who are leading the charge against pluralism, are themselves not reactionary, but due to the strange twists of the Mobius Band of the politics of identity, find themselves in favour of censorship, non-platforming and 'safe spaces' where the right not to be hurt or offended trumps free speech, experimentation and curiosity are deemed public relations liabilities, and the fear of social media backlash to provocations operates as an effective tool of self-censorship.[2] This is a paradoxical situation, in which the Left's traditional struggle for communitarian unity is replaced by a demand for recognition not as the 'other' but on the basis of difference from all the other 'others' (Kruks, 2001; Brown, 1995).

For its part, philosophy does not fare any better than politics. Contemporary reality is saturated with post-modern traits and antics because the philosophical project of postmodernism failed to make its mark on it. Postmodernism's daring ambition was to produce a genuinely secular philosophy, that does not take its bearings from the idealistic foundations of Western philosophical standard. The goal of 'overturning Platonism' (Deleuze, 1983), was not the tantrum of self-indulgent *les enfants terribles* (although it did become the playground of some terrible children) (Sutton, 2018), rather it was an urgent and deeply political attempt to hold rationalism and humanism to account for their role in the barbarisms of the 20th century. Because rationalism seems to be an equal opportunities employer in terms of mass-murder, concentration camps, nuclear bombs and other raptures of technological progress, dividing them fairly equally between the Left and the Right political extremes, Post-modern philosophers explored alternatives to the dominant narrative that makes reason and logic the cornerstone of Western philosophical world view (Golding, 2010). Their goal was to by-pass the Cartesian *I think therefore I am*, because the *I* of the *I think* somehow always happens to be white, Western and male, who, due to his exceptional thinking prowess, is simply destined to assume the role of Top Gun, the conqueror of nature, women, indigenous populations and everything else that happens to be on his warpath.

This promise of a pluralist, non-binary philosophy that challenges the established political order on both sides of the political divide, came crushing down with the Twin Towers on September 11, 2001.[3] In the ensuing global war, that is marketed as the West's righteous struggle against the Muslim antichrist, atheism and the 'end of grand narratives' (Lyotard, 1984) came to be seen as dangerous and unaffordable luxuries. The promise of a philosophy that is free from the metaphysical anchorage in the logic of identity, had to be quickly abandoned. When the declared enemy are the elusive Taliban tribesmen on Honda mopeds and balaclava-clad Islamists criss-crossing deserts in armed pickup trucks, sympathy for the nomad becomes a dangerous game.[4] And when the President George W. Bush declared after 9/11 'you are either with us or with the terrorists' (CNN.com, 2001), the creative possibilities of becoming-other seemed dangerously close to treason. The war effort required total mobilisation of intellectual resources, and said mobilisation did not bode well for the tantalising promises of becoming-sunflower, and of the paradoxes of libidinal economy and desiring machines.[5]

The principle of identity and its discontents

During these hazy, dot.com years between September 11, 2001 and the financial crash of 2007–2008 a new alliance was forged among the political class and the representatives of a newly minted philosophical school known as 'speculative realism'.[6] For the speculative realists, the excesses of postmodern philosophies of Deleuze, Derrida, Heidegger, Irigaray and Lyotard have gone too far in challenging the basic premises of rational thought and scientific positivism, undermining the presuppositions of logic and dialectics, and even blurring the boundaries between science and myth (Heidegger, 1978). Speculative realism returned philosophy to the rational-scientific foundations that first Freud then Heidegger thought to undermine by aligning it instead with art, poetry, music, Eros and the libido. Politically this was a smart move, as in the bonfire of the universities that followed from the global recession, the dialectical and analytical departments fared much better than their continental and post-modern counterparts. Politics without philosophy is nothing more than ideology (Boyer, 2001), for that reason aspiring politicians read PPE (Philosophy, Politics and Economics) in Oxford and Cambridge, and every new turn of the austerity screw is accompanied by the stoic sigh 'it was the right thing to do'.[7] Speculative realism, with its foundations in scientific certainty, truth and dialectics, was the fitting background music to the zero-sum war game that followed on from September 11. Instead of paradoxes it offered certainty, instead of the post-modern condition it offered truth, instead of rhizomatic becoming, deterritorialisation and nomadic war machines it offered the logic of identity as the linchpin of science and the rational basis of the state.[8]

The question of identity fuels the fiercest arguments on both sides of the political divide, as the conservatives seek to articulate identity as the fulfilment of individual destiny, and the right to consume goods and services, while the liberals seek to enlarge the notion of identity to encapsulate a growing number of ethnic, sexual and racial norms (Rose, 1996).

In its simplest form, the problem of identity can be expressed in a formula $A = A$, where A can be anything you like, a table, a Stradivarius violin, a molecule of hydrogen, the universe or you. To say that the A is equal to A means that it is not, and can never be anything other than A. For that reason, $A = A$ means that $A \neq B$ (known since Aristotle as the principle of non-contradiction) (Irwin, 1990). The power of identity lies in its ability to divide the world into autonomous, separate and clearly defined entities: a table is a piece of furniture with a flat top and one or more legs for eating, writing or working, a violin is a stringed musical instrument played with a horsehair bow (Webster Dictionary, 2018). So far so clear cut, yet a problem immediately arises when we imagine a table with strings stretched over its surface, and a bow moved across them: while it is not a Stradivarius, can we be certain that the table is not at the same time a little bit of a violin? And what becomes of a violin when I place it on a leg and eat my dinner from it? If a table and a violin present such unsolvable epistemological problems, how much more complex the situation becomes when the A is not a piece of furniture but a person who is not-quite-white, not-quite-straight, not-quite-black and not-quite-fe/male. Trying to force identity into the rigid framework of scientific certainty can be extremely injurious to one's health, as can be evidenced by anyone who was ever told in no uncertain terms that they are a filthy B who has no place among the pure-bred A's. It is a bitter irony of the identity argument, that one of the most sophisticated lines of reasoning against identity comes from Heidegger, who certainly was no stranger to indulging in a bit of racial purity himself.

> Everywhere, wherever and however we are related to beings of every kind, we find identity making its claim on us. If this claim were not made ... there would then also not be any science. For if science could not be sure in advance of the identity of its object in each case, it could not be what it is ... Thus, what is successful and fruitful about scientific knowledge is everywhere based on something useless.
>
> (Heidegger, 2002, pp. 26–27)

As Heidegger tersely explains, identity is simultaneously science's greatest achievement and the very limit beyond which it cannot go. Without identity there can be no science, as behind every definition lies the assumption that $A = A$. Equipped with this formula science can go about its business: water = H_2O, zebra = an African wild horse with black-and-white stripes and an erect mane, $E = MC^2$. Yet, the universal reach of the identity principle is also its fundamental weakness, for, while there is nothing that cannot be expressed as $A = A$, this all-powerful mechanism relies on the notion that the '=' (equals sign) represents an objectively given reality. For were it not the case, no scientific argument could make a claim for universal validity. Yet, what is the '=' if not a mental construct, something we can think of, but find it impossible to pinpoint its whereabouts. And if the '=' is something that exists only in our minds (and does it really mean the same thing for each and every one of us?), can we really trust it to base the whole edifice of science and culture on it? Could there be a minuscule, teeny-weeny chance that our mental image of '=' is simply wrong? It certainly can feel that way when we look at the melting ice caps, the pollution of air and water, the plasticisation of the oceans and white supremacist marches, for the infallible logic of identity operates behind the scenes in all these manifestations of the power of positive thinking. Behind the certainty of the '=' lies an image of the human mind as this infallible synthesiser from which all other images are emerging (Colebrook, 2014, p. 22). It is hardly surprising therefore, that postmodernism's challenge to the domination of the logic of identity received such a short shrift both from scientific and political quarters.

The animosity towards postmodernism united the proponents of the Left and of the Right, suggesting that they might not be so different after all. For the Left, postmodernism always was defeatist and a-political not only because it denied the existence of an objective reality that could be manipulated at will, but also because of its rejection of class-struggle as the universal engine of progress. On the Right, postmodernism was seen as anti-state, anti-science and anti-capital, an epistemological strategy aimed at rescuing the Left after the bankruptcy of Marxism and the breakdown of socialist states that flowed from the collapse of the Berlin Wall (Hicks, 2004).

This state-sanctioned condemnation of all things post-modern found further succour with the scandal of Heidegger's Nazism and antisemitism (Oltermann, 2014), while Derrida, along with his followers and inspirations was accused of dangerous nihilism, for deconstruction seemed to erase the distinction between Nazism and non-Nazism (Wolin, 1993). The result of this intolerance towards ambiguity, and the renewed demand for clarity, rigour and coherence hastened a return to the certainty of dualistic thinking and to binary oppositions in which all grey areas, equivocations and complexity are erased.

However, this rejection of post-modern equivocation and the return to the dominant discourse of binary oppositions did not succeed in driving out fascist and Nazi ideologies, rather the expulsion of ambiguity ushered in a new age of ostensibly clear-cut distinctions between 'truth' and 'post-truth', and a host of other debates over fake news, populism and contempt for parliamentary democracy. Crystallised around the figure of Donald Trump in the USA and Brexit in the UK, the binary opposition between 'leave' and 'remain' or 'globalists' and 'nationalists' has never been more explicit, yet despite the clearly drawn battle lines these warring factions have a lot in common, as they both operate from within the same proto-rational structure known as the principle of identity, which they are unable to see and to critique, because doing so would require them to abandon the very foundations of their positions.

The Diogenes cure

Caught in between these antagonistic positions are illegal immigrants, snowflakes, pussies, walking wounded, passport-less and stateless, citizens of nowhere, artists, anarchists, dreamers. Those who – like the inhabitants of the Gaza strip – look at the world through gaps in a barbed-wire fence, those who – like Europeans living in the UK, have no voice in deciding their future. Also caught in between are the misfits, the non-binary and the whistleblowers, those for whom the bell tolls, the fifth column, enemies of the people and those who – for whatever reasons – are still attached to the notion that hope comes not from choosing between truth and post-truth but from asking whose interests are served by the idea of truth in the first place. And then there are those who have felt in their bones long before 'fake news' became part of the imperial language, that 'news' is always fake, for when was there anything new in the if-it-bleeds-it-leads news cycle?

For those who are still clinging to a conviction that there is something that escapes the binary opposition between the enemy and the foe, and that this something might actually be the key, or at least a lucky charm, hope comes unexpectedly from the words written 200 years ago by Søren Kierkegaard who, in his own dark night of the soul, found encouragement in the kindred spirit of Diogenes 'the dog'.

Diogenes was a Cynic philosopher, famous throughout the ancient world for his uncompromising personal conduct. As a firm believer that actions speak louder than words, during cold winters he hugged marble statues in order to harden his body (Laertius, 2008), an exercise that he probably found useful after being captured by pirates and sold into slavery. When he finally settled in Corinth, he enthusiastically adopted a lifestyle of extreme austerity, living in a barrel (according to some sources in a big jar), begging for his food, defecating in the open and masturbating in the marketplace. When the good people of Corinth chided him for pleasuring himself in public, he replied 'But why are you scandalized, since masturbation satisfies a need, just as eating does?' (Laertius, 2008, p. 47). From the surviving fragments of Diogenes' life and teachings, an image emerges of a way of being that nowadays is more readily associated not with philosophy but with performance art. As Foucault observed, the tradition of Cynic philosophy lives on in the practices of those contemporary artists who adhere to the idea that artist's life should constitute a testimony of what art is in its truth (Foucault, 2011, p. 187). Marina Abramović allowed the audience of her *Rhythm 0* (1974) performance to cut her with a knife, and a loaded gun was pointed at her head. In another performance, *Rhythm 5*, she set herself on fire. In Bas Jan Ader's performance *In Search of the Miraculous* (1975) he attempted to cross the Atlantic in a small boat, his body was never found. Paul McCarty's 1976 performance *Class Fool* included self-injury and self-molestation in a ketchup splattered classroom. Tehehing Hsieh spent one year (1978–1979) in a 3.5 by 2.7-metre cage (*Cage Piece*). In another performance, *Time Clock Piece* (1980–1981) he punched a time clock every hour on the hour for a year. By using violence and self-mutilation as a rebellion against the 'symbolic', these artists testify that the role of art is one of reducing existence to its basics, blurring and even removing the boundaries between art and life. Like many contemporary performance artists, Diogenes made his body the site and the object of his art, believing that the philosopher must establish a relation with reality that is not based on logic, discourse or argument, but on the practice of living as a form of truth-telling.

According to Kierkegaard (who got this story from Lucian):

> When Corinth was threatened with a siege by Philip and all the inhabitants were busily active – one polishing his weapons, another collecting stones, a third repairing the wall – and Diogenes saw all this, he hurriedly belted up his cloak and eagerly trundled his tub up and down the streets. When asked why he was doing that, he answered: I, too, am at work and roll my tub so that I will not be the one and only loafer among so many busy people.
>
> (Kierkegaard, 1985b, pp. 60–61)

Picture the scene: a bustling metropolis is urgently preparing for an impending catastrophe, whether natural or man-made: a fast-approaching devastating tsunami, a ballistic missile or the inauguration of a democratically elected dictator, whatever it is, it is not turning back, the doomsday clock's hand is pointing to few seconds to midnight and counting. Everyone is doing what people do in such circumstances: some amass provisions, some stockpile weapons, others barricade the door, pray, make love, get high, cuddle the children or whatever else people do to take their minds off the fact that in a day, month, or even a year, everything friendly, homely and comforting will be taken away, and what will come in its place does not bear thinking about.

And in the middle of all this commotion, Diogenes, who of course cannot be trusted with a useful task, is busily rolling his barrel up and down the street. What does he think he is doing, and how can this be of any help to us, if our job description does not include the ability to make fire by rubbing two sticks together? Before answering, one thing has to be made clear. Diogenes is not what is usually called 'mad'. He is not insane, which literally means unhealthy. On the contrary, contemporaries report that despite the hardships of his life, or perhaps precisely due to the severe restrictions he placed on himself, Diogenes was of vigorous and radiant health, his body fit and trim, his eyes bright, his skin clean and supple. He is in good physical condition both on the inside and on the outside. As Epictetus explains, Diogenes *must* be fit and good looking because true to his philosophical method he is teaching how to live a good life not by analysing syllogisms, but through instructing by example:

> It is also necessary, however, that the Cynic should have the right kind of body, because if he comes forward looking like a consumptive, all thin and pale, his witness would no longer carry the same weight. For he must not only prove to laymen, by displaying the qualities of his mind, that it is possible to be virtuous and good without having the things that they set such store on, but he must also show through his bodily qualities that a plain and simple life lived in the open air has no deleterious effects even on the body. 'Look, both I and my body bear witness to that truth'. That was the way of Diogenes, for he would walk around radiant with health, and would attract the attention of the crowd by the very condition of his body.
>
> (Epictetus, 2014, pp. 651–652)

On one level, Diogenes' rolling his barrel up and down the high street is an activity like all others: someone else might be at the same time dragging home a shopping trolley full of cat food, for even this is preferable to starvation, and besides others are less likely to be tempted by it. Another might be joining the queue at the train station, as the latest rumour is that some trains are still running, someone else might be searching for a working cash machine with money, as all their life's savings are in the bank, and it is closed. Like so many others, Diogenes too is frantically active, but unlike the rest, his activity is knowingly and demonstratively futile. He is not looking for a solid wall to shelter himself behind it; he is not trying to find a place to hide, as he clearly knows that in this life there is nowhere to hide, and he is also not trying to attract attention to his vulnerability and extract pity from the passers-by.

On the other hand, he is not assuming the role of a street preacher, the one that stands in the middle of the highway proclaiming that the end is nigh, that time has come to focus on the things that matter in this moment of reckoning – finding God, confessing sins and in general saving one's soul from damnation. In the midst of the binary choice between saving one's body and saving one's soul, Diogenes chooses neither, he refuses to accept both dominant narratives, the first that says that in this dog-eat-dog situation, fists and bullets speak louder than words, that the fittest will survive and all others will perish in agony, but he also rejects the opposite narrative that we are all doomed, that the only thing worth saving is the soul, because everting physical, material and carnal is about to be comprehensively annihilated.

To make things even more puzzling, Diogenes also does not adopt the so-called 'philosophical' attitude, the one that would require him to say with a sigh, 'well, it was fun while it lasted, but now that the world is coming to an end, I will calmly await my destiny. What matters to me is not that I am about to die, but that I will not give in to fear and remain serene and at peace with myself to the end'. Not for Diogenes is this form of passivity; he is not giving up on life; he is not prepared to be lead to his death like a lamb to the slaughter. No, man, he is right there, in the midst of things, with all the other people, running around like headless chickens.

What is remarkable is that in this moment of reckoning, Diogenes refuses all the available choices, and yet, out of this black-or-white situation, where one either tries to save the body or the soul, he manages to carve another dimension that pinches something from both the prepper-survivalist and the preacher-philosopher, without giving in to neither.

In rolling his barrel in the middle of all the panic and desperation, Diogenes not so much participates in this event as he *imitates* it. His path is not one of a man of action, but it is also not a rejection of action. Perhaps it could be described as counteraction, or as performative action that challenges the established consensus around the 'proper' way to react. He is neither for survivalism nor against it; he is not so much ridiculing the other people as he is *reflecting* them to themselves. By witnessing, reflecting and imitating Diogenes shows his love of humanity as fearless truth-telling.

By rolling his barrel Diogenes performs a kind of public broadcasting service; when everyone else is losing their heads, he is holding up a mirror that reflects back, to those who can see it, that there is another way to deal with the situation. Diogenes demonstrates philosophy as practical action. When he starts to roll his barrel, it becomes a form of truth-telling, truth as performance, a form of live art, of life as a manifestation of truth. If Diogenes is sending a message, it is a sublime message, that life is a reality show in which Diogenes is the star, and that this show is being shown live; simultaneous recording and broadcasting from a city under siege. After all, as Freud taught, beyond the reality/pleasure principle lies the domain of the death drive, which is also the domain of the sublime. What this means is that the task of art (and of philosophy) is inseparable from a resounding rejection of the symbolic order (Ruti, 2012). By pursuing his lifestyle choices beyond social limits, Diogenes rejects accepted norms of behaviour, breaching the reality principle and letting laughter and jouissance enter a situation that is clearly not a laughing matter.

Both the survivalists and the preachers are rational people, both respond to the unfolding situation in the way that seems most logical to them. When the proverbial shit hits the fan, trying to save one's soul is not less (or more) rational than trying to save one's body. And this is precisely what concerns Diogenes, namely, that if the choice is between two rational responses, then this is not a choice at all, it is a choice in name only, a simulacrum of choice. Diogenes communicates this not by trying to stop people in their tracks to teach them the errors of their ways, but by creating a simulacrum of his own, one that mimics the survivalist's attempt to outsmart destiny by producing a tongue-in-cheek version of it. He is not criticising rational decision making, but holding a mirror to rationality, holding it to account, exposing its futility in the face of a situation that has nothing rational about it. When everyone else is following the logic of identity that asserts that force will be met with an opposite and equal force, Diogenes draws attention to the fragility of the equal sign.

The key question that the Cynic philosopher elucidates in his performance-provocation is the question of humanity's response to the sublime. It is precisely at a moment of grave danger, when the sea level is rising, the bushfires are raging, the nuclear warhead is armed and the dark clouds gather, that it is urgent to ask how and why we are human. Running away from danger, or baring our teeth and claws, are natural, but not specifically human responses. Wild horses run away when they are ambushed, and antelopes lower their antlers to face an attacking lion. Other animals, of a more philosophical disposition, choose to remain completely still, hoping to be mistaken for a stone or a twig. All these are rational responses to a threat, but they are not specifically human.

It might be, as common sense wants us to believe, that this is indeed the way of the world, that we are the descendants of antelopes and lions, that we must eat or be eaten, and this is all there is to it. But Diogenes does not believe in this kind of evolutionary positivism. Because if it is really the case that our destiny is to fight or flight, why then this overwhelming sense of dread, why are we clinging so anxiously to the newsfeed, to MSNBC, to the latest scoop, why aren't we simply going about our business like the deer, peacefully munching grass until such time when the wolfs pounce?[9] Yet, on the other hand, we are also not made of spirit alone, as the evangelists and the Buddha make us believe, for we so dearly love this sack of skin and bones, that we feel reluctant to part company with it despite the promises of eternal life in God's bosom.

According to Diogenes the siege of the city is a privileged moment when these questions come into a sharp relief, and all rational beliefs are severely tested and found wanting. For as we have seen, lions and deer are capable of rational decision making, and in a moment of danger they exhibit the same responses as the industrious people of Corinth. What is it then, that makes humans different from deer? What is it that makes our situation so specifically tragic and what, if anything, can give us hope in such time?

What Diogenes seems to be saying through his performance is that rational logic is only good for dealing with situations that are themselves rational, but when the perimeter of rationality is being breached, when the avian flu is spreading like wildfire and robotic militias are given their marching orders, the rational response is not the one to reach for, as right now the main problem is not how to survive, but what is it to be rescued.[10]

For Diogenes, this is not food, water, gold bullion or assault rifles, not even the loved ones and your own skin, but the uniquely human ability to make a record, to create an image, a picture, and in this way to produce an alternative reality that sidesteps the lion/gazelle binary. This reality is sublime because it is irreconcilable with rational logic, and because it reminds us of something that was lost when this logic became the iron law of nature. What matters here is that Diogenes pursues his calling of philosophy and of truth-telling beyond the norms of ordinary behaviour. He is showing what is possible to achieve when one is prepared to step out of habitual self-interest and to create a room for transcendent truth (Ruti, 2012, p. 88). Diogenes demonstrates the concrete possibility of revolutionary action by showing how truth demands one to break free from the norms and conventions of society.

By rolling his barrel Diogenes transforms the situation into an image of the situation, suggesting that it, too, is an image. The situation was not of his choosing, because it is, like everything else that is external, outside his sphere of influence and not in his power to change. In the words of Epictetus, who respected the teachings of Diogenes,

> Some things are within our power, while others are not. Within our power are opinion, motivation, desire, aversion, and, in a word, whatever is of our own doing; not within our power are our body, our property, reputation, office, and, in a word, whatever is not of our own doing.
> (Epictetus, 2014, p. 571)

There is no point in asking why me? Why now? Who will win? As none of this has any bearings on the outcome. We can just stop signing online petitions, going on marches and composing snarky below the line comebacks, not only because these are all futile, but also because these are exactly the responses we are programmed to have. This is how we are being kept busy, with one eye on the Twitter feed, as if the euphemistically named smartphone is our own little private war room, and the other eye permanently rolled in indignation. This is how the conman is tricking us every time: we had to watch the right hand, but we were busy watching the left. So outraged we were about racism, sexism and lies that we forgot to notice that it is our own staring down the screen that is changing society more rapidly than any single political movement driven by hate or greed ever could.

For Diogenes it was already clear that the greatest danger lies not in the armies of Philip as they lay siege to the splendid city of Corinth, but in the city's dwellers conveniently forgetting what is in their power to change and what isn't. While the disaster cannot be averted, humanity does not need to be surrendered so easily. Rolling his barrel, Diogenes is not making survival his goal, rather he is mimicking the human response to danger, and in so doing allowing us to take a break from pressing 'refresh'. With the only recording device at his disposal being his own body, he makes himself into a *living sculpture*. From time immemorial sculpture is a technology that transcends identity by allowing to contemplate the heroic deeds of the past, and in this way to come a little closer to an understanding of what being human might actually entail.

What kind of production is Diogenes engaged in? He is not producing fortifications or food supplies. These actions, while important, have a clear goal in mind: surviving the siege, defeating the invaders, not going down without a fight. But precisely because they are goal-oriented, they put the human actor in the service of the goal, and a human being who is in the service of anything that is outside of their own sphere of influence is already enslaved. To be a slave of Philip's soldiers or to be a slave to the principle of identity (the equals sign) is the same thing. This is a point that bears repeating: slavery does not begin when the invaders tear down the door of your house, put you in irons and make you watch your children being led away. No, slavery begins before the first gun is being fired, when you are still free to choose, and you choose to obey the fight or flight instinct that makes you no different from an animal. The production Diogenes is engaged in is of an entirely different order. He is labouring not to resist the external enemy, but to resist the internal voice that tells him that $A = A$.

If, as Clausewitz has taught, war is the continuation of politics by other means, then the military preparations of the citizens of Corinth are political labour (Clausewitz, 2006). But for Diogenes, the ostensibly pointless act of rolling the barrel demonstrates that there are two forms of political agency: labour whose goal is politics and labour that is itself political.[11] It is the later form of labour, which has no political goals because it is itself a purely political act, that Diogenes offers to his fellow citizens as a lesson in what it means to be *bios politicos* – a political, rather than a common animal. In so doing, Diogenes complex gains the role of the political in the forming of the sublime as a therapeutic-political agency.

Notes

1. The political implications of the non- representational are developed by Lyotard in relation to questions of law and language-based schemas in *The Differend*, and in relation to the politics of the other in *Heidegger and 'the Jews'*.
2. See for instance: 'Philosopher's Article On Transracialism Sparks Controversy (Updated with response from author) – Daily Nous'. http://dailynous.com/2017/05/01/philosophers-article-transracialism-sparks-controversy/ (accessed 16 April 2018)
3. Terry Eagleton argues that postmodernism was caught off-guard by the emergence of a new grand narrative – fundamentalism – in the wake of 9/11. 'What's Next After Postmodernism?'
4. On nomadism see Gilles Deleuze and Felix Guattari *A Thousand Plateaus* (2003).
5. On Becoming Sunflower see Golding, Johnny. 2010. *Fractal Philosophy, Trembling a Plane of Immanence and the Small Matter of Learning How to Listen: Attunement as the Task of Art*. For Libidinal Economy see Jean-Francois Lyotard, *Libidinal Economy*, Trans. Iain Hamilton Grant (London: Continuum, 2004). Desiring Machines is a concept from Gilles Deleuze and Félix Guattari, *Anti-Oedipus: Capitalism and Schizophrenia*, Trans. Robert Hurley, Mark Seem and Helen R Lane (London: The Athlone Press, 1996). On paradoxes see Gilles Deleuze, *The Logic of Sense*, Ed Constantin Boundas, Trans Mark Lester and Charles Stivale (London: Continuum, 1990).
6. See for instance: Quentin Meillassoux, *After Finitude: An Essay on the Necessity of Contingency*. Many SR materials are available online, for instance 'Brief SR/OOO Tutorial | Object-Oriented Philosophy' (2009).
7. See for instance a tweet of the Prime Minister (2010–2016) David Cameron, 'David Cameron on Twitter: "It Was the Right Thing to Do ..."', Web, https://twitter.com/David_Cameron/status/969260789776486401 (accessed 13 April 2018).
8. On Rhizomatic becoming, deterritorialisation and nomadic war machines see Deleuze and Guattari, *A Thousand Plateaus*.
9. On existential dread see Kierkegaard (1985a). *Fear and Trembling*.
10. 'Leading AI researchers boycott Korean university over its work on "killer robots" – The Verge'.
11. On the difference between 'political art' and 'making art politically' see Bishop (2004).

Acknowledgement

This chapter is inspired by the writings of Claire Colebrook, Epictetus, Johnny Golding, the late Gillian Rose, Robert Paul Wolff, as well as the political events of recent years.

References

Bishop, C. (2004) 'Antagonism and Relational Aesthetics'. *October*, 110, pp. 51–79.
Boyer, A. (2001) 'Ontological Materialism and the Problem of Politics'. *PLI – The Warwick Journal of Philosophy*, 12, pp. 174–199.
Brown, W. (1995) *States of Injury: Power and Freedom in Late Modernity*. Princeton, NJ.: Princeton University Press.
Clausewitz, C. von (2006) *On War*. Trans Michael Howard, Peter Paret and Beatrice Heuser. New York: Oxford University Press.

Colebrook, C. (2014) 'Death of the PostHuman: Essays on Extinction, Vol. 1'. In *Death of the PostHuman*. University of Michigan Library, Ann Arbor: Open Humanities Press.
Deleuze, G. (1983) 'Plato and the Simulacrum'. *October*, 27, pp. 45–56.
Deleuze, G. (1990) *The Logic of Sense*. Ed Constantin Boundas. Trans Mark Lester and Charles Stivale. London: Continuum, 1990.
Deleuze, G., and Felix G. (2003) *A Thousand Plateaus*. Trans Brian Massumi. London: Continuum.
Deleuze, G., and Félix G. (1996) *Anti-Oedipus: Capitalism and Schizophrenia*. Trans Robert Hurley, Mark Seem and Helen R. Lane. London: The Athlone Press.
Diogenes Laertius (2018) *Lives of Eminent Philosophers*. Ed Tiziano Dorandi. Oxford: Oxford University Press.
Epictetus (2014) *Discourses, Fragments, Handbook*. Ed Christopher Gill. Trans Robin Hard. Oxford: Oxford University Press.
Foucault, M. (2011) *The Courage of Truth: The Government of Self and Others: Lectures at the Collège De France 1983–1984*. Trans Frédéric Gros, François Ewald, Alessandro Fontana, Arnold I Davidson and Graham Burchell. Basingstoke, Hampshire; New York, NY: Palgrave Macmillan.
Golding, J. (2010) 'Fractal Philosophy, Trembling a Plane of Immanence and the Small Matter of Learning How to Listen: Attunement as the Task of Art'. In Ed Stephen Zepke and Simon O'Sullivan, *Deleuze and Contemporary Art*. Edinburgh: Edinburgh University Press.
Golding, J. (2012) 'Ana-Materialism and the Pineal Eye: Becoming Mouth-Breast (or Visual Arts after Descartes, Bataille, Butler, Deleuze and Synthia with an s'. *Philosophy of Photography* 3 (1), pp. 99–121.
Heidegger, M. (1978) 'What Is Metaphysics'. In Ed David Farrell Krell, *Basic Writings: From Being and Time to the Task of Thinking*. Wiltshire: Taylor & Francis.
Heidegger, M. (2002) *Identity and Difference*. Trans Joan Stambaugh. New York, NY, Evanston and London: University of Chicago Press.
Hicks, S. R. C. (2004) *Explaining Postmodernism: Skepticism and Socialism from Rousseau to Foucault*. Tempe, Arizona and New Berlin/Milwaukee: Scholargy Publishing.
Irwin, T. (1990) *Aristotle's First Principles*. Oxford: Oxford University Press.
Kant, I. (2007) *Critique of Judgement*. Oxford: Oxford University Press.
Kierkegaard, S. (1985a) *Fear and Trembling*. Middlesex, England: Penguin Books.
Kierkegaard, S. (1985b) *Fragments, Johannes Climacus*. Ed E. Hong. Princeton, NJ: Princeton University Press.
Kruks, S. (2001) *Retrieving Experience: Subjectivity and Recognition in Feminist Politics*. Ithaca: Cornell University Press.
Lacan, J. (2007). *The Ethics of Psychoanalysis 1959-1960. Book VII*. London: Routledge.
Lyotard, J-F. (1984) *The Post-modern Condition: A Report on Knowledge*. Trans Geoff Bennington and Brian Massumi. Manchester: Manchester University Press.
Lyotard, J-F. (2004) *Libidinal Economy*. Trans Iain Hamilton Grant. London: Continuum.
Meillassoux, Q. (2009) *After Finitude: An Essay on the Necessity of Contingency*. London; New York, NY: Continuum.

Rose, G. (1996) *Mourning Becomes the Law: Philosophy and Representation*. Cambridge: Cambridge University Press.
Ruti, M. (2012) *The Singularity of Being: Lacan and the Immoral Within*. New York, NY: Fordham University Press.
Webster's New World College Dictionary (Fifth edition) (2018). Boston, MA: Houghton Mifflin Harcourt.
Wolin, R. (1993) *The Heidegger Controversy: A Critical Reader*. Cambridge, MA: MIT Press.

Online resources

'Brief SR/OOO tutorial | Object-Oriented Philosophy'. https://doctorzamalek2.wordpress.com/2010/07/23/brief-srooo-tutorial/ (13 April 2018).
'CNN.com – Transcript of President Bush's Address – September 21, 2001'. http://edition.cnn.com/2001/US/09/20/gen.bush.transcript/ (14 April 2018).
'David Cameron on Twitter: "It Was The Right Thing To Do … "'. https://twitter.com/David_Cameron/status/969260789776486401 (13 April 2018).
Oltermann, P. (2014). 'Heidegger's "Black Notebooks" Reveal Antisemitism at Core of his Philosophy'. https://www.theguardian.com/books/2014/mar/13/martin-heidegger-black-notebooks-reveal-nazi-ideology-antisemitism (12 January 2020).
'Leading AI Researchers Boycott Korean University Over its Work on "killer robots" – The Verge'. https://www.theverge.com/2018/4/4/17196818/ai-boycott-killer-robots-kaist-university-hanwha (16 April 2018).
'Philosopher's Article On Transracialism Sparks Controversy (Updated with response from author) – Daily Nous'. http://dailynous.com/2017/05/01/philosophers-article-transracialism-sparks-controversy/ (16 April 2018)
Sutton, B., 'John Baldessari Lends His Voice and Conceptual Art to The Simpsons'. https://hyperallergic.com/435688/the-simpsons-john-baldessari/ (12 January 2020).
'What's Next After Postmodernism?', http://www.leftvoice.org/What-s-Next-After-Postmodernism (14 April 2018).

Index

Note: page numbers containing n refer to notes.

Abram, J. 92, 102
Abramović, Marina 160
abstract nouns 51, 52
absurd, the 8, 144, 147–148
Adams, Tessa 1, 10–12
addiction 85–87, 89
Ader, Bas Jan 160
Adorno, Theodor 3–4, 8, 80–81
aesthetic object 7, 51–52, 61
aesthetics 10, 97–98; and the body 1–2; contingency of 49; of existence 154–155; Jung's avoidance of 17–18; and object relations 15; and political sublime 152, 153, 154–155; and psychoanalysis 12–13, 17, 18, 19, 62–63, 65; of theatre 41, 42, 43, 44; and therapeutic encounter 51–52; and transformational object 62–63; and unconscious 13
affective experience 13, 42, 71, 74, 94, 98
alpha function 71
Ambassadors, The (Holbein) 20
anthropology 46
Antigone 99–100, 102, 107–108
anxiety 38–39, 72
Apollonius 25
Arendt, Hannah 79
Aristotle 46
art 3–4, 6, 10, 12–20, 73, 138, 154; and beauty 13, 18; and elitism 39; extraordinariness of 38; and Freud 18; and Jung 15–16, 17–19; and nature 21; performance 160; and politics/realism 19–20; and projective identification 14, 15, 16; and psychoanalysis 12–15, 17–18, 20; social basis of 14–15;

successful/unsuccessful 14; and viewer/intercourse 14, 16
art criticism 13, 17, 19
art history/historians 13, 15, 20
artist 15–17; and collective psyche 6, 19; internal world of 13; as objective 16, 17; reverence for 18, 19; role of 15–16; sublime purpose of 16, 18, 19; as visionary 16, 18, 19
Asklepios 46–47, 48
Athens (Greece) 46, 47
attentiveness 51, 52
Augustus, Emperor 33
authenticity 4, 42, 83
auto-eroticism 106, 108, 116
autocracy 23, 32, 33, 34
autonomy 2, 3, 4, 14, 15, 19
awe 9, 52, 66–67, 73, 74, 75, 76, 96, 97, 107, 144

Badiou, Alain 113
BCPSG (Boston Change Process Study Group) 69–70
beauty 2, 10–11, 13, 18, 49, 51, 52, 106, 111, 138, 146; and ladder of love 80; Longinus's dismissal of 23, 24; political reading of 63; and sublimation of desire 107, 116
Beckett, Samuel 140, 141
Berger, John 45, 49, 82
Beyond the Pleasure Principle (Freud) 68–69
Bion, Wilfred 4, 71, 72, 76, 96, 99, 140
Bloom, Harold 27
Bluets (Nelson) 83–84, 87–89
Boal, Augusto 44

body 1–2, 80, 106, 111; and art 16, 17; and language 112–114; and mind 87–88; and sublime 97, 115; transgender 106, 108, 109–110, 120; and violence 4
Bollas, Christopher 62, 63
Borromean Knot 73
boundaries 40, 97, 110, 118, 119, 122, 123–124, 136, 156, 160
breast 14, 15
Brecht, Bertold 43–44
Burgoyne, B. 73
Burke, Edmund 2, 5, 35, 153
Bush, George W. 156

Callimachus 24
cancer 66–67, 73
Carson, Anne 83
Cassius Longinus 22
Catch-22 (Heller) 138–151; absurd in 8, 144, 147–149, 150; beauty of writing in 146; context of *see* post-modern fiction and psychoanalysis; Doc Daneeka's death in 146, 147; humanism in 145, 149; humour in 146, 147, 149, 150; Kid Sampson's death in 146–147; love in 144, 150; Michaela's murder/Aarfy's lack of remorse in 146, 148–149; post-modern elements of 145, 149–150; scepticism of grand narratives in 145, 150; sense of self in 150; Snowden's death in 145, 146, 150; structure/pace of 146; sublime in 144, 145, 146–149, 150–151
Catholicism 38, 47, 48, 84, 85, 86, 115; and Reformation/Inquisition 115–116
Catullus 24
children/childhood 52, 92, 96–97, 101, *see also* mathematics classroom
Christianity 47, 48, 80, 87, 111
Cicero 23
Civitarese, Giuseppe 99, 102–103, 104
Clapham, Miles 93, 94, 99, 104
comedy 6
concrete thoughts 66, 71
consent 2, 26
containment 38, 71
contradiction 21, 34–35, 37, 39, 40, 100, 122, 136–137
countertransference *see* transference/countertransference

creative process 13, 38, 47; and play 95, 100, 102, 104; and sublimation of desire 107
Critchley, Simon 107
critical theory 3
Cynic philosophy 160, 161, *see also* Diogenes

Danish Girl, The (film, dir. Hooper) 109
Days of the Commune, The (Brecht) 43–44
de Certeau, Michel 115
death 73, 79, 80, 81, 82
death drive 119, 163
Deleuze, Giles 155, 156
dementia 10, 11–12
democracy 32–33, 40, 154, 155; contempt for 159
Demosthenes 23
depressive position 13, 14, 66, 71–72, 101
Derrida, Jacques 103, 117, 156, 158–159
desire 7, 55, 79, 80, 82, 84, 86, 87, 117–118; as beyond language 99; and repression 116–117; sublimation of 107–108, 112–113, 114, 116; as will 97
despair 59, 106
dictatorship *see* autocracy
Diogenes 8, 153, 155, 159–165; fitness/healthiness of 161; futile activity of 160–165; and identity 163, 165; life of 159–160; and performance art 160, 165; and rejection of rational choice 162, 163, 164–165; and sublime 162, 163, 164; truth-telling by 162–163, 164, 165
Dionysus 46, 47, 48
Dionysus of Halicarnassus 22
displacement 29
dogma 65
Dostoyevsky, Fyodor 143
dramatherapy 6–7, 37, 39, 41–42; and contradictions/contingency of everyday life 49–50; and dramatic distancing 40; and ritual 46, 47; therapeutic relationship in 38, 41
dramatic reality 39, 40, 42
dreams 46–47, 48; waking 71, 75
Dylan, Bob 75–76

Eagleton, Terry 1, 2, 4, 49, 166n3
Eco, Umberto 113

education 8, 123–125; and boundaries of cleverness 123–124; and classroom design 124–125; and knowledge diffusion 1225, *see also* mathematics classroom
ego 62, 63, 84, 99, 108, 141
Eliot, T.S. 12
Emerson, Ralph Waldo 51, 64
empathy 41, 66, 67, 110, 147, 148
enactments 69, 71, 74–75
Enlightenment 8, 99, 152
Epictetus 161, 164
Epidaurus (Greece) 47, 48
ethics 64, 93–95, 96, 99–100, 103–104; and political sublime 152, 153–154
ethnographic approach 122, 126, 137
Euripides 30
everyday, the 1, 5, 7, 9, 35, 37, 114, 137, 150–151; and attentiveness 51; and beauty 11; in *A Fantastic Woman* 108–110, 116; messiness of 6, 39, 49–50; and play 92, 97, 103, 104; as problematic construct 106; and repression 6; and theatre 38, 39, 40, 41, 42, 43, 45, 46; in *The Untamed* 116
existential thought/experience 73–74, 76, 83
existentialism 64

failure 52, 122, 123, 124, 131
Fairburn, Ronald 84
fairy tales 100–101, 102
fantasies 75, 76, 118; of love 81, 84, 88; of Other 106
Fantastic Woman, A (film, dir. Lelio) 106, 108–112; everyday in 108–110, 116; final scene of 119–120; and St Francis 111, 119; liminal space/boundaries in 109, 110; magic realism in 108, 110; music in 109, 111, 114, 116, 119, 120; prejudice/discrimination in 106, 110, 116, 120; sublime/sublimation in 109, 110–112, 116; transgender identity in 106, 108, 109–110, 120
fate 63, 70, 73, 82
father 27, 53, 111
Feagin, S. L. 63
fear 38–39, 40, 52, 153
feelings 6, 24, 42, 43, 71; and sex 55, 58, 60
Felman, Shoshana 99, 103, 104

feminism 122
Ferenczi, S. 74
Ferro, A. 71
fiction *see* literature
financial crisis (2008) 156, 157
Finnegan's Wake (Joyce) 142, 151n1
Foucault, Michel 4, 154, 160
Francis, St 111, 119
Frankfurt School 72
Frazer, James 46
freedom 3, 4, 5
Freud, Sigmund 4, 18, 20, 82, 92, 98, 101, 113, 139, 156; on death drive 119, 163; and Longinus 21, 25–26, 27, 32, 34; and oceanic feeling 5, 74; on psychoanalysis as translation 112; and reality 67–69, 71, 73; on sublimation of desire 107
Frie, Roger 143
friendship 96, 99, 100
Fromm, Erich 72

Gainsborough, Thomas 45
Gibbon, Edward 26
Glazer, Jonathan 117
Glyndebourne opera 39
God 19, 80, 106, 111, 114, 120
Gorgias of Leontini 25
Goytisolo, J. 82
Grace 111, 114, 116, 120
Grainger, Roger 37, 40
Gramsci, Antonio 152
grandeur 6, 22, 23, 28, 48
Gravity's Rainbow (Pynchon) 140
Greece, ancient: ritual in 46–47
Grotstein, J. S. 72
guilt 54, 101, 102

Hamlet (Shakespeare) 42
Hawking, Stephen 91–92, 98–99, 100, 102
Heidegger, Martin 79, 86, 156, 157–158
Helen of Troy 25–26
Heller, Joseph *see Catch-22*
Herodotus 29, 30, 35n4
Herzog, Amy 111
Hippocrates 46–47
Holbein, Hans 19–20
holding 66, 82
Holland, Mary K. 143, 145
Homer 23, 26, 26–28, 29, 34, 35n2
hope 38, 39, 41, 45, 48, 49

Index

Horace 25
horror 66, 67, 153
Hsieh, Tehching 60
Hughes, Robert 49–50
humanism 145, 149
hupsos 24, 26, 28, 35
hysteria 4, 112

Ibsen, Henrik 40
icebergs 74
ideal 6, 8, 123
ideal subject 122, 126, 131, 132–133, 134
identity 91, 99, 143; gender 109, 110, 120; loss of 119; politics of 155, 156–159, 160
idolatry 53, 54, 56, 64, 65
Iliad (Homer) 26, 27
Imaginary, Lacanian 72–73, 111
Imago group 13, 15, 127
infant/infancy 15, 17, 52, 102
infantile wishes 67, 68
infant–mother relationship 62, 63
intersubjectivity 66, 69–70, 71, 73, 75
introjection 14, 15
Italian Renaissance 13

Jakobson, Roman 113–114
Jameson, Frederic 44–45
Johnson, M. 40
jouissance 106, 108, 112, 114, 116, 118, 134, 163
Joyce, James 141–142, 151n1
Jung, Carl 5, 15–16, 17–19

Kant, Immanuel 2–3, 5, 35, 152, 153–154
Keats, John 76
Khan, M. M. R. 75
Kierkegaard, Søren 80, 159, 160
Klein, Melanie 5, 12, 13, 14, 15, 101; and reality 66, 68, 71, 72, 76
knowledge 88, 96–100, 104, 113, 143; crisis of 154; and identity 158; and pedagogy 124, 125, 128; self- 38, 92, 95, 97, 100
Kristeva, Julia 106, 108, 114–115, 116

Lacan, Jacques 3, 21, 25, 28–30, 33, 99, 108, 113, 124, 126; and post-modern fiction 139–140; Real of *see* Real, Lacanian; on reality principle 153; on representation 123; on sublimation 107; topographic model of 72–73, 111

Lady of Shalott, The (Tennyson) 81–82
Lakoff, G. 40
landscapes 45
Landy, Robert 42
language 122, 140; and ethics 93–94; limitations of 51–52, 56, 57, 58, 61–62, 64, 65, 98; poetic, mythical 102–103; and semiotics 113–114; as sublimation of desire 112–113, 114–115, 116, *see also* speaking; translation
laughter 96, 97, 100–101, 163
Lawn, M. 125
learning disability 52, 53, 57
Leikert, Sebastian 98, 99
Lenormand, Marie 100
liberalism 154, 155
libido 14, 15, 84, 107, 114, 140, 156
literary criticism *see On the Sublime*
literature 6, 8, 21, 23, 139; post-modern 8, 31, 35n7; and psychoanalysis 139, *see also* post-modernist fiction and psychoanalysis
longing 84, 85, 86, 87, 89, 116, *see also* desire
Longinus *see On the Sublime*
loss 7, 52, 60, 85, 86–87, 88, 108, 116; and mourning 87, 89, 106
Lourdes (France) 47, 48
love 5, 9, 52, 79–89, 92; addictive 84; Christian/divine 80–81, 111, 114, 115, 119, 1120; as container 82; and convergence of time 75–76; ladder of 80; and longing/loss 84, 85, 86, 87, 89, 106; and mind–body dichotomy 87–88; as narcissistic 108; and philosophers 79–81; rejection of 79; and Romantic poets 81–82; and sublime 7, 81, 89, 114; and truth 7, 79–82, 89; and wisdom 79, 81–82
Lyotard, Jean-Francois 3, 143, 153–154, 156, 166n1

McCarten, Anthony 91
McCarty, Paul 160
Macksey, R. 21, 35n3
magic realism 108, 110
Maier-Katkin, D. 79
Marquez, Gabriel Garcia 84
Marriage of Figaro, The (Mozart) 40, 41
Marx, Karl 43
materialism 37, 45, 49
materiality 2, 3, 49

mathematics classroom 8, 122–137; Balwinder subject of ridicule in 134, 136; and Balwinder's family–school relations 129; and Balwinder's popularity 131–132, 135; Balwinder's relation to/position in 126–127; and Balwinder's self-subversion 132, 133–136; and competition 125, 126, 127–128; ethnographic approach to 122, 126, 137; failure/interruption in 122; and ideal subject 122, 126, 131, 132–133, 134; intrusion of head teacher in 127–128; and moral character 124, 125, 126; public scrutiny in 125, 126, 127, 128, 134, 137; and shame 124, 125, 127; as social technology 125; socio-historical context of 122, 123, 124, 136, 137; sublime in everyday in 137; as sublime object 122, 123, 126–127, 130, 136; and TCB system 124–125, 127, 136; and teacher's ambivalence towards Balwinder 128–131
meaning-making 66, 67, 69, 71–72; and play 94–95, 96
Meltzer, Donald 13–14, 15, 16
metanarratives 40, 142
metaphor 28–29, 30; and theatre 40, 41, 46, 47, 49
metonymy 28–30, 35n5
Miller, Paul Allen 99
Milner, Marion 13, 15, 16–17, 103
mind 139–140, 142, 158
mind–body dichotomy 87–88
miracles 94, 103
mise-en-scene 14, 42
Mitchell, Stephen A. 70, 82
Mitchell-Boyask, R. 46
morality 100–103, 107
mother 53, 54, 56, 58–59, 60, 62; abandonment by 85, 87; and transformational object 62–63
mountains 11
mourning 87, 89
Mr and Mrs Andrews (Gainsborough) 45
music 23, 31–32, 109, 111, 112, 114, 119, 120
mutuality 69
myth 103, 104, 156

Nancy, Jean-Luc 117
narcissistic desires/fantasies 67, 89, 108

National Theatre 40
natural sublime 2–3, 44–45, 73, 138; and icebergs 74, 76; and landscapes 45; Longinus's dismissal of 23, 24, 27, 28; and mountains 11
naturalistic acting 42–43
nature 2–3, 6, 7; and art 21; Longinus's dismissal of 23, 24, 27, 28; and terror 2
Nazism 43, 158, 159
Nelson, Maggie 83–84, 85, 87–89
neo-liberal ethics 8, 152
neoteric school 24
neurosis 68–69, 72, 73
Newman, A. 101, 102
news media 159, 163, 164–165
Nietzsche, Friedrich 51, 52, 61, 62, 64
9/11 attacks 156, 157, 166n3
now moments 70, 76

'O', Bion's concept of 72, 76, 96
object relations 15, 154
objectification 3
objectivity 23, 67–68, 71, 94
oceanic feeling 5, 74
Odysseus 2–3, 11
Odyssey (Homer) 26–27, 29, 31
Ogden, Thomas 71, 84
Olsen, Regine 80
On the Sublime (Longinus) 21–35; autocracy in 23, 25, 32, 33, 34; background of author 22; comparison in 28; five elements of sublime in 22; and Freud 21, 25–26, 32, 34; genius in 23, 32, 33; and Homer 23, 26–28, 29, 34; and *hupsos* 24, 26, 28, 35; ideal reader in 23; and Lacan 21, 25, 33; literary criticism in 21, 23, 24–25; and metonymy 29–30; and natural sublime, dismissal of 23, 24, 27, 28; nature/ nurture in 22; Oedipal element in 27; and Plato 32–33, 34; political sublime in 32–35; power relations in 25–26; pre-eminence of literature in 23; repression in 6, 25, 26, 27, 29, 34; sexual interpretation of 26, 32; silence in 31–32, 34; similes/metaphors in 26–27, 28–29; and sublime in the everyday 6, 21–22, 24, 29, 32; sublime as objective in 23; unconscious in 21, 27, 28–29
opera 39, 40

ordinariness 49–50, 51, 110, *see also* everyday life
otherness 9, 14, 72, 73, 103, 117, 119; and liberal democracy 155
Overton, Tom 45

pain 5, 40, 53, 87, 99, 122; and music 111, 112; and pleasure 2, 7
panopticon 4
paranoid-schizoid position 13, 66, 71–72
Pendzik, Susana 39
perception 37, 46, 98, 152
performance art 160
philosophers 32–33, 40, 89, 115; poet- 7, 82–84, 88, 89; and truth 79–81, 87
philosophy 80, 123; of aesthetics 1–2; Cynic 160, 162, 163, 164; postmodern 155–157; and psychoanalysis 93, 113
Picasso, Pablo 15, 17, 18
Plato 32–33, 34, 80, 87, 119
play 71, 91–104; and comportment/non-rationality 94–95; as creative 95, 100, 102, 104; and emancipation 99, 100; as ethical 92–95, 96, 103–104; and everyday 92, 97, 103, 104; and fairy tales 100–101, 102; as healing 92, 100–101; and laughter/jokes 96, 97, 100–101, 102; and myth 103, 104; as non-compliance 100–101, 102; psychoanalysis as 71, 92–93, 98–99, 102–103; and relationships 7, 95, 96; and rules 92; and safety/trust 93, 97; and self-knowledge 96–100, 101; and sublime 7, 92, 96–98, 103–104; and surprise 97, 98–99; and tickling 96–97, 99, 102, 103, 104; and transformation 96, 97, 98, 100, 104; and truth 7, 100, 102–103, 104; and wonder 7, 94, 95, 96, 97
pleasure principle 68, 69
pluralism, challenge to 155, 156
poet-philosophers 7, 82–84, 88, 89
poetry 73; and love 81–84; Roman/Greek 24–25; silence in 31
political sublime 63–64, 152–165; and aesthetics of existence 154–155; as break with reality 152–153; and Diogenes *see* Diogenes; Kantian/postmodern 152, 153–154; and Longinus 23, 32–35; and performativity 153, 162; and technology/social media 152
politics 5, 8, 155–159; and anti-pluralism 155, 156, 159; and art/theatre 6, 19–20, 43–45, 47, 48, 49; and global crises 158, 163; identity 155, 156–159; populist 42–43, 159; and postmodern philosophy 155–156, 158–159
pornography 54–57, 59; idolisation of 53, 54–56, 61; and quantity/explicitness 61; as transformational object 62, 63
positivism 67, 156, 163
post-modernist fiction and psychoanalysis 8, 139–144, 150; and Beckett 140, 141; and detachment 143; and Joyce 141–142; and Lacan 139–140, 141; and lack of engagement 140–141; and language 140, 141; and metanarratives 143; and sublime 144, *see also Catch-22*
postmodern sublime 3, 63–64, 144, 154
postmodernism 3, 31, 63–64, 142; political 153–157; reaction against 158–159
Pound, Ezra 83
power 39, 40, 57; political 2, 47; and sublime 25–26, 33–34, 52
power relations 25–26
primary process 13
projection/projective identification 14, 15, 16, 40, 45, 68
psychoanalysis 66–67; and aesthetics 5; and avoidance of aesthetics 17–18, 19; as dogma 64–65; and ethical moments 92–93, 96, 99; and fiction 8; and knowledge 96; and learning disability 52, 53; and mind–body 4; and philosophy 113; as play 71, 92–93, 98–99, 102–103; as pornography 61, 64, 65; and post-modernist fiction *see* post-modernist fiction and psychoanalysis; and sublime 63–64, 66, 73, 75; and surprise 98–99; and transformation 5, 71; as translation 112; and translation of sexual desire 107, *see also* therapeutic relationship
psychosomatic experience 46, 48, 97, 98
Pynchon, Thomas 140

Rancière, Jacques 38
Real, Lacanian 67, 72–76, 111, 140; and convergence of time 75–76; and erotic

transference/countertransference 74–76; and Imaginary/Symbolic registers 72–73; and natural sublime 74; and sublime 72, 73–76
realist drama 43–44
reality 67–73; alternative/virtual 153, 164; as dream 71–72; and enactments/play 69, 71, 74–75; intersubjective 69–70, 71, 73; and meaning-making 66, 67, 69, 71–72; as objective/external 67–69; and projection 68; and symbolisation 67, 68
reality principle 68, 69, 152–153
reason 153, 156; limits of 3, 154
Reason 3; and the body 1–2
Redmayne, Eddie 109
Reformation 115–116
relationships: and play 7, 95, 96, 101–102; and political context 43; sexual 14, 52, 55, *see also* love; therapeutic relationship
religion 73, 76; and ritual 10, 38, 46, 47, *see also* Catholicism
representation 1, 61, 62, 83, 122, 123; dramatic 42, 43; limits of 3, 123; and love/loss 7; pictorial 17, 18; symbolic 13
repression 6, 25, 26, 27, 29, 34, 68, 101, 107, 116–117
reverie 65, 66, 71, 75
Ribout, Theodore 42
ritual 6, 10, 38, 45–48, 49; and dramatherapy 46, 47; in traditional societies 46
road works 10–11
Roberts, Rhys 28
Rodman, Robert 65
Romantic poets 81–82, 87, 88
Royal Opera House 40
Ruskin, John 19

sacred 1, 10, 11, 48, 52, 62; and profane 16
Sapho 23
schizophrenia 141
school classroom *see* mathematics classroom
science 46, 64, 99, 103, 138, 156; and identity 158
Searles, H. F. 74
Segal, Hanna 13, 14, 17
self 72, 73, 138, 150; loss of 74

self-knowledge 96–100, 101, 113
Sellars, Peter 39, 40, 41
semiotics 113–114
sex 53–54, 57–58; addiction to 85–87; and art 14; as defence against intimacy 86, 87; and talking/writing 112–113; in therapeutic relationship 75, *see also* pornography
Shakespeare, William 40, 42
shame 8, 32, 124, 127
Sharma, Simon 45
shock 3, 20, 60, 66, 145
shudder 3
signifier/signified 123, 124
silence 31–32, 34, 99
simile 26–27
smartphones 152, 165
social media 152, 155, 165
socio-historical context 122, 123, 124, 136, 137
Socrates 33, 80, 119
Soper, Kate 49
Sophocles 88
speaking: and experience, distance between 51–52, 56, 57, 58, 61–62, 64, 65; as sublimation of desire 107, 112–113
speculative realism 156–157
Stanislavski, Konstantin 42, 43
Stokes, Adrian 12–15, 16, 17–18; and Klein 12, 13, 14
subjectivity 2, 3, 6, 7, 20, 22, 38, 45, 49, 94, 122, 123–124, 138, 154; and reality 69, 71, 72, 73
sublimation 4, 18, 24, 80, 101; in *A Fantastic Woman* 109, 116; of desire 107–108, 112–113, 114, 116; and sublime 106–108; through music 111–112
sublime 1, 5–9; and art *see* art; and awe *see* awe; as beyond representation 52; and contradiction 37; and divine/spiritual 106; as ethical moment 93–94; etymology of 24; as exceptional 5; and fear 38–39; and Grace 111, 114, 116, 120; and Lacanian Real 72, 73–76; in Longinus *see* Longinus; and love 7, 81, 89; and metonymy 29–30; and nature *see* natural sublime; and opportunity 41; and perception 98; and politics 6, 8; postmodern 3, 63–64, 154; psychological fiction of 6; and

representation 3, 123–124; and shift in perspective 7, 99, 138; and shock/surprise 3, 5, 76, 97, 98–99; and subjectivity 3, 6, 7, 20, 22, 122, 146, 149, 150; and sublimation, compared 106–108; and theatre/dramatherapy 6–7, 38, 39, 44; as therapeutic 5; three aesthetic qualities of 97–98, 99; and tragedy 99–100; and transformational object 62–63
sublime object 122, 123, 126–127, 130, 136
submission 2, 119
surprise 3, 5, 76, 97, 98–99
surrender 7, 97, 98
symbolic equation/representation 13
Symbolic, Lacanian 72, 73, 75, 111, 114
symbolisation 67, 68, 71
symbolism 28–29; and depressive position 66, 71
Symposium (Plato) 80, 119

Tantalus 84
TCB (teacher–classroom–batch) system 124–125, 127, 136
Tennyson, Alfred Lord 81–82
Teresa, St 106, 108, 114–116; and Grace 114, 116; *jouissance* of 114; sublimation of desire by 114–115, 116
terror 2, 5, 11
terrorism 156, 157, 166n3
theatre 6, 29–30, 37–50, 85; aesthetics of 41, 42, 43, 44; and affective memory 42; and anxiety in performing 38–39; artifice/constructedness of 41–42, 44; audience as protagonist in 44; classical 45–46, 47, 49; as collective art 38; and contradiction 37; and elitism 39; and everyday life 38, 39, 40, 41, 42, 43, 45, 46; materialism/context of 37–38, 39–42; and metaphors 40, 41, 46, 47, 49; and naturalism/realism 42–45; and politics 6, 42–43, 48, 49; and projective identification 45; and ritual 45–48; silence in 31–32; sublime in 38–39, 40, 41, 44, 45, 48–49
Theory of Everything, The (film, dir. Marsh) 91–92, 98–99, 100, 102
therapeutic action 66
therapeutic relationship 38, 41, 51–63; as aesthetic object 51–52, 61; aesthetic/sublime in 62–63; and ethics 93; and idealisation of pornography 54–55; and intersubjectivity 69–70, 73; and Lacanian Real *see* Real, Lacanian; and mother's illness 53, 54, 56, 58–59; and now moments 70; and speaking/experience, distance between 51–52, 56, 57, 58, 61–62, 64; and sublime 66, 73, 75; transformative potential of 51; and translation 112, *see also* transference/countertransference
tickling 96–97, 99, 102, 103, 104
Tiresias 88
Todd, Jane Marie 112
togetherness 6, 29, 30
tragedy 99–100
transcendence 4, 10, 47, 73, 76, 122
transference/countertransference 42, 69, 70; erotic 74–76
transformation 4, 5, 6, 10, 20, 71; and art/theatre 41; and play 96, 97, 98, 100, 104; and therapy 66
transformational object 62–63
transgender 106, 108, 109–110, 120
transitional experiences 66, 71
transitional space 92, 94, 98
translation 113–114; psychoanalysis as 112
trauma 5, 68, 99, 104, 107
Truman Show, The (film) 152
Trump, Donald 40, 159
truth: and love 7, 79–81, 82, 83, 88, 89; and play 7, 100, 102–103, 104; and politics 159, 163–164, 164

ugliness 10, 13, 52, 106, 108, 116
Ulysses 15
unconscious 13, 69, 108, 113, 139–140
Under the Skin (film, dir. Glazer) 117, 118–119
Untamed, The (film, dir. Escalante) 106, 108, 116–119; alien creature in 117, 118; desire in 117–118, 119; and loss of identity 118, 119; repression/violence in 116–117; sublime in 117, 118

Vega, Daniela 109
Vernant, Jean Pierre 47, 48
violence 4, 52, 56, 108, 116, 117, 118
Virgil 24

Wallace, David Foster 143
Warner, Marina 100–101
Wiles, David 47
Winnicott, Donald W. 40, 42, 62, 64–65, 71; and play 92, 94, 96, 98, 100, 101, 102
wisdom 7, 79–80; and love 79, 81–82; and truth 79–81; and truth/love, combined 7, 79

Wittgenstein, L. 64, 83, 93, 94, 95, 96, 99, 103
wonder 7, 64–65, 89, 94, 95, 96, 97; and pain 99

Žižek, S. 33, 123
Zupančič, Alenka 112–113

For Product Safety Concerns and Information please contact our EU representative GPSR@taylorandfrancis.com
Taylor & Francis Verlag GmbH, Kaufingerstraße 24, 80331 München, Germany

www.ingramcontent.com/pod-product-compliance
Lightning Source LLC
Chambersburg PA
CBHW070724020526
44116CB00031B/1772